THE CONDOTTIERI

THE CONDOTTIERI
Soldiers of Fortune

Geoffrey Trease

210 illustrations, 16 in colour

THAMES AND HUDSON · LONDON

Printed and bound in Great Britain by Jarrold and Sons Ltd, Norwich

ISBN 0 500 25027 8

Contents

Preface

Any work of this nature, designed for the general reader, must inevitably owe an incalculable debt to the scholars whose patient researches have not only uncovered the raw materials but have tested, assessed, and interpreted them as no non-specialist is competent to do. The modest intention of this book is no more than to parade the most interesting of the condottieri against the background of their times, telling their stories and exploring their diverse characters. If some of the stories have been told before, it may be just because they are rather good stories.

The primary sources are the countless letters, contracts, and other contemporary documents preserved in the archives of Italy, together with the chronicles, histories, biographies, and similar works compiled at the time or soon afterwards, the writings of Machiavelli offering the most familiar example. These are the materials that have occupied several generations of academic specialists, without whose labours no study of the subject could proceed. As far back as 1844 such researches made it possible for E. Ricotti to publish the four volumes of his *Storia delle Compagnie di Ventura in Italia*, a classic work to which all subsequent writers on the subject must owe much, directly or indirectly, whatever the revisions of judgment prompted by such important later books as W. Block's *Die Condottieri* (1913).

For the individual life-stories no one could avoid drawing liberally and gratefully upon the early modern biographers such as Dennistoun, Temple-Leader, and Oscar Browning, and Oman's classic *Art of War* is still indispensable. Among present-day scholars those whose writings have proved particularly helpful have been D. M. Bueno de Mesquita, E. R. Chamberlin, J. J. Deiss, J. R. Hale, and Daniel Waley. All these works will be found listed in the *Guide to Further Reading* at the end of this volume, together with many others which its author has consulted on one point or another with profit and appreciation, now warmly acknowledged.

'So Italy having fallen almost completely into the hands of the Church and of a few republics, and the priests and other citizens being unused to military service, they started to hire outsiders as soldiers.'

MACHIAVELLI

2 When the condottiere Guidoriccio da Fogliano recaptured two rebel towns for Siena in 1328, the city commemorated him with this fresco by Simone Martini in the Palazzo Pubblico. Richly accoutred, he rides through a bare landscape between palisades.

8

The remembered riders I

Still they ride, throughout Italy, defying us to ignore them.

In Venice it is Bartolomeo Colleoni's harsh face, framed in its open helmet, that glares down at the traveller in the little square of San Giovanni e Paolo. As Verrocchio's colossal bronze is commonly rated the finest equestrian statue in the world, Colleoni is sure of his immortality. One of the statues to be named in the same breath with this is at Padua, not many miles away, in the Piazza del Santo: Donatello's masterpiece, the first great bronze of the Renaissance, the first to be cast since ancient times. This time the rider is Erasmo da Narni, the commander whose subtlety won him the nickname of Gattamelata, 'the Honeyed Cat'. In the Duomo at Florence it is Hawkwood, the Englishman, who rides on for ever in Uccello's painting.

The complete list would be a long one. In small cities and great, on every scale from a medallion to a mural, these adventurers confront posterity. Roberto Malatesta has somehow found his way into the Sistine Chapel. And though Carmagnola, for obvious reasons, is not individually commemorated in the Venice that condemned him as a traitor, his victories could not be ignored when spirited subjects were needed for the ceilings of the Doge's Palace.

'A famous condottiere,' says the guide quickly, intent on his schedule. His tone discourages the question, 'But what was a condottiere?' The word surely is in general currency. It no longer requires to be singled out in italics as a foreign intruder. The condottieri were mercenaries, soldiers of fortune. What more need be said?

In fact, a great deal. Neither of these apparent synonyms conveys the full significance of the condottiere, a unique phenomenon confined to a particular period, the Italian Renaissance. It is not at all idle to ask, what exactly *was* he? And what claim have these grim-visaged riders on our interest, apart from the fact that by a happy chronological coincidence

11

3 Michele Attendolo, who led the Florentine forces at the battle immortalized by Uccello's three paintings of *The Battle of San Romano*.

4, 5 The two most famous equestrian statues of the Renaissance were erected in honour of condottieri. Donatello's Gattamelata (left) was made between 1447 and 1453. The condottiere, 'Honeyed Cat' (real name Erasmo da Narni), was a baker's son from Umbria who rose to become a Venetian nobleman. Donatello's bronze figure was the first equestrian statue to be cast since antiquity, and it retains a calm classical dignity. Verrocchio's Colleoni (right) belongs to the next generation and conveys a new and terrifying impression of power. Bartolomeo Colleoni began his career as one of Braccio da Montone's men, but as with Gattamelata it was in the service of Venice that he made his fortune.

they furnished subjects for Leonardo da Vinci, Piero della Francesca, and so many other artists of the Renaissance?

There have been mercenaries and soldiers of fortune since at least the days of ancient Greece, persisting down to our own day – witness the Congo in the 1960s. But normally they have been foreigners enrolling either singly or in small groups, subordinate to the commanders of the government employing them. Sometimes their groups have been larger and their own leaders have made a mark on history – one thinks at once of Xenophon and of the Gothic and Vandal adventurers such as Alaric and Stilicho who began as mercenary generals to the later Roman emperors. But neither these men nor picturesque individuals like the Scotsman, Tam

12

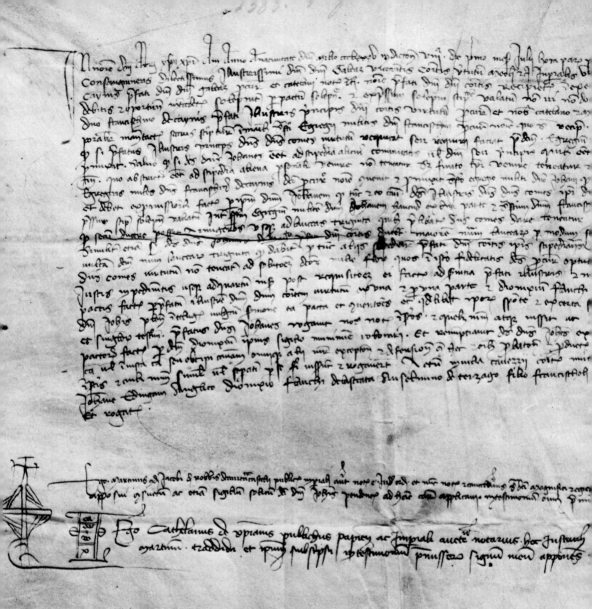

6 Contract (*condotta*) between Sir John Hawkwood and Gian Galeazzo Visconti, dated 1 July 1385. Hawkwood (spelt here 'Haucud') agrees to hold himself at the disposal of Gian Galeazzo, the newly proclaimed lord of Milan, promising to come to his aid, when needed, with thirty lances for a fee of 300 florins a month. If he brings more men, the fee is to be raised proportionately. The situation at this time was an electric one. Less than two months earlier Gian Galeazzo had deposed his

14

uncle Bernabò Visconti. Bernabò was Hawkwood's father-in-law, but the latter was heavily in debt and the prospect of profit overcame his scruples. Five months later, however, Gian Galeazzo murdered Bernabò (or at least was accused of doing so). Hawkwood threw up the agreement and was soon in the service of Florence leading an expedition against his former employer. This contract, therefore, was an abortive one, but is typical of the kind of bargain made between prince and condottiere.

7 Supposed portrait of Roberto Malatesta, from a fresco by Rosselli. The Malatesta family represents an important type of condottiere. Lords of a small independent principality, Rimini, they combined political with commercial advantage by using their armies on behalf of other rulers. Roberto, who died in 1482, was the son of the most famous of the Malatesta, Sigismondo, the patron of Alberti and Piero della Francesca.

Dalyell, who led Muscovite armies against Turks and Tatars in the seventeenth century, can be truly equated with the condottieri.

Medieval conditions throughout western Europe were particularly favourable to the development of mercenary forces, and conditions in Italy, as will be seen, continued that development to its most sophisticated level, the condottiere system. In those centuries the modern standing army and the legionary organization of ancient Rome were equally inconceivable. On the other hand, forces could not long be maintained in the field on the basis of the feudal levy, a method perhaps over-emphasized in bygone classrooms because it offered teachers such neat lesson-material. What was the use of a mere forty-day spell of duty, save in a brief emergency? It was a problem that had worried Harold when William the Conqueror's

16

sailing was delayed – and William could not have invaded England with a forty-day army. When he came, his ships were packed with mercenaries from many distant places. Thereafter the kings of England came to rely more and more upon paid volunteers, English, Welsh, and foreign. The campaigns against Scotland and France could only be waged by the hard-bitten prototypes of Shakespeare's Fluellen and Corporal Nym.

Thus there evolved the system of the indentured retinue, whereby a nobleman with a taste for war would engage to serve his sovereign for a period of time, and with an armed force, far beyond his feudal obligation. His 'retinue' would consist of so many knights, so many men-at-arms, and so many mounted archers. The total might run to a thousand men or more, each grade with its own rate of pay, ranging from four shillings a day for an experienced knight banneret down to threepence for an archer who could not provide his own horse. Besides this pay, the soldier looked forward to loot and ransom-money. The conditions for these were very precisely laid down, and it may be imagined that the mercenaries watched each other after a victory as keenly as waiters in a restaurant. The commander usually claimed a third of the proceeds and another third went to the King of England, but in Spain the royal share was only a fifth.

The indentured retinue was thus very like the 'free company' which was soon to evolve from it, subject to many of the same rules and conventions, and its commander, with his contract from the king, his grant from the Exchequer, his personal pay, and his percentage of the profits from plundering a camp or capturing a high-born adversary, had much in common with a condottiere. But the great English earls who contracted their services to the Plantagenet kings in this way were not true condottieri, for they remained subjects and were fighting their sovereign's war, either under his personal leadership or under some illustrious deputy like the Black Prince. War was made worth their while but they were not, in the completest sense, professionals.

That complete professionalism was the keynote of the condottiere system.

The word derives from the Latin *conducere*, via the Italian verb *condurre* with its connotations of 'conducting', 'organizing', and 'supplying'. Thence, through the past participle *condotto*, comes the associated noun, *condotta*, which in this period came to mean the contract made between a free-lance commander and the government – any government – that employed him.

These *condotte* were precise agreements (like the English indentures) but their terms were capable of almost infinite variety. They could be for a short period or a long one or even for life. They could be in the nature of retaining fees, leaving the condottiere free to accept temporary engagements elsewhere by mutual consent. They might stipulate an aggressive campaign or a purely defensive role, in which case the pay would be lower. They might be purely negative, the condottiere undertaking, for a suitable consideration, that for a certain period, whatever other governments he chose to serve, he would not fight against the one whose money he was now accepting. As an obvious corollary in such cases he would have to insist, when negotiating subsequent *condotte* with those other governments, on a clause excluding hostile activities in certain directions.

Further clauses would settle the numbers, types, and equipment of the troops he was to provide, and he could expect the most searching periodical inspections to check that he had fulfilled the terms, and was not trying to fob off ignorant civilians with a stage army. If other condottieri were to be employed in the same campaign, he would need to know whether he was to rank as senior commander or to take orders from a rival. Subsidiary rights, such as his share of loot and ransom-money, would be set down in black and white. A *condotta* was, indeed, as individual and variable as a contract between author and publisher, with a comparable complexity of options, undertakings, dates of payment, rights, and responsibilities. 'Advance' had two meanings for a condottiere, and there was one that he preferred to precede the other.

If we are to attempt an analogy with modern professions, however, it might be better to compare the condottiere with the lawyer or the football-player. Each earns his livelihood by engaging in a succession of contests. The lawyer serves one client after another, the footballer transfers from club to club. In court or on the playing-field, he faces adversaries who may have been his friends and colleagues a little while before – and who may be so again in the near future. With the condottiere this professional *camaraderie* was transferred to the battlefield, which was often, but not invariably, much less bloody in consequence. There are some exaggerated stories of condottiere warfare, tales of hour-long battles in which no one was seriously hurt, and which ended with courtly handshakes worthy of Wimbledon. They should not be swallowed uncritically, since they come largely from Machiavelli, a military theorist notoriously biased against the mercenary system. But obviously the condottiere was looking for a livelihood, not a hero's grave, and having done his best he was not going to fight on to the death. Surrender held no terrors: as in all warfare at this time there was an accepted ransom routine, and a respectably established condottiere, even if temporarily short of cash, could often regain his freedom on credit as soon as the battle was over. Similarly, if he was victorious, he had every incentive to take prisoners rather than butcher the

18

8 Niccolò da Tolentino, one of the Florentine captains at San Romano. Castagno's painted monument, of 1456, is based on Uccello's similar monument to Hawkwood

(*ill. 107*).

DOMINVS PHLIPPVS HISPANVS DESCOLARIS   RELATOR VICTORIE THEVCRO3

fugitives. This was the general rule, but it would be a mistake to suppose that there were no exceptions. There *were* desperate battles and heroic exploits and forlorn hopes that were crowned with success. Condottiere warfare had its conventions but it never became either a ballet or a game of chess.

The question naturally arises, why did this special and rather artificial system evolve in Italy and never really establish itself anywhere else? The answer is complicated. Only in Italy was there the combination of political and economic factors which, coinciding with a certain stage in the development of military techniques and with certain conditions elsewhere, encouraged the ascendancy of the condottiere.

Most other countries, however afflicted by civil wars and dynastic rivalries, acknowledged one central authority. England, Scotland, France, Denmark, Portugal, Castile, Aragon, and most other European kingdoms had some ruler whose resources dwarfed any that could be mustered by a self-made adventurer. In the Italian peninsula there was nothing like that. The Holy Roman Emperor, for all his traditional claims, was a shadowy figure beyond the Alps, rarely and then ineffectively displaying himself in the Mediterranean sun. His ancient rival, the Pope, was for much of the fourteenth century an *émigré* at Avignon, and subsequently, after his restoration to Rome, only one of a group of temporal rulers, struggling to hold his share of the country. Southern Italy, true, was a kingdom – the backward 'Regno', ruled or more often misruled from Naples – but for much of the time this region was so riven with strife that its weak rulers were as dependent on condottieri as were any of the little duchies and republics into which the rest of the peninsula was fragmented.

Even the most miniature of these autonomous states required its own military forces from time to time to prosecute war with its neighbours. There are some illuminating examples in Daniel Waley's valuable study, *The Italian City-Republics*, of the early employment of mercenaries before the full condottiere system came into being. What is now a mere suburb, Fiesole, he records, 'had recourse to them . . . in 1124 when struggling to preserve her independence against her close neighbour Florence'. Waley describes how the Italian republics originally relied on their own civic forces. The 'nobles and other prosperous citizens' were compelled to 'maintain a suitable horse for cavalry service', and the rest of the male population from fourteen to seventy was in theory liable to serve as infantry. But by the mid thirteenth century the help of mercenaries, French, German, and Italian from other regions, was regularly invoked. 'The civic militia and infantry "host" lived on', says Waley, 'into the fourteenth century, reinforced but not superseded.'

21

9 'Pippo Spano' – Filippo Scolari – left his native Florence to take service under Sigismund of Hungary, rising to a position of wealth and honour.

If other countries found the feudal levy inadequate for their military needs, it may be imagined how the economically advanced city-states of Italy, such as Florence and Milan, found the mobilization of a civic militia not only an insufficient provision but also a burdensome distraction from the normal business of trade, manufacture, and finance. They had a particular incentive to delegate their military duties to outsiders who specialized in war.

Yet another incentive was provided by the chronic internal dissensions to which these states were subject. The old struggle between Papacy and Empire, that had divided Italians into Guelfs and Ghibellines respectively, might now be over, but the party divisions lingered, the names about as meaningful as 'Republican' and 'Democrat' in America today, yet still serving to distinguish the factions kept active in each community by class interest and family jealousy. Party conflict really *was* conflict, with coups, conspiracies, and riotous assemblies rather than orderly debates, votes, and elections. Such an atmosphere fostered the use of mercenaries. For even if the citizens had been keen to leave counter and work-bench to march against a neighbouring town, and even if they had had the training and temperament to make effective soldiers, no ruling party would have cared to hand out arms to the whole population, its opponents and its supporters alike. If this was true where a government had a rough-and-ready majority, it was even more so where a tiny clique, or a single leader, seized power and was determined to hold it by strong-arm methods.

The government, therefore, whatever its political complexion, found it prudent to keep the arms in the hands of impartial outsiders, who, so long as they received their pay, had no motive for turning those arms against their employers. Experience had taught the Italians that, if they had to trust any one, it might be wiser to trust a stranger than a fellow citizen. They had voluntarily continued a practice originally imposed upon them by the Emperor Frederick Barbarossa: the *podestà*, or chief magistrate, of a city was an eminent person enlisted from outside, who could have no hope of seizing power for himself and was supposedly impartial and incorruptible. This supposition was fortified with practical safeguards. Thus, the *podestà* of Verona was appointed for a single year, with an attractive salary, free lodging, and maintenance – but he was expressly forbidden to bring his wife and family with him, to dine out in the city, or to accept gifts. When, in due course, instead of recruiting their mercenaries themselves and putting them under a native commander, the councillors of a city began to hand over the whole business of defence to a condottiere on contract, making him Captain-General, they were merely adapting an arrangement that had proved satisfactory in the civil sphere.

These then were some of the factors determining the appearance of the condottiere in Italy. The great trading prosperity of the northern cities there and the lead they gave in the development of banking meant that for them (unlike some parts of Europe) it was easier to find money than men – though their resources, it is fair to remember, were by no means inexhaustible, and there were critical moments when even Milan and Florence faced financial crisis. Still, roughly speaking, it was states such as these that could provide money, while other lands – Germany, France, England, and the poorer regions of Italy itself, such as Romagna – had a surplus of fighting men. Warfare, too, was at a stage of its evolution when a relatively small number of well-trained, well-equipped men-at-arms and archers, properly led, could beat a multitude of patriotic amateurs. Such a force could be hired as a unit, at a predictable cost and for a specified period, by agreement with one or more condottieri. It was a thoroughly businesslike arrangement, with an irresistible appeal to the commercial genius of the Italians.

Who, and what sort of men, were these mercenary captains? Wherein lies their interest? For it is scarcely in the battles they fought, in the mostly petty and often meaningless campaigns that ebbed and flowed across the peninsula.

The first fact to establish is that there was no condottiere type. A gallery of the outstanding commanders is remarkable for its human variety: national origin, class, character, and motive are almost infinitely diversified.

Hawkwood, the reserved Englishman, dependable, strictly professional, and devoid of political ambitions, could quickly have adjusted himself to a British officers' mess in the twentieth century. He is the best-known figure from the early period, when the condottieri were foreigners – Germans, Swiss, Provençals, Bretons, Burgundians, Gascons, and the like – soldiers rendered redundant by the outbreak of peace in other lands.

Before Hawkwood died, near the close of the fourteenth century, the Italians were taking over. They came from almost every region. Romagna, backward and poor, was a natural nursery for the fortune-hunting soldier: it produced the Sforzas, Alberico da Barbiano, and many a lesser man. Colleoni and the dal Vermes came from Lombardy, Carmagnola and Facino Cane from Piedmont, Gattamelata from Umbria, as did Braccio da Montone, Biordo Michelotti, and the Piccinini. Less notable, perhaps, was the contribution made by Rome, Naples, and the south, but there was many an impoverished nobleman from those parts, a Colonna or an Orsini or a Sanseverini, who supplemented an inadequate inheritance by hiring his sword to the warring states further north.

23

Many condottieri shared that kind of social origin, being younger sons of great houses or, like the Malatestas of Rimini and Federigo Montefeltro of Urbino, lords of states too miniature to offer full scope for their energies. Biordo Michelotti was an exiled Perugian aristocrat who crowned his career by returning to rule the city that had driven him out. Alberico da Barbiano, a rung lower in the social scale, showed that a feudal knight, no less than a feudal lord, could adapt himself to the new way of life imposed by economic changes. Attendolo Sforza, father of the renowned Francesco, was Alberico's neighbour in Romagna and about his equal: it is untrue, as is sometimes said, that the Sforzas were peasants. But the great, though hapless, Carmagnola was a peasant, and Gattamelata was a baker's son. In their profession talents truly *were* 'the passport to glory'. At least one eminent ecclesiastic, the bellicose Cardinal Vitelleschi, has been numbered by scholars among the condottieri, and his record in many respects justifies his inclusion.

In disposition, tastes, and ambitions, these men were as diverse as their backgrounds. Sigismondo Malatesta was reckoned a monster of depravity, his neighbour and professional adversary, Federigo of Urbino, a pattern of humanity: both were passionate art-lovers and lavish patrons. Some condottieri, like Hawkwood, hoped for nothing but a peaceful and comfortable old age: when Cecchino Broglia was fighting for Milan against Florence in 1398, the agent of Lucca then in Florence hinted that nothing too aggressive need be feared and that the Milanese commander was open to offers, indeed 'looking out for a good feather-bed on which to rest in his declining years'. The shrewd Florentines were quick to make up a financial feather-bed. Yet other mercenary captains, by contrast, were consumed with the lust for power. They risked and sometimes lost their lives in bids to seize the *signoria*, or lordship, of a city and establish their own dynasty. Francesco Sforza, who played patiently but boldly for the dukedom of Milan, was the most conspicuously successful of these.

So there were treacherous condottieri and honest ones, avaricious and open-handed, illiterate and cultivated, calculating and impetuous, these last most attractively exemplified by the heroic Giovanni delle Bande Nere, Giovanni 'of the Black Bands', the outstanding condottiere of the sixteenth century and the best that Florence herself ever produced.

In any study of these men it is impossible to separate them from their employers, the Popes and Papal Legates, the Milanese dukes and Venetian doges, the Queen of Naples, the Florentine financiers, and the worried little committee-men in a dozen lesser cities who sought to achieve military security without wasteful expenditure. Nor can the backgrounds against which the condottieri acted their parts be ignored: Sforza must be

10 Sketch of a proposed monument to Francesco Sforza by Leonardo da Vinci.

seen riding his charger through the doors of Milan cathedral, Carmagnola meeting his death in front of St Mark's, Hawkwood's camp-fires twinkling from the heights of Fiesole, Federigo Montefeltro discussing Plato in his library at Urbino.

In fact, in reconstructing the lives of the mercenary captains, we re-create the life of Renaissance Italy as a whole. Oscar Browning was not stretching reality when he called his history of the period ending 1530 *The Age of the Condottieri*. But by concentrating on them as men, as individuals and as a special category, it may be possible to survey the familiar landscape from a fresh point of view.

What (it is only sensible to ask) do we know of the condottieri 'as men'? Our century has a healthy distrust of heroic legends.

We know more than might be expected. Though the condottieri themselves were handier with the sword than with the pen, except in matters of business, the period is well documented. The archives of Italy are stuffed with relevant state papers. Scholars have deciphered the confidential reports and offers that flew to and fro. Often the whereabouts of these grim-faced cavaliers can be plotted day by day, as they made their forced marches and stealthy detours through the hills, from the date-lines on their correspondence. The contracts are there, the strength of contingents, the rate for the job, the names of insignificant individuals like Antonio, who beat the kettle-drum in Hawkwood's company. It is by no means 'all' down there in black and white, but a surprising amount is, even to the small sums of money advanced to a man-at-arms or archer who could not wait for pay-day.

Less objective, but in some ways more informative, the contemporary chronicles put flesh on the bare bones of the business records. They add colour, if often it is the colour of prejudice, which the historian must allow for. The same battle may look oddly different in the chronicles of the two warring cities, but are not two eyes valuable for getting matters into focus? As to discrepancies in numbers of troops engaged and casualties, it was Galeotto Malatesta who realistically advised: 'Take the mean between the maximum given by the exaggerators and the minimum by the detractors – and deduct a third.' Herein lies the essential charm of the Italian Renaissance for the modern reader. We are dealing with sceptics like ourselves, men with a sense of humour to which we can respond.

So, looking up at Donatello's and Verrocchio's heroic bronzes, or admiring the warm colours of Uccello's stylized *Battle of San Romano* – probably a less decisive victory than the artist thought it tactful to depict for Lorenzo de' Medici's bedroom – we find ourselves speculating about the minds that once operated inside those helmets, the hearts that pulsed beneath those cuirasses. What were the facts?

11 Leonardo's drawings of warriors in fantastic classical armour are clearly related to condottiere monuments like that of Colleoni, upon which Leonardo may have worked when he was Verrocchio's assistant. But it would be hazardous to connect them with any historical figure.

The first Free Companies　2

'The father of all condottieri', according to the Florentine chronicler, Giovanni Villani, was Roger di Flor, the son of a German falconer in the service of the Emperor Frederick II. This verdict ignores some earlier soldiers of fortune sometimes loosely described as condottieri, notably the Emperor's supporter and son-in-law, the self-made Ezzelino da Romano, whom Dante consigned to the seventh circle of Hell. Certainly it was Roger di Flor who pioneered the true condottiere system, under which a free-lance general with a ready-made army offered his services wherever he chose.

Roger was born at Brindisi, a port that had flourished under the Emperor's patronage. His mother belonged to a leading family in the town. Frederick II, 'Stupor Mundi', was by then already dead. Roger's father was killed fighting for his grandson against Charles of Anjou in 1268. The boy, still quite small, grew up on the Brindisi water-front very much like the countless other free-ranging, mischievous boys who down the ages have infested the harbours of the world. One winter's day, when he was eight, he trespassed aboard a Knight Templar's war-ship that was moored close to his mother's house. Clambering about the vessel as though he belonged to it, he attracted the indulgent eye of the captain. 'Come with me and I'll make a man of you,' said the latter, if the very credible tradition may be accepted. It was a fair offer to an impecunious and venturesome orphan. When the ship sailed, Roger was on board.

During the next decade he grew to manhood in the service of the Order, then at the zenith of its influence. The Templars, despite their modest alternative title of 'the Poor Knights of Christ', owned property from Ireland to Cyprus and were the great financiers of Christendom. Roger learned more than seamanship in this congenial atmosphere, though to do him justice he learned that too, and ultimately gained command of the

12, 13, 14 Background to the first condottiere: the Emperor Frederick II (left) was a man of exceptional talents and very wide interests. Among them was falconry, upon which he actually wrote a book (below). One of his falconers, a German like himself, lived to serve his son Manfred and grandson Conradin, and was killed when the latter was defeated in 1268 by Charles of Anjou. He left a small son, Roger di Flor, destined to become 'the father of all condottieri'.

15 Charles of Anjou, brother of
St Louis of France, conqueror
of Naples and Sicily, the ruler
against whom the people of
Palermo rose in revolt on the
occasion known as the Sicilian
Vespers, in 1282.

biggest vessel in their fleet. When the Saracens captured Acre in 1291 he
rescued numerous Christian refugees and conveyed them to safety with
their treasures. Possibly he displayed too much private enterprise and too
little discretion. At any rate, he was denounced to the Pope for dishonesty
and apostasy. The Grand Master attempted to arrest him and seized such
assets as he had not presciently transferred elsewhere. Having lost his naval
command and been expelled in absence from the Order (which was itself
to be disbanded amid great scandal a few years later) Roger fled to Genoa,
acquired a ship of his own, and set up as a pirate, a profession for which he
now possessed the basic qualifications.

Before long, with perhaps a wistful regard for outward respectability,
the ex-Templar took service with the Aragonese King Frederick of Sicily,
then at war with the Angevin King Charles of Naples, to whom Roger
had previously offered himself in vain. He did well for his new master,
was promoted Vice-Admiral, and won the loyalty of the tough Catalans
who fought under him. But the twenty-year conflict that had opened
with the massacre of the 'Sicilian Vespers' ended in 1302 with the Peace of
Caltabellotta. Roger was redundant. So were his Catalans. King Frederick
wanted them out of his island, yet for reasons of internal Spanish politics
they would have been unwise to go home. Roger and his men realized
that their future, if any, lay together.

16, 17, 18 Roger di Flor learnt the art of war with the Templars, the knightly Order pledged to defend Christendom from the Moslems. Left: the seal of the soldiers of Christ, 'Sigillum militum Christi'. Below: Templars in battle, from a manuscript, and a Templar knight depicted in a medieval Spanish relief.

19, 20, 21 Throughout the thirteenth century the Holy Land, 'Outremer', was the scene of an unending struggle between Crusaders and Saracens. Right and bottom: Crusader knights in battle. In 1291 Acre, seen (below) in a Venetian map drawn some thirty years later, fell. Roger di Flor helped evacuate the town.

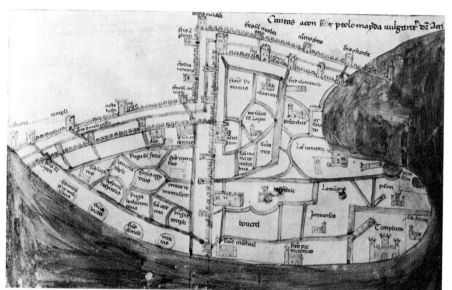

Thus came into existence the Catalan Grand Company that was to figure so incongruously in the medieval history of Greece. Roger knew that his late master, King Frederick, had tried to get rid of his unwanted mercenaries by offering them for an Angevin attempt to overthrow the Emperor of Byzantium, Andronicus II. If they could not find work fighting against Andronicus, what about fighting *for* him, against either the Turks or anyone else? The Byzantine emperor jumped at the chance. Roger received what the Italians would have called a *condotta*. He undertook to sail to Constantinople with a ready-made fleet and army. His men would be paid double the usual rate, with four months' pay in advance on reaching the fortress of Monemvasia in southern Greece. Apart from all financial considerations Roger would be given the title of Grand Duke, the status of Lord High Admiral, and the hand in marriage of Maria, the emperor's niece. He set out with alacrity, his command amounting to thirty-six ships and over six thousand men. Pausing only to pillage Corfu, then held by the hated Angevins, they reported punctually for duty in Constantinople. The promised money and Maria were duly handed over.

'Would that Constantinople had never beheld the Latin Roger!' Such was the understandable lament of the historian, Pachymeres.

For a short time the adventurer gave satisfactory service. That autumn he led the Grand Company into Asia and gave the encroaching Turks some brisk punishment before taking up winter quarters at Cyzicus on the Sea of Marmora. The winter was always an anxious season for the employers of mercenaries. When soldiers could not occupy themselves with the looting and raping of an enemy population, they were apt to make do with the people they had been hired to protect. Roger himself had the instincts of a pirate and did not set the best of examples. The next spring, however, he marched out with his cut-throats again and relieved the city of Philadelphia in Lydia, which was fighting for its life against the besieging Turks. His success, and his marriage into the imperial family, encouraged dreams of grandeur. Knowing the inherent weakness of the Byzantine power, he considered carving himself a principality. The emperor was in a quandary, not daring to discipline his uncontrollable general, whose troops were spreading terror among his subjects. To make matters worse, they were continually receiving reinforcements from the West, as the news got round that there were good pickings to be had. The emperor recalled Roger to the European side of the Straits. Roger obeyed cheerfully, for the Catalans had worked over that part of Asia Minor and were ready to start on the untouched Greek cities beyond the narrow seas. He made his headquarters at Gallipoli, and went up to Constantinople to complain about his rate of pay. For a little while he and the emperor

22, 23 When in 1302 Roger found himself with
an efficient body of fighting men but without an
employer, he offered his services to the Emperor
of Byzantium (above: the earliest surviving view
of the city). It was the first example of a ruler
employing a self-contained, ready-made army,
but one which Roger's employers, Andronicus II
and Michael Palaeologus (right) lived to regret.

24 Tomb monument of Cangrande della Scala, Verona. The Scaligers ruled Verona from 1260 to 1387. Cangrande (died 1329), Dante's patron, added Vicenza and Padua to his territory.

played a typically Byzantine game of intrigue, and one that a Westerner like Roger was ill-advised to try. Andronicus flattered him and conferred upon him the ancient and exalted title of 'Caesar' – the falconer's son was in fact the last person on whom it was conferred. But simultaneously, with the aid of his son and co-ruler, Michael Palaeologus, the emperor was planning his liquidation. Roger was lured to Adrianople, where on 4 April 1306 he was assassinated and his cavalry escort wiped out. It was by no means the end of the Catalan Grand Company, as the Byzantines had hoped, and as those interested must read elsewhere, but it was the end of this prototypal condottiere.

In Italy there had been mercenaries for a long time, mainly Germans, originally attracted to the service of successive Emperors and then often remaining in the pay of Italian rulers. Native soldiers of fortune were less conspicuous, though Castruccio Castracane (1281–1328) was remarkable. Exiled in boyhood from Lucca, he served Philip IV of France, the Scaligers of Verona, the Visconti of Milan, and the Venetian republic, before joining the Emperor Henry VII in his invasion of Italy in 1310 and four years later seizing power in his home-city of Lucca, which he ruled as a despot until his death. Castracane has thus more in common with the later condottieri who concentrated on political and territorial advancement for themselves than the leader of a nomadic force such as Roger di Flor.

The latter's true imitator in Italy was a Swabian knight, Werner of Ürslingen, who had previously served the Scaligers. Long afterwards, when the condottiere system was getting out of hand and various states were trying ineffectively to limit or abolish it, the preamble to an agreement of 1385 refers to 'this plague of the Companies, first devised within our memories by Duke Werner of Ürslingen, some forty-three years ago'.

25 Cangrande's nephew was Mastino II. He employed the German Werner of Ürslingen, who was largely responsible for introducing the condottiere system to Italy.

A little before that date, 1342, Mastino della Scala of Verona had faced the hard truth that he was not the man his uncle, the legendary Cangrande, had been. He must content himself with reduced circumstances. Accordingly, he made a humiliating peace with the enemies leagued against him and paid off the mercenaries he no longer needed. These, instead of dispersing, found a natural leader in Werner, who seems to have been outstandingly ruthless even in that tough assemblage, liking to boast of himself as 'the enemy of God and of compassion'. He had no difficulty in arranging with Pisa, then under serious threat from her traditional rival, Florence, to employ the whole company for the next three years. When that time was up, and the fighting with Florence had been brought to a successful conclusion, he refused to disband his troops, and the intimidated Pisans had to make what would now be termed a 'redundancy payment' before the Germans, more than ever united by self-interest, consented to ride away. They were now fully their own masters. They assumed the name of the Great Company in evident imitation of the Catalans, whose profitable operations had continued in Greece under various leaders since Roger's assassination. Werner himself, doubtless aware of the high-sounding Byzantine titles Roger had borne, styled himself Duke of Spoleto, a dubious claim based on the fact that a Conrad of Ürslingen had been given the title a century and a half before.

For the next few years the Great Company wandered through Italy like bandits, plundering or extracting protection-money from communities too weak and disunited to stand up to them in the open. The mercenaries, for their part, were not strong enough to storm a walled city or patient enough to beleaguer it. So in practice they stripped the surrounding countryside, the *contado*, of everything the inhabitants had not been able to take with them when they fled to the shelter of the town. Even monasteries were not spared. Two or three times in a single year, the monks might have to pack up their treasures and join the stream of refugees. Laggards caught outside the gates, men, women, or children, might be murdered, raped, or held to ransom. How much purely wanton damage the mercenaries committed before moving on – the burning of farms, hacking down of vines, and slaughter of cattle – depended largely on what inducement they were offered by the wretched inhabitants parleying from the battlements.

In 1348 Werner and his Great Company hired their services to King Louis the Great of Hungary for an attack on Naples. Louis's younger brother, Andrew, had married their cousin, Queen Joanna I of Naples, who, finding him in many respects unsatisfactory, was widely believed to have connived in his murder. Some even credited her with weaving the

26 Queen Joanna I of Naples. Her (alleged) murder of her husband induced the latter's brother, Louis of Hungary, to engage Werner of Ürslingen to invade Naples. With his 'Great Company' he ravaged the kingdom for three years before peace was made and he was able to retire to a life of ease.

cord used to strangle her husband and hang him from the balcony, and no one is more likely to have accepted this sensational version than her indignant brother-in-law. When she proceeded to marry the murderer, the Hungarian king wasted no more time and invaded Naples, Werner playing an important role in the operation. Joanna and her current husband (she was to have four altogether, but no children) sought refuge with the Pope at Avignon. Her subjects were left to the tender mercies of the Great Company. To add to the general misery, this was the year that traders brought the Black Death to Italy from Constantinople. Its impact on Florence is recorded for ever in the pages of Boccaccio. Conditions were much the same elsewhere. In Italy, as in other European countries, about a third of the people perished. Louis's soldiers were not immune. It was hard to carry on a war when, however slight the battle-casualties, there was another foe, invisible and inexorable, striking down the most impregnably armoured warrior. In 1351 Louis made peace with Queen Joanna and allowed her to return to Naples. Werner, in the meantime, had made his fortune out of the chaos. He resigned his command of the Great Company and rode home across the Alps to Swabia, where he enjoyed a few years of opulent retirement before dying in 1354.

The Great Company saw no reason to disband. They chose themselves another leader, and since they were by no means an exclusively German association – their membership now including men from half a dozen nations – it is not surprising that they elected a Provençal adventurer, Montreal d'Albarno. The Italians called him Fra Moriale, since he had once been a Knight of St John, until his expulsion doubtless for as good a reason as Roger di Flor's from the Templars. Morally, there can have been little to choose between him, Roger and Werner. It was in these first days that the condottieri earned the reputation for iniquity that their successors never quite lived down, though many later mercenaries were patterns of virtue compared with their employers and in some cases demonstrably reduced the horrors of war rather than accentuating them.

Montreal had taken over the contract made between Werner and Louis, and for the moment he held his ground at Aversa, just north of Naples. But the King of Hungary had now made peace and withdrawn, and within a year Queen Joanna, restored to her capital, was able to muster enough force to expel the Great Company. Montreal rode north into the Papal States, which not unnaturally (with the Popes in apparently permanent exile at Avignon) were in a state of chronic confusion most advantageous to a soldier of fortune.

The Great Company was well organized, indeed a far better fighting machine than most governments could put into the field against it. It numbered seven thousand men-at-arms and two thousand crossbowmen. They were paid regularly and, however savage when the looting started, were strictly disciplined so long as Montreal needed their obedience. There was a council of the most respected leaders: even the strongest of condottieri were seldom fools enough to ignore the opinion of their lieutenants. Secretaries and accountants guaranteed fair shares, just as a provost-marshal, regular judges, and a portable gallows ensured order.

Thus, Montreal was not 'selling his sword' to this lord or that republic. He was selling the services of an army, nine thousand men, a unit he controlled as perfectly as the actual weapon in his hand. He could withdraw those services as soon as promise them, transfer them to the other side or merely threaten to, using every trick of the bargainer. He had no scruples whatever about abandoning one client for another, no shame about blackmailing any community into the payment of protection-money. In 1353 he brought off the classic achievement of the unprincipled condottiere: leading his men on a circular tour of central Italy, he extracted 16,000 florins from Pisa, the same from Siena, 25,000 from Florence, and twice that sum from Rimini. It is impossible to express these amounts, or the others that will necessarily recur in this narrative, in modern values. The florin, originally minted in Florence in 1252, began as a gold coin when the use of that metal was resumed in western European currency in the thirteenth century. Its rival, the ducat, was first issued by Venice in 1284, though the word had been previously applied to an Apulian silver coin more than a hundred years earlier. In due course both florins and ducats were minted in silver as well as gold, and issued by other states, so that, what with variations in weight, alloy, and other factors (not to mention the ever-shifting value of modern money), these medieval sums are untranslatable, and their significance for our purposes is mainly in relation to each other.

Whatever the modern equivalent of Montreal's exactions, the total must have represented a fortune easily gained, and after that it is not surprising that over-confidence brought its reward in the following year. He had committed the Company to fight for the allied lords of Padua, Ferrara, and Mantua against Giovanni Visconti, the despotic Archbishop of Milan. Montreal felt so sure of himself that, leaving his army in Lombardy, he paid a quick visit to Rome to collect some money due to him. He could rely on the lieutenants he had left in command and he feared nothing in Rome, where that oddly extravagant character, the senator Rienzi, had just been restored to power. Was not Rienzi dependent upon him, having recently borrowed funds from the Great Company's treasury?

In this Montreal suffered one of those rare lapses into *naïveté* that can be the fatal undoing of the normally astute scoundrel.

Rienzi, the once brilliant, now bloated and infatuated demagogue, fated to be lynched himself a few weeks later, was eager to celebrate his return from the political wilderness with some strikingly popular action. Perhaps he remembered his old pledges that banditry should be suppressed and murderers executed. No less probably he remembered his borrowings from the Great Company. At all events, he saw to it that Montreal was arrested as soon as he reached Rome, tried as a notorious brigand and murderer, and promptly beheaded.

Montreal's death destroyed the unity of the Great Company. He had no obviously outstanding successor. Two commanders seem to have been elected, a German, Conrad of Landau, or Lando, and a German-Swiss, Annechin Bongarden, or Bonstetten. These names appear in the records in a confusing variety of forms. The contemporary Italian clerks and chroniclers shrugged their shoulders despairingly over the barbaric syllables they heard spoken with differing intonations and which often they had never seen written down. Nothing defeated them more completely than the English 'Hawkwood', which figures in the documents in a dozen guises, some bearing no discernible relation to the real name.

Landau had two sons, Eberhard and Lucius, dedicated to the same sanguinary profession. Neither Conrad Landau nor Annechin Bongarden was able to keep the army together. It required an exceptional commander to unify that polyglot mass of Germans and Flemings, Catalans and Castilians, Hungarians and Provençals – and even Italians. The Company began to split up, and split again. Landau and Bongarden reverted to their natural status, captains of their own mercenary bands.

The year 1354 had removed another eminent figure as well as Montreal and Rienzi. It saw the death of Giovanni Visconti, who had so notably combined the archbishopric of Milan with the political leadership of that state. His temporal power he left divided between his three nephews, Matteo, Bernabò, and Galeazzo, a classic situation full of potential problems, only simplified by the death in the following year of the eldest and weakest brother, reportedly accelerated by the other two. Even so, the Milanese domains had a ruler too many, and neighbouring states tried to turn the discord to their own advantage. Landau took service with Gonzaga of Mantua and rode almost to the gates of Milan, but he over-estimated the flabbiness of the citizens, who rushed to arms with something of their ancient spirit, marched out, and, aided no doubt by their sheer numbers, drove the mercenaries away.

Landau's not very notable career ended on 22 April 1363, in a skirmish on the bridge at Canturino. He was fighting then against a new adversary that had just appeared in Italy, the *Compagnia Bianca*, the White Company, predominantly English but bearing no real relation to the fictitious body created by Conan Doyle. In that year the White Company was joined by Sir John Hawkwood, and for a short time Bongarden served with him in uneasy partnership. But Hawkwood was a very different stamp of man from the condottieri before him. A new era opens with his arrival on the stage.

The English captain 3

'A poor knight,' Froissart called him about 1360, 'having gained nothing but his spurs.'

Hawkwood was some fifteen years older than the courtly chronicler. He was born in 1320 or not long after, in the turmoil of Edward II's degenerating reign, but by the time he was old enough to understand the word 'king' it meant the new sovereign, Edward III, whose French wars were to give Hawkwood's life its whole direction, and whom he always regarded, even from the most distant Italian battlefield, as his true lord.

His was the classic situation of the younger son, with his own way to make in the world.

His father, Gilbert Hawkwood, is described as a tanner. Tanners often owned some land and enjoyed considerable local status. In this case the family home was Hawkwood Manor at the Essex village of Sible Heding-ham, near Colchester and within about fifty miles of London. There was, confusingly, an elder son John. People used only a small selection of first names in those days, and it was common enough, when a child died young, to baptize a subsequent infant with the same name. It is harder to under-stand why Gilbert Hawkwood should want two co-existent Johns. Per-haps the second christening took place when the elder boy was unwell, and was conducted in a pessimistic spirit, bearing in mind the high rate of juvenile mortality.

At all events, when Gilbert made his will in 1340, an act usually, if unwisely, deferred until one's death-bed, the John Hawkwood who in-herited the manor was not the future condottiere but his elder namesake. There were other children to provide for. Agnes and Jane were already married, but Alice and Margaret had still to find husbands. There was Nicholas, who in the end became a priest. The younger John, who was appointed an executor of the will – he would still be under twenty – received a modest legacy and, like the other unmarried members of the

family, was to be maintained at home by his brother for one year. This gave him leisure to decide upon a career.

That was the year of King Edward's shattering victory at Sluys, a naval battle decided (just as Crécy and Poitiers were to be) by the marksmanship of the English archers, which littered the French and Spanish decks with corpses until men leaped overboard and drowned to escape transfixion by those murderous shafts. The story of that triumph would have lost nothing in the telling by the time it reached the Essex villages. Along with the whole national mood of the period, it may well have tipped the scales and turned the youth's mind to soldiering.

He could, of course, have adopted a trade. There is a legend, but no supporting evidence, that he became a tailor. It is hard, knowing his subsequent doings, to imagine his submitting to the long apprenticeship required in this and other crafts. For twenty years, though, his biography is virtually a blank. There is no reason why, poor and unknown, he should have left any trace in the chronicles. Nor is there any reason to reject the general tradition that, by about 1343, he was fighting in France, that he was with the Black Prince at Crécy in 1346 and again at Poitiers ten years later,

42

27, 28 Edward III's victory over France and Spain at Sluys (left) in 1340 marked the decisive advent of the longbow, the weapon which made England invincible at Crécy, Poitiers and Agincourt. Right: Edward endows his son, the Black Prince, with the province of Aquitaine. During these long campaigns in France the English captain, Sir John Hawkwood, learnt the tactics that he was later to use with such success as a condottiere in Italy.

and that he distinguished himself sufficiently to have a knighthood conferred on him in the field.

What is beyond question is that in those campaigns of the so-called Hundred Years War, which in fact dragged on with short interruptions from 1338 to 1453, Hawkwood learned the tactics that made the English invincible in the open field and himself so dreaded a commander when he applied them in a country where they were still unknown. He must also have proved his personal courage or he would not have been given his spurs, and he must have demonstrated his ability to lead men or he would not have emerged later as the captain of their choice. What he had clearly not done was amass much capital, either in loot or ransom, the accepted methods by which soldiers augmented their uncertain pay. 'A poor knight', insists Froissart. Hawkwood was never good at filling his own pockets. Although in Italy he was to show himself a keen bargainer, extracting large sums from various employers, he was often short of money. As his tastes were never extravagant, it must be concluded that most of these amounts went to the regular payment of his followers, another explanation for his popularity with the rank and file.

The Treaty of Bretigny in 1360 found Hawkwood in the prime of life, approaching forty, above medium height, broad-shouldered and powerful, traditionally with brown hair, brown eyes, and a ruddy English complexion, possessing 'nothing but his spurs'. That treaty, bringing an uneasy peace between France and England, likewise brought unemployment to thousands of his kind, English and Welsh, French and Flemish, the now surplus troops of both kingdoms. It was all very well for the great English barons to obey their king's instructions, disband the indentured retinues they had led to France in his service, and return to their estates at home. These commanders, says Froissart urbanely, 'departed in courteous manner out of those fortresses they held . . . and gave leave to their men of war to depart'. But where were the landless and penniless to go – men like Sir Robert Knollys and the Welsh captain, John Griffith, and Hawkwood himself, not to mention all the nameless men-at-arms and archers who found themselves stranded in the country of their late enemies?

The question found an obvious answer. They did what Roger di Flor and the Catalans had done in Sicily half a century earlier. They formed themselves into free companies for which, no doubt, the officially dis-

29 Mercenary troops were liable to supplement their pay by pillaging friendly as well as enemy territory.

banded retinues provided a ready-made basis. Their noble employers were replaced with captains of their own choice whom they knew and respected. They already had a pattern of organization and a code of rules governing such vital matters as the sharing of spoils and ransom. M.H. Keen's detailed study, *The Laws of War in the Late Middle Ages*, shows clearly that this code was not (as a modern reader might pardonably imagine) a special invention of the free companies. They merely observed the practices sanctioned in all armies of the period. Similarly, though there was no international law universally accepted, Keen shows that there was a whole body of conventions about the waging of hostilities and the treatment of enemies. These affected, if they did not always determine, the conduct of free companies just as they did that of more legitimate forces.

Where the free companies differed, after the Treaty of Bretigny, was in their lack of authority to exist and wage war. They continued to ravage France as though peace had never been signed, terrorizing the inhabitants and at least gravely embarrassing their late employers. Edward III had to send officers to seek out those lawless captains who were his own subjects, give them notice to quit France, arrest them if defiant, or – more feebly and probably more frequently – take their names.

Fortunately for Hawkwood, who always preserved a deep respect for his sovereign and seems never to have blotted his copy-book at home, he had moved southwards a year before the king's commissioners began their difficult task. Froissart tells how one great horde of mercenaries, which he puts at sixty thousand, first swept through Burgundy and then, in December 1360, went down the Rhône 'to visit the Pope and have some of his money'. This Pope was Innocent VI, fourth of the French-born pontiffs who for the previous half-century had found Avignon a healthier domicile than Rome.

Hawkwood went to Avignon with this horde. He is definitely heard of there in 1361. At Avignon he must have learned a good deal about the confused condition of Italy. The Pope himself, anxious to get all these un-invited guests off his doorstep, was recommending them to go there. They could fight for the Duke of Savoy against Milan.

At Avignon, too, Hawkwood and his comrades could see a shop-window, as it were, of the attractions waiting for them beyond the Alps. The papal city had become in itself a miniature Italy, sparkling with the wealth and luxury of the south. Tuscan merchants came regularly by sea and river from Pisa. Others were permanently established in Avignon, like Francesco di Marco Datini, later famous as 'the merchant of Prato', whose biography has been so brilliantly written by Iris Origo. Therein she catalogues some of the items that must have set the soldiers' fingers itching

30, 31 Francesco Datini (left), the merchant of Prato, controlled a business that reached to every corner of Europe. Above right: unloading goods before a fortified town in the time of Datini.

– the valuable crucifixes and mitres, the 'innumerable silver and gold candlesticks, chalices, bowls, basins, goblets, cups, plates, salt-cellars, forks, and spoons', along with 'the silks and brocades of Lucca, the veils of Perugia and Arezzo, the painted panels and gold and silver-ware of Florence' and all the other tangible evidence that Italy was the ideal hunting-ground for plunder.

Datini dealt also in arms, and since he had the businessman's impartial habit of selling if possible to both sides it is not excessively fanciful to picture him bargaining with Hawkwood or at least some of the other visitors encamped outside the gates. He imported much of his military stock from Milan, famous as a centre for the arms trade, but he also ordered lances, swords, daggers, and spurs from Florence, Bologna, and Viterbo, and sent one of his partners to Lyons to buy light steel helmets, or basinets, 'in the latest style'. Sometimes he imported blades from Germany and handles and scabbards from Italy, employing journeymen to produce the finished article. He had a Flemish craftsman, Hennequin of Bruges, who was kept busy making up coats of mail. The necessary components, studs, buckles, wire, and sheets of metal, could be assembled from various sources. Datini carried a large, but doubtless not a wastefully large, stock. The 1367 inventory of his Avignon shop lists forty-five basinets, sixty breastplates, twelve coats of mail, and twenty-three pairs of gauntlets. He was a shrewd dealer and lost no chance of profit, large or small. If a customer could not afford to buy, Datini would hire equipment – on

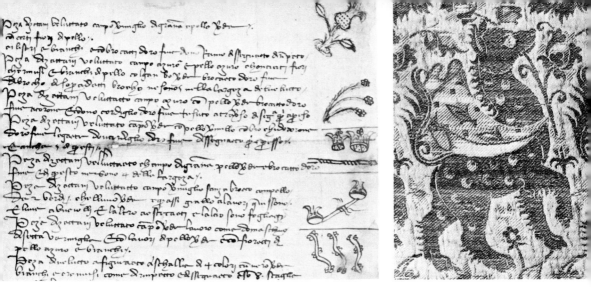

32, 33 International trade: a page from Datini's order-book mentioning brocade, and (right) Italian brocade exported to Sweden.

34, 35 A typical goldsmith's shop (below), and one of its products, a reliquary cross probably bought at Avignon.

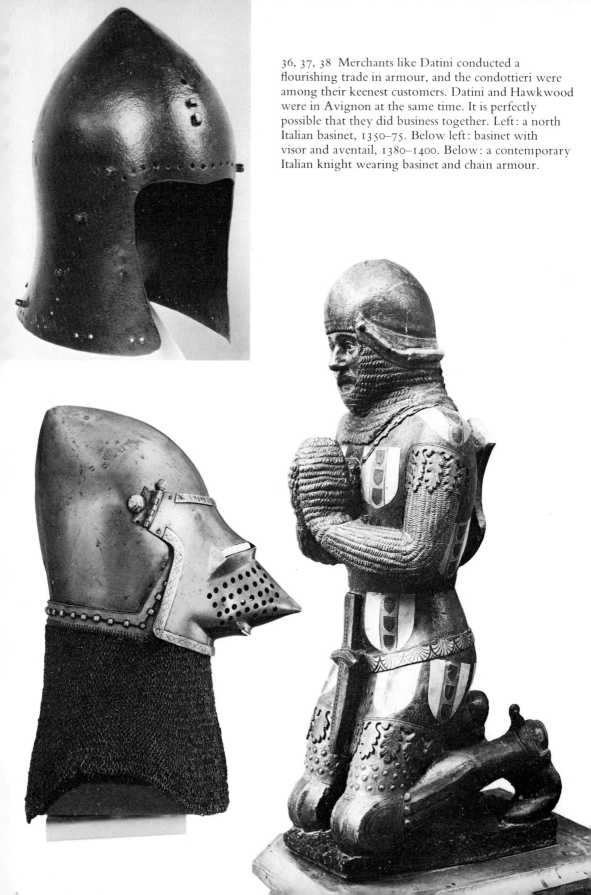

36, 37, 38 Merchants like Datini conducted a flourishing trade in armour, and the condottieri were among their keenest customers. Datini and Hawkwood were in Avignon at the same time. It is perfectly possible that they did business together. Left: a north Italian basinet, 1350–75. Below left: basinet with visor and aventail, 1380–1400. Below: a contemporary Italian knight wearing basinet and chain armour.

adequate security, we may be sure, for otherwise, by the very nature of the goods, it would have been a risky transaction. But in 1369 it is certainly on record that he hired a basinet and an old pair of gloves to the Sieur de Courcy, who was temporarily embarrassed. Much later, in 1382, just before he returned to his native Prato, the merchant heard that a mercenary band had been dispersed in Liguria. At once he ordered his Pisa agent to Genoa, with instructions to buy up any arms that were going cheap. 'For', he said, 'when peace is made, they often sell all their armour.'

39 A Milanese basinet, 1390–1410. Such protection made it difficult to kill a fully armoured knight, whose fate when defeated was normally to be held to ransom.

40 Pope Clement V (left), himself a Frenchman, was induced by the King of France to leave Rome in 1309 and settle at Avignon. For the next seventy years this small town was the seat of the Papacy.

41 Clement died in 1314 and was succeeded by John XXII, seen here receiving delegates from the Eastern Church at Avignon. During this period the town became one of the richest in Europe and a flourishing centre of trade.

42 The Palace of the Popes at Avignon, built during the mid fourteenth century and now forming one of the most splendid examples of medieval domestic architecture.

Whether or not Datini ever did business with Hawkwood, his accounts and correspondence throw much light on the mundane question of how, and whence, the warrior obtained his equipment. Clearly there was a brisk traffic all the time, new and second-hand, with an element of the pawnshop if necessary. When the stricken field was tidied up after a battle, the victors knew where to dispose of the metallic litter that was surplus to their own needs. Similarly, when peace came, however temporary, and the soldier had to travel in search of his next employment, he might well desire – or be compelled – to dispose of some of his heavier battle-gear. He would not want to take to the road defenceless, but he would not himself have the transport for all that steel as well as his personal kit and any loot he was still trying to sell. So, keeping a dagger and such other minimal equipment as common sense suggested, the ordinary mercenary soldier might sell the rest of his armament and rely upon his next employer to advance the cash when he had to equip himself again. In practice, however, the average man would not need to be doing this continually, for though one *condotta* might be short, for a mere six months or even three, it was often extended or at least converted into a half-pay *condotta in aspetto*, an option or a retaining fee. Tried comrades would stick together, if not in big companies at least in little bands, and would prefer to sell their services collectively as a going concern. But for one reason or another – if a man had been wounded, or a prisoner, or unemployed for a time, or otherwise compelled to raise cash by selling his armour – there was sufficient turnover to keep armourers and merchants happily in business.

Datini was far from being the wealthiest merchant in Avignon. The city must have tantalized the mercenaries, packed as it was with Italian goldsmiths, bankers, and luxury traders of every kind, and dominated by a papal court so opulent that even the cardinals' mules had golden bits – Petrarch declared that soon they would be shod with the same metal. 'What a city to sack!' was the thought going through many minds. But not all the papal funds had been lavished on frivolity. Much had been spent to give Avignon some of the strongest fortifications in Europe, and the Palace of the Popes was itself a massive citadel. It is unlikely that many of the soldiers were allowed within the gates at one time, and the free companies did not attempt strongly defended cities, having neither the heavy siege artillery nor the commissariat for such ambitious operations.

None the less, Innocent VI could have derived no pleasure from contemplating the vast encampment across the river, and he was quite prepared to pay an immense sum to the mercenaries to induce them to go away quietly. He also had to grant them a plenary indulgence, which must indeed in this case have covered a multitude of sins. One division of the host, numbering about six thousand horsemen and some infantry, marched away through the Maritime Alps to serve the Marquis of Montferrat in his current dispute with the Visconti of Milan. Another large party was hired to go to Spain, under the command of Bertrand du Guesclin, and remove Pedro the Cruel from the Castilian throne. A third section moved off into the Rhineland, where 'these villains commonly called English' were only driven out by the combined endeavours of eleven cities led by Rudolph of Habsburg. This description, 'commonly called English', is a reminder that the free companies were a mixed bunch and their victims were not deeply interested in their origins. Many a Breton and Gascon had been fighting for Edward against the King of France. As for the Irish, Scots, and Welsh, who in the Mediterranean world could distinguish them from their equally uncouth fellow islanders?

43 A fortified town, a military camp and an army with banners advancing from the hills: this vignette of condottiere life is part of Simone Martini's fresco shown in *ill. 2*.

Hawkwood's closest associations seem to have been with the party that went into Italy, but for some reason he did not immediately go with them. Froissart says that he turned back and that he fought at the Battle of Brignais in April 1362. 'Perhaps,' suggests the modern historian, Fritz Gaupp, 'it did not suit him to accept a junior position under the French Marquis of Montferrat.' Presumably he was by now a commander of repute, and subsequent events show that he had his own very definite and distinctive methods of waging war. Had he entered Italy with the first wave, it is improbable that his doings would have gone unrecorded.

Instead, the English – who quickly won for themselves the name *Compagnia Bianca* because they maintained their armour bright and spotless – began by serving under a German leader, Albert Sterz, who conveniently combined a knowledge of their language with experience in Italy, a country completely new to them. Their employment in the north did not last long, though long enough to dispose of Conrad Landau. Later in 1363 they accepted a contract to fight for Pisa, then at war with Florence. Both sides considered engaging them, and the Florentines regretted afterwards that they had not seized the chance. 'To avoid the immediate burden of expense,' wrote the chronicler Velluti, 'in the end, to our shame and loss, we spent six times as much, while if we had only engaged the Englishmen on our side we Florentines would have been lords and victors in the war.'

In their first year or two in Italy the English had won a reputation for toughness and ferocity – even their indifference to cold weather impressed the shivering natives – and the Pisans were anxious to exploit that reputation at the earliest possible moment. The Florentines were in their territory, and they looked to the arrival of the English for a quick deliverance. The English, however, had paused on the way, near Piacenza, to provide themselves with horses and arms. The ingenious Pisans therefore dressed up a company of their own men to look like Englishmen, sent them out of the city secretly, and welcomed them in again with the maximum display of banners, blowing of trumpets and furore of organized cheers. Impressed by this, the Florentines prudently retreated.

Soon after this, the English did in fact arrive, and it was not long before some of the Pisan citizens began to have doubts about the wisdom of their investment. The truculence of the foreign soldiers was well up to specification, but it was apt to be directed at friends as well as foes. If the Italians could not distinguish a Briton from a Breton, the White Company were not very interested in the finer points of difference between a Pisan and a Florentine. They were allocated quarters but would not keep within the bounds assigned. Anxious husbands and fathers began to send their wives

53

and daughters for prolonged visits to Genoa and other friendly cities that did not enjoy the protection of foreign soldiers. They arranged false alarms to keep the Englishmen occupied, sending them clattering out into the countryside to repel imaginary raiders, so that at least they returned to the city healthily tired.

This was how matters stood when, towards the end of the year, Hawkwood rejoined his old comrades. For the time being Sterz remained in command, but when a new agreement was negotiated between the White Company and the republic of Pisa, in January 1364, the soldiers insisted that Hawkwood be named as Captain-General.

Sir John's career as a condottiere had begun.

44 Walled towns could safely defy the mercenary armies. Siege equipment was costly and cumbersome. A manuscript of 1326 (above) shows a giant crossbow firing a metal bolt.

45 The soldiers (left) in the Lorenzetti's *Allegory of Good Government* at Siena might have stepped from the ranks of Hawkwood's White Company.

Pisa, in Hawkwood's time, was no longer the aggressive naval power that had once swept the Saracens out of Corsica, Sardinia, and the Balearic Isles, and ruthlessly smashed her nearest commercial rival, Amalfi. Those had been the great days when the Pisan merchants had shipped fifty-three full cargoes of soil from Jerusalem and spread them out in the Campo Santo, so that citizens could await Judgment Day in the world's most hallowed earth without the tiresome necessity of going to the Holy Land to die. This era of opulence and glory had ended, eighty years before Hawkwood's arrival, in the annihilating sea-battle of Meloria, when the Genoese carried off eleven thousand Pisan prisoners, and the bitter saying ran, 'Who would see Pisa, let him go to Genoa.'

None the less, Pisa in 1364 was still a city-state to reckon with, a valued ally for anyone in conflict with Florence. Both places were on the Arno. Pisa held the river-mouth and was then much nearer the sea, which has been retreating ever since Roman times, when it was only two miles away instead of the present seven or eight. Florence was about fifty miles up-country, where the Arno comes swirling down from the Apennines. With Pisa thus commanding access to the Mediterranean, it was inevitable that the two cities should be rivals and that the Val d'Arno should be the troubled scene of continual petty wars between them.

Six miles of ramparts enclosed Pisa. It was a prosperous place, had recovered its confidence since the disaster of Meloria which no one was old enough to have experienced, and could not foresee that its days of real independence were numbered. Hawkwood saw, more freshly, the architectural splendours that attract the visitor today. The Leaning Tower leaned – it always had done – but not at such an alarming angle as it does now. Tomaso Pisano had recently put the finishing touches to a job begun nearly two centuries earlier. The Baptistery had probably just acquired

46 Pisa about 1380 – a conventionalized panorama from one of the frescoes in the Campo Santo.

the Gothic dome and other additions made by Cellino di Nese, not altogether agreeable to modern taste but doubtless hailed at the time as evidence of civic progress and piety. The white marble of the Romanesque cathedral shimmered in the winter sunshine. Santa Caterina, San Francesco, Santa Maria della Spina, San Paolo a Ripa d'Arno, and other churches showed that God was not forgotten amid the chink of coin. Nor was good learning. Scholarship has long flourished there, and the influx of students from Bologna, twenty or thirty years before, had resulted in the establishment of a university.

Such was the city in which Hawkwood set up his headquarters in the new year of 1364. There is no reason to suppose that he had much of an eye for the students, jostling in and out of their lecture-rooms, or for the artistic achievements of the Pisani that confronted him on every side. His mind was on the spring campaign against the Florentines and the welding of his new command into an effective fighting force.

It is time to look at the organization and equipment of the White Company.

56

It was the English who introduced into Italy the term 'lance' as a method of reckoning troops. But if we hear that Hawkwood led a thousand lances into such-and-such a battle, it would be quite wrong to picture him charging the enemy with a thousand lancers galloping behind him as in some nineteenth-century battle-scene.

His men would have been on foot to do the actual fighting. And there would have been two thousand of them on the field, with a thousand pages holding their horses at a safe distance in the rear.

It took two men to hold the lance (the actual weapon) so that it would sustain the impact of a charging enemy. Hawkwood had seen, on the bloody battlefields of France, how chivalry could commit suicide when cumbrously armed horsemen flung themselves against dismounted men closely arrayed in favourable positions. He knew how the Black Prince had won his victories. The men-at-arms bunched closely, turning themselves into human porcupines, bristling with slanted points, no shields, four strong hands gripping each lance. In defence, they were forerunners of the British squares at Waterloo. In attack, pressing slowly and weightily forward, they were more like the ancient phalanx of Macedon. When the enemy finally broke, the pages could race forward with their chargers, and they could safely mount for the pursuit of the fugitives.

The essential complement of the man-at-arms was the archer on the flank. He was reckoned quite separately from the 'lances' but in the new English mode of warfare his contribution was vital.

The longbow, the traditional weapon of Robin Hood, most probably originated in South Wales and was adopted by the English with devastating success, first against the Scots and then against the French. Compared with it, the kind of short bow used by William the Conqueror's archers at Hastings was little more than a dangerous toy, while the crossbow favoured by most nations, though lethal and useful enough if its owner was operating at leisure from behind battlements, was far too slow – as was bloodily demonstrated at Crécy when the Genoese crossbowmen engaged by the King of France were mown down by the English archers.

Similar archers formed an essential part of the White Company. Their bows were as tall as themselves, or a fraction taller. To shoot, they rested the end on the ground, held the notched arrow to the right ear, and thrust the bowstave forward with the left hand, putting their full strength into the action. The long arrow flew with immense velocity and its penetrative power was appalling. It would go through armour and skewer a knight to his saddle. An archer could loose six shafts a minute if he had them stuck ready in the ground at his feet. A first-class man could have the sixth in the air before the first hit its target, and shoot up to twenty a minute. He was the machine-gunner of the Middle Ages. Not only was the longbow quick and deadly, it was accurate, and it was centuries before the musket could match it in range. It has been said that not until the American Civil War and the advent of quick-firing rifles did any army possess a weapon to equal Robin Hood's. Earlier in the nineteenth century some thoughtful person had suggested to the British War Office that the longbow might be considered for revival, but the imaginative suggestion had been pigeon-holed with characteristic complacence.

Why, one wonders, *did* no other nation take up the longbow? And why did the English let it fall into disuse?

It is one of the puzzles of history. In part, the answer may be that neither archer nor weapon could be produced quickly. There was an art in getting just the right taper to the bow, from middle to end, and in seasoning and treating the Spanish yew from which the best bows were made. The bowyer was a craftsman. The bow would be twelve months in his workshop. Then, properly cared for, it would last a lifetime and longer. The fletcher brought equal seriousness to the making of the long shaft, the fitting of the head and the goosefeathers, so that it would fly true and strike deep. And to become a good shot entailed patient and regular practice at the butts, which was enjoined by the English kings, who banned the crossbow and anything else likely to distract their subjects from this pastime. When Henry VIII became king in 1509 he frowned on hand-guns for the same reason, but he could not keep the tradition of the longbow alive. England was entering a long era of peace at home and did not send large land forces abroad. By the time of the Civil War (which either army, Cavaliers or Roundheads, could have won hands down if they had been the only side with the longbow) the mysterious crafts of the bowyer and fletcher had decayed, and there would have been few Englishmen who, even given the weapon, could have toppled a charging Prince Rupert or a Cromwell at two hundred yards. Yet to one of Hawkwood's bowmen it would have been child's play.

The same considerations probably explain why the French, Italians, and others never took to the weapon whose efficacy was so gruesomely demonstrated to them. They explain too, incidentally, why the impact of Hawkwood's tactics was not even greater than it was, and why he did not carry all before him. His experienced English archers were limited in numbers. As time took toll of those veterans of Poitiers, he could not recruit fresh marksmen from far-off England, nor could he train local talent in the same skill. The replacement of their weapons must have been difficult also, though we do hear of his obtaining some bows of good quality from Lucca.

Even if Hawkwood could have enrolled an unlimited number of archers, he would still have needed his 'lances'. Only in Sherwood Forest could a question be settled by the longbow alone. Ordinarily, if a decision is to be imposed upon the losing side and ground permanently held – especially a narrow-streeted town administered – the long-range weapon has to be supplemented with one that can be used at close quarters. Just as the machine-gun has often required the support of bayonets, so the longbow had to be used in conjunction with sword and lance. And as none of them was of much use against a fortified city adequately defended, and Italy was a land of such cities, it is not so hard to understand why Hawkwood, eminently successful though he was, never deceived himself that he was invincible.

Thus, the White Company was a balanced combination of men-at-arms and archers. It carried sectional scaling-ladders so that a mere wall would not keep it out, but it had no heavy equipment to batter down strong fortifications.

47 In 1363 Edward III made archery practice compulsory on Sundays and holidays. It was kept up in England until the days of Henry VIII.

48 Scaling-ladders were carried by mercenary companies, but were powerless against strongly fortified positions.

49 The fourteenth-century order of battle: trumpeters, followed by the captain and

As a unit, the 'lance' was a trio, the traditional trio of knight, squire, and page, but the senior member, in Italian the *caporale*, was not necessarily a 'knight' in the strict chivalric sense. A man had to win his spurs, and we often hear of quite seasoned commanders being knighted.

Five lances formed a 'post', five posts a *bandiera*, that is, seventy-five men-at-arms and pages. A commanding personality might have his own following of several or many lances, who would enlist with him *en masse*. A prominent condottiere would not need to recruit his whole army in ones and twos. He attracted these petty captains and their gangs. In

lamorofa

cavalry, with foot soldiers at the rear. The army is that of Siena, fighting in 1363.

negotiating a *condotta* he was in the position of a modern contractor, knowing just where to turn for sub-contractors. Such, at least, was Hawkwood's position as time went on and he became known throughout Italy. To begin with, he was in a strange country, closely bound to the fellow adventurers who had preceded him from France.

The *caporali* and their squires rode chargers. They and their horses tended to be less heavily armed than the men-at-arms of other nations, except the Hungarians who were more like mounted archers. But whereas the Germans, Burgundians, and Italians heaped massive defensive armour

61

50 An English knight at home: Sir Geoffrey Luttrell with ladies of his family.

upon the knight, leaving the squire with inferior equipment, the English pair wore much the same. The English knight gained mobility by wearing less steel, and this suited him as he was going to fight on foot and did not intend to hurl himself on horseback at the enemy array. Equally it suited the horse, and so did its own lighter protection. It did not itself have to meet the brunt of the battle – the *ragazzo*, or page, would be keeping it safe behind the lines until it was needed for triumphant pursuit or prudent departure. In the main, its function was to carry its master up and down the mountain-valleys of Italy. Hawkwood was to become famous for his forced marches, and they were made possible by the sensible equipment of his men and their horses.

At first, the Italian employers were apt to look askance at what appeared, especially to an unmilitary merchant and city councillor, the inadequate armament of these Englishmen. Was the taxpayer getting his money's worth? The *condotta* usually laid down in the most precise terms exactly

62

51 An Italian knight at war: a fourteenth-century relief.

how many men were being supplied and how they were to be equipped.
Inspections were regularly carried out by commissioners to make sure
that the terms of the agreement were being kept. It did not take the
English long to convince their employers that, however unconventional
their tactics and equipment were in certain respects, they knew what they
were doing and they represented a good investment.

The archers, besides the longbows slung across their backs, carried
swords and knives. Their protective armour consisted of an iron helmet,
breast-piece, and gauntlets. Like the pages, they usually rode a pony or
nag when on the march. Thus, as a general rule, Hawkwood's Englishmen
may all be thought of as mounted infantry, whereas other mercenary
armies divided more traditionally into horse and foot. Foreign men-at-
arms, before the 'lance' was adopted as the common unit, were reckoned
in twos rather than threes. Two men, the knight and his squire, constituted
a *barbuta*, the word originally meaning a helmet of a particular shape.

63

Whatever misgivings the Pisan councillors may have felt when they first surveyed the lightweight armour of the English, they can hardly fail to have been impressed by their dazzling smartness. The Florentine chronicler, Filippo Villani, was soon to write of them with understandable exaggeration: 'Each had one or two pages, and some had more. When they took off their armour, the pages set to polishing it, so that when they appeared in battle their arms seemed like mirrors and were therefore more terrible.'

A favourite contemporary detergent was the marrow from the leg-bones of a goat. Greased with this, the armour did not rust, and could soon be polished to the blinding brightness expected of the White Company.

Villani ruefully makes it clear that these were no parade-ground dandies but most formidable fighters. 'Bound and compact,' he writes, 'with lowered lances, they marched towards the enemy, raising a terrible outcry, and it was almost impossible to split their formation.' But, he suggests with a Florentine's resentment, 'they triumphed rather through the cowardice of our men than because of their own valour'.

He admits their discipline in battle but sniffs at their free-and-easy behaviour off-duty. 'They were all young men' (this seems unlikely – Hawkwood was in his forties and there is no reason to doubt that many of the Company were his contemporaries) 'and therefore hot and impetuous, quick with weapons, careless of safety. In the ranks they were prompt and obedient to their superiors, but in camp, because of their uncontrolled spirit and audacity, they sometimes sprawled about in a casual and unguarded fashion.'

One can only sympathize with Hawkwood in his efforts to impose some kind of order upon this horde of debonair individualists. For all his mounting prestige and authority it is doubtful if he ever completely solved the problem. Certainly as late as 1377, by which time he was fighting for the Florentines, his troops compelled him against his will to take up winter quarters in friendly territory rather than an enemy area which they had presumably already stripped of valuables. Within a few weeks the Signoria, the government of Florence, were complaining to him that fifty of his soldiers had ridden into Corliano and plundered the inhabitants as if they were enemies. Similar outrages were occurring daily, which they were sure would distress him. It was for the general to end this scandal at once, they suggested. He should proceed to the spot immediately. His presence and tact would be enough to restore order.

Like the Pisans fourteen years earlier, the Florentines found that the mercenaries were troublesome servants, especially when insufficiently occupied with their proper business of war. It was in 1377, also, that a

Florentine councillor warned his colleagues: 'With the English it is essential to move carefully, so that no scandal develops. As they will have to remain in our employment for a considerable period, we must handle them and behave towards them so as not to annoy them. For, if they are compelled to march against their will, they will do things to the commune that we shall not like at all – in fact quite the contrary! For the moment they have to be stationed here. We must endeavour to arrange that they move out voluntarily.'

The employing government liked to decide, whenever possible, where mercenary troops should be quartered. On hostile territory, ideally. If not, somewhere where they would do least harm and be in no position to assist a revolutionary coup by seizing the key positions. Above all, not in the capital city in any considerable numbers – though that was just where they did like to have the condottiere himself, in the quiet season, if he was not positively required elsewhere. They preferred him to be where they could quickly get hold of him (in any sense) if a crisis arose.

This tendency was not invariable. In his latter years Hawkwood was so implicitly trusted by the Florentine government that they used him and his troops to put down internal disorders, a duty seldom confided to mercenaries. And in cities where one man had made himself a dictator – often a man who had built up his power as a condottiere – he naturally felt safer with a bodyguard of hired strangers than if he armed the citizens whose liberties he had taken away.

The local population not only feared for its property and political rights, it was concerned (as already mentioned) for its womenfolk.

52 Mercenary companies might bring victories to the towns that employed them, but were equally likely to bring problems as well. Outrages by soldiers against women and civilians are among the effects of Bad Government in the famous fresco by the Lorenzetti brothers at Siena.

Celibacy was neither a rule nor even a habit with the mercenaries. The free companies were free in more ways than one. They seem to have had a considerable camp-following, ranging from women they had abducted to enthusiastic volunteers, and including even nuns who had been snatched from the cloister and were no longer fitted for conventual life. At the Battle of Brentelle in 1386 the Paduans captured, *inter alia*, two hundred and eleven courtesans in what might excusably be termed the enemy baggage-train. These girls they crowned with flowers and provided with bouquets – it was fittingly midsummer, and a delightful sequel to an unexpectedly easy battle, the Venetian condottieri having been bribed to retreat. The courtesans were led in procession into Padua and entertained to breakfast by Francesco Carrara in his palace. Life evidently was not all rape and ruin.

Of Hawkwood's own personal life, before he came to Italy and for some time afterwards, nothing certain is known. His long-vanished tomb is said to have depicted two wives. The nameless first one may well have been with him at Pisa, where he usually lodged at Martino's inn, a house respectable enough for the Emperor's daughter to stay there when she passed through the city a year or two later. By 1377 he had two small sons, whom the Bolognese held as hostages against him, and whom he redeemed with anxious promptitude. It is thought that he may also have had a daughter, Fiorentina, by this first marriage. But there is no scandal, no legend of amorous excess attached to his name, and in a period when bastardy caused no embarrassment there were no likely lads boasting (as they surely would have done) that the martial blood of 'Giovanni Acuto' ran in their veins. A stable married life was not impossible for a condottiere, as there is plenty of evidence to prove. For the rank and file it was perhaps not so easy.

The White Company was organized very much as the Great Company had been. Like Montreal, Hawkwood had a staff to assist him. His principal lieutenants were the German, Sterz, whom he had supplanted, and an aristocratic Englishman, Andrew de Belmonte, whom the Italians called 'Dubramonte', and credited with royal blood, because his gentle manners contrasted with those of his more barbaric followers. It was perhaps for this reason that Andrew had a romantic affair with a certain Monna Tancia, wife of one Guido, Lord of the Forest, but the identities and fates of these characters are no longer traceable.

The company treasurer was a highly important figure. This was William Turton, to whom, as 'Guglielmo Toreton', the chamberlain of the Pisan republic paid over the contracted sums. The names of many a humble soldier, 'Marco' and 'Marcuccio', the trumpeters, and others, are preserved in the Pisan accounts, though their original form and nationality are often obscured by the spelling of the native clerks. There was a surprising amount of paperwork and the treasurer needed the help of a considerable staff. There were negotiations with employing governments, reports, requests, instructions, and complaints. There were applications for permission to march through the territory of friendly or neutral states – a recurring necessity in a land that was a jigsaw puzzle of interlocking principalities. Within the company there were the accounts, the pay due to each member according to his grade, and a record of any monies advanced. The troops were apt to gamble and otherwise fritter away their earnings. If they got into debt, they might pawn or sell their arms and equipment, thereby becoming useless to their employers. Florence, at this same date, was meeting the difficulty with her own mercenaries. She opened a credit fund in February 1362, making interest-free loans of public money to embarrassed warriors. If a knight borrowed from the fund, two constables, or high-ranking officers, had to stand surety for him. The constable himself was good for six times as large a loan, if he needed it.

Altogether, Hawkwood and his administrative staff had to combine the functions of lawyers, diplomats, accountants, and paymasters. It could not have been done without taking on Italians. Sterz, with his knowledge of Italy, must have been indispensable in those early days. But Hawkwood himself became, in time, fluent in the language of the country in which he was to spend the rest of his life.

53 A condottiere in his tent. This Bolognese miniature (illustrating Caesar's wars against Pompey) was painted in 1373 and reflects with reasonable accuracy what contemporary conditions would have been like.

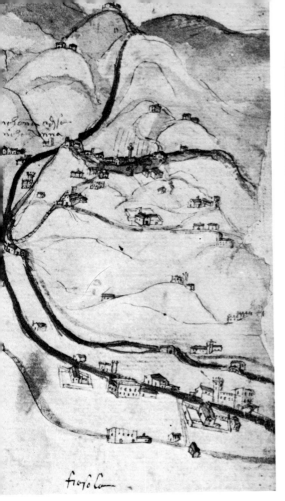

54, 55 The hill of Fiesole from which, in March 1364, Hawkwood (above) looked down upon Florence. The portrait is part of Uccello's study for the painting in Florence Cathedral (*ill. 107*).

Deep snow covered the Tuscan hills that February of 1364 and some of Hawkwood's men, underestimating the cruelty of the Italian winter, perished incautiously in the cold. It was only on the second day of the month that 'Giovanni Auti' (as the Pisans chose to spell his name) rode forth with his army. His total strength was about three thousand five hundred horsemen and two thousand infantry, his own company being combined with the rest of the Pisan forces.

It seems that they were not enough. The Florentines had invested heavily in the war. They had engaged large numbers of German mercenaries, commanded by Henri de Montfort and Pandolfo Malatesta, the latter being one of those petty lordlings from the Adriatic coast who so frequently became condottieri to supplement their meagre revenues. Hawkwood's men came off badly in the opening skirmishes against them.

68

In March, however, the Pisan forces were doubled. Annechin Bongarden, veteran of the Great Company, joined Hawkwood with three thousand *barbute*, that is, six thousand men-at-arms, also Germans or Swiss. In April their combined forces advanced on Prato, twelve miles north-west of Florence. Their probing patrols met with a smart rebuff. Hawkwood and Bongarden then feigned a withdrawal, and tried another approach. Pushing through difficult country, by densely wooded valleys and steep passes, where often they had to lead their horses, they seized the heights of Fiesole and looked down upon Florence itself, lying only three miles away at their feet. This must have been the Englishman's first glimpse of the city he was to serve so faithfully. It was not yet the proud city of the Medici – their day was yet to come – but it was a splendid enough sight within its circuit of ramparts, with Giotto's newly finished campanile and a soaring forest of other towers, but still lacking, of course, Brunelleschi's dome.

For the present, however, Florence was just an enemy city, and Hawkwood observed with satisfaction the alarm caused by his appearance so close and on the same side of the river. Barricades were being hastily constructed in the suburbs outside the Porta San Gallo. Malatesta had relinquished his Florentine command. De Montfort had to shoulder the main burden of the city's defence.

56 Florence in the fourteenth century.
Prominent in the centre is the Baptistery.

·CIVITAS·   ·FLORENTIE·

It was the end of April. What better date for the assault than May Day, that traditional occasion for festivity? Hawkwood and Bongarden, along with Sterz, Belmonte, and the other principal captains it was usual to consult on such an important decision, agreed that 1 May would be very suitable.

In Florence, too, it was normally a holiday. Apart from the May Day festivities with which most peoples hailed the advent of summer, there were civic celebrations to mark the installation of the new 'priors', or magistrates – these being not monastic priors but leading members of the various trade guilds. In most years they were inducted with much ceremony and municipal entertainment. But on May morning 1364, the bells rang only to sound the tocsin and the trumpeters had no breath for fanfares.

The attackers carried the outer barricades and swept forward to the gates of the city proper. Hawkwood and his colleagues can scarcely have entertained any hope of capturing Florence. The idea would not have occurred to them. They were not equipped to batter their way in, and even if they had managed it, those narrow streets would have been impossible to carry in the face of a desperate population. Far too many people would have been hurt. It never paid to drive the enemy to desperation. The capture and looting of a prosperous suburb, however, would have the ideal effect of satisfying the soldiers, annoying the enemy, and looking well in the next dispatch to Pisa. To the mercenary a knock-out victory too often spelt unemployment.

This is not to say that the fighting was not brisk for some time. The English archers took shelter in the houses outside the Porta San Gallo and enjoyed a shooting match with the Genoese crossbowmen on the city wall. There was some rough hand-to-hand work. Henri de Montfort made a spirited effort to drive off the attackers and was himself badly wounded. Hawkwood's forces retired when they were ready – when, that is, they had collected all the loot worth taking, and when smoke was beginning to drift across the scene from the houses they had set on fire.

Returning to their camps at Fiesole and Montughi, they compensated themselves for the delay in their festivities. 'During the night,' writes Matteo Villani, 'they had their celebrations and several of the leaders were knighted. Companies of twenty-five or a hundred danced with torches in their hands, which they threw to one another when they met. There were more than two thousand of these torches, and the bearers shouted and yelled, those who were near the walls hurling abuse at the commune of Florence, which was heard by the men on guard.' Hawkwood's men were having a high old time in the piazza of Fiesole, singing, playing

57 The Florentines' most powerful weapon against any mercenary army was money. Most condottieri had no hesitation about changing sides if offered sufficient inducement. Hawkwood was an exception, but even he could not hold the White Company together against the temptation of higher pay. This fresco shows fourteenth-century money-changers with their books, quill pens, and piles of coins.

games, and forming processions with coloured lanterns. Villani adds that for a joke they sent down a drummer and a trumpeter to one of the other gates, on the south-eastern side of the city, and sounded a false alarm, which made all the people turn out of doors in near-panic, believing that the enemy was storming the ramparts.

The besiegers stayed in the area for a week, pillaging and doing wanton damage to the young crops. The Florentines hit back with the most potent weapon in their armoury, the florin.

They approached the various mercenary captains with attractive proposals. In all, they spent 100,000 florins to split the forces arrayed against them. Bongarden, after some heated argument with Hawkwood, pocketed 9000 for himself and 35,000 for his men, and promptly deserted the Pisan cause. Some of the English were a little more squeamish. They began by agreeing to a five-month truce. Belmonte, of the reputed royal blood and romantic love-affair, took 5000 florins. Having neutralized the White Company, the Florentines tried to win it over completely, offering a six-month contract if it would turn about and fight its present employers.

Most of the English could see nothing against this. They urged Hawkwood to accept, but that unenterprising knight would have nothing of it. He had made a bargain with the republic of Pisa and he was committed. The army then re-elected Sterz as its commander. Only eight hundred men remained with Hawkwood. So the White Company began to break up. 'If they had not divided among themselves,' wrote a Pisan chronicler, 'they would have become masters of all Tuscany and all Italy, so fierce and proud were they.'

Hawkwood, left with the shadow of an army, could do little. Henri de Montfort was able to carry out reprisals by raiding and burning almost up to the gates of Pisa. The arrival of Milanese troops caused him to withdraw again. Soon, through the Pope's mediation, a sulky peace was agreed. Pisa lost on the settlement, but Hawkwood at least had saved his honour.

Bongarden and Sterz combined to form the Company of the Star. Within a few months of their deserting Pisa they were in the pay of Siena, the Florentines' other traditional enemy to the south. The Sienese chronicler records various amounts, large and small, handed out in the late summer and autumn of 1364. Among the lesser sums was the payment of 400 florins for Bongarden's horse, wine, and other perquisites. A large fee went to Bongarden's counsellor for what were darkly referred to as 'certain favours', and the Company seems to have charged extra for 'guard duties' and for 'injury sustained by some of the members'. One wonders what precisely was included in the basic fee. Ironically, in the light of the expensive Florentine corruption a little while before, there was a bonus of 10,000 florins for making a raid into Florentine territory.

And before long the Company of the Star was on its way south to Naples, in quest of fresh adventures and advantages.

58 Mercenary captains receiving their pay, a miniature from a Sienese official record of the fifteenth century. Financial arrangements were made with the captains only, who were then responsible for paying their own troops.

A man and his masters   5

Fidelity was the keynote of Hawkwood's character.

It was his fate to serve some monstrous employers, but he fought for them as a modern lawyer fights for his criminal clients, with a cool professional integrity unaffected by his private opinions. Having accepted a case, he could be relied upon to do his best. He was incorruptible.

The more one learns about him, the more he seems to resemble a type familiar in our own century and the last. He was reserved in manner, revealing his plans only when it became necessary. He could be harsh, but was not wantonly cruel like so many of his contemporaries. He looked after his men and inspired great loyalty. He had no bent for politics, but the professional soldier's common bias towards established authority, what he calls 'law and order' and its critics call 'reaction'.

Thus it was in the service of an unlovable little dictator that he remained in Pisa after the settlement with Florence. The city had been in desperate straits during the last months of the war, having no money to pay the soldiers who had remained loyal. An ambitious citizen, Giovanni dell' Agnello, went to Milan to negotiate a loan from Bernabò Visconti. The two men made a private deal. Pisa would get the money only if Agnello were elected Doge of Pisa and the dependent city of Lucca. Agnello, in turn, gave a secret undertaking to the Milanese ruler that he would always act as his satellite. The Pisans were in no condition to argue. They accepted Agnello as their doge.

'Never was a ruler more odious or overbearing,' says Matteo Villani. 'When he rode forth he carried a golden staff in his hand and wore magnificent clothes. Back in the palace, he placed himself at the window where the people could see him, as if he were some sacred relic – swathed in cloth of gold, leaning on cloth of gold cushions. He permitted, indeed compelled, all who addressed him to kneel as though to a Pope or emperor.' Another writer, Sercambi, hints that he murdered his first

73

59 Hawkwood's master in the mid 1360s, Giovanni dell'Agnello, Doge of Pisa, comes to meet Urban V at Leghorn in 1367. The Pope prudently declined to land.

wife as socially inadequate for his new role, and took a second bride of noble birth, but 'we will say no more of this lady, for she was so unhappy with such a husband that she did not stay a year with him'.

This was the man Hawkwood served for the next few years. To this period belongs the famous incident in 1367 when Pope Urban V broke the long Avignon exile by venturing on a visit to Rome. Agnello rode in state to welcome him when his ship sailed into Leghorn. Hawkwood escorted his master with a thousand men-at-arms in glittering array. Distrusting this show of force, Urban refused to come ashore, and put to sea again as soon as possible.

The doge had by this time contrived to clear out his political opponents and got himself voted into office for life. But in 1368 he fell, quite literally. The Emperor Charles IV had come to Italy and was passing through Lucca. As this city also came within his sway, Agnello hastened there to do the honours in person. The welcome duly took place at the city gates. They all moved on to the Piazza San Michele, where Agnello was handed a letter from Pisa. He stepped on to the portico of the cloisters to read it, but was so closely surrounded by his friends and followers that the portico collapsed under the weight. Agnello broke his thigh. Many of his party had broken legs and other serious injuries. Never has an unpopular government collapsed more suddenly. A delighted nobleman galloped post-haste to Pisa, barely fourteen miles away, where the citizens rushed through the streets crying: 'Long live the Emperor! May the doge die!' Agnello did not die, but he had to seek refuge with his

74

60 The walled city of Milan in the fourteenth century. Here Hawkwood came in
1368, remaining in Milanese service for the next four years, and fighting first the
Emperor Charles IV and then the Pope.

patron in Milan, and when the Emperor made his state entrance into Pisa
some weeks later it was a constitutional government of the old pattern
that welcomed him to the palace Agnello had taken over as his permanent
home.

Where was Hawkwood, it is natural to ask, at this crisis of his employer's
fortunes?

He was far away, and in no position to help. The reason can be explained
only by going back some months.

Earlier in the year Hawkwood had ridden northwards to Milan, on loan
as it were to Bernabò Visconti, who seemed likely to need all the troops
he could muster. For the Emperor's visit to Italy was by no means welcome.
It was a threat to the independence of the Italian cities. In theory they
were still subjects of these Holy Roman Emperors who, at ever-lengthening
intervals, would make the long journey from their domains in Germany
and Bohemia and try to assume in Italy the authority which had been
real in the days of Frederick Barbarossa in the twelfth century. A man
like Bernabò Visconti, who felt himself equal with the sovereign princes
of Europe, had no desire to bow the knee and revert to the status of a
vassal.

Bernabò was with one exception (and that a cardinal and papal legate)
the most ruthless of all the varied masters Hawkwood was to serve. It is
worth noting in general that even the most ruffianly of the condottieri
seldom matched the atrocities committed by the princes and churchmen

75

who engaged them. Burckhardt comments on the unmistakable 'likeness
. . . between Bernabò and the worst of the Roman emperors', and on his
obsession with boar-hunting: 'whoever interfered with it was put to
death with torture; the terrified people were forced to maintain 5000
boar-hounds, with strict responsibility for their health and safety'.

This autocrat was renowned for his virility. At one count he was
credited with thirty-six living children and eighteen women in various
stages of pregnancy. His beautiful wife Beatrice – whose far from negligible personality caused her to be known more usually as 'Regina' – was
one of the famous della Scala family of Verona. She could scarcely complain that her husband's outside interests robbed her of the attention that
was her due, for she was kept busy bearing his children, the total number
of whom varies with the historian. It seems to have been at least fifteen,
so she was probably well pleased for him to express some of his boundless
vitality in other directions. He showed a kindly solicitude for his bastards,
no less than for his boar-hounds, but he did not vex Regina by according
them equal status with her children. He was generous in arranging good
marriages for his illegitimate daughters, to well-established condottieri
and suchlike, but something superior was done for the girls begotten in
wedlock. They were found blue-blooded husbands, a King of Cyprus, a
Duke of Austria, two Dukes of Bavaria, and a Count of Württemberg.

Such social aspirations were inconsistent with any acknowledgment
of subservience to the Emperor. So when, that spring, Charles IV came
marching down through the Alps with a considerable army and the warm
support of the Este family and other opponents of the Visconti dynasty,
Bernabò was determined to display his power. He had recently built a
new fortress to command the crossing of the Po at Borgoforte, just south
of Mantua, and here he resolved to challenge the Emperor's passage.
Unfortunately, a quarrel arose between his German mercenaries and the
Italians he had sent to make up the garrison. Bernabò had to hasten there
in person to assert his authority and to install Hawkwood and his Englishmen in their places. The cosmopolitan nature of the armies at this time is
well illustrated by the Borgoforte affair: while the garrison now combined Englishmen, Germans, Italians, and Burgundians, the Imperial
army of twenty thousand men advancing against them included Germans,
Bohemians, Swiss, Poles and other Slavs, together with Bretons, Gascons,
and Provençals in a supporting papal contingent (Pope and Emperor
being for the moment in harmony), and the anti-Visconti Italians.

It was May. The river was running high, fed by the melting snow of the
Alps, rushing across the Lombard plain in numerous tributaries. Hawkwood calmly awaited the attack upon the bridge-head. If he had (as we

76

61 Bernabò Visconti, lord of Milan, one of the most ruthless tyrants in a ruthless age.

believe) fought at Crécy twenty-two years before, it may have given him some pleasure to recall that on that occasion the Emperor had been a young man on the losing side, and had been taken wounded from the field.

Charles evidently appreciated the difficulty of a frontal attack on such a position. Downstream, where he had set up an entrenched camp, he had a fleet of galleys and other craft to support him. The state of the river suggested an even better way of outflanking the fortress. Why not send sappers to demolish the embankments upstream, and divert the water into Hawkwood's defences? How far this scheme was carried out is uncertain. At least it had no immediately decisive result. But as soon as darkness fell Hawkwood countered by breaching the downstream embankments, so that the floods went swirling through the tents and trenches of the Imperial camp, and all over the low plain stretching towards Mantua, to which city, eight miles away, Charles had to scurry for shelter. His losses in equipment and provisions were so great that he gave up the idea of trying to force his will upon the Milanese, and he agreed to Bernabò's terms. So it was that, by the end of the summer, he was able to pay his peaceful state visits to Lucca and Pisa, as already recorded.

Hawkwood's frustration of the Emperor at Borgoforte enhanced a reputation already growing throughout Italy. His triumph could not have come at a better moment for the Visconti family, who were about to crown two years of patient negotiation with another status-building marriage, between Bernabò's niece, Violante, and the King of England's son, Lionel, Duke of Clarence, an advantage for which Milan was prepared to pay a dowry of 2,000,000 gold florins and hand over the lordship of numerous towns and castles in Piedmont.

It is generally believed that Hawkwood was present at this wedding, as Petrarch was, and a host of other notables. The dates make it possible: the Plantagenet bridegroom did not reach Milan until the end of May, the marriage ceremony following a few days later at the doors of Milan cathedral. And it would have been strange indeed if the English con-dottiere, who had just scored such a useful victory for Milan, had not been bidden to this particular festivity. The bridegroom was the Black Prince's younger brother and may well have known Hawkwood personally, not merely by repute. In any case, among all those hundreds of noblemen and knights who had attended the duke from England there must have been many old comrades whose eyes lit up on seeing Sir John.

It was a handsome wedding, mounted regardless of expense, designed to demonstrate to the world in general and to the English visitors in par-

62 Lionel, Duke of Clarence, came to Milan in 1368 to marry Bernabò's niece, Violante Visconti.

63 By the middle of the fourteenth century, the Visconti of Milan had succeeded in imposing their rule within a wide radius of their capital. This relief from a Visconti tomb shows subject cities, each presented by its patron saint, paying homage to Milan.

ticular the greatness of the Visconti family and the opulence of the Milanese bourgeoisie, whose interests they had represented and taken care of so satisfactorily for several generations.

Milan itself was about twice as large as Florence, a city of well-paved streets and splashing fountains, grand palaces and alluring shops, and a population of about two hundred thousand. Its cloth-merchants went as far as England for their fine wool. Silk was woven here too. Milanese armourers were renowned for their craftsmanship, just as some of the most prized war-horses were bred in the well-farmed countryside around. Nor was the Milanese territory confined, like that of lesser states, to this countryside or *contado* within a modest radius of the city. The precise boundaries varied with the fortunes of war. Roughly, though, they ran up into the Alps and embraced all the northern Italian lakes, with only Garda a disputed area, where Visconti ambitions came up against the interests of powerful eastern neighbours, the della Scalas of Verona and the Gonzagas of Mantua. At this date Milan had no seaboard: Genoa was still independent and did not fall under Visconti domination until a generation later.

Even so, it was a sufficiently impressive domain in 1368. As it was, so to speak, a standing set throughout the long dramatic chronicle of the condottieri – Hawkwood and his successors spent half their professional lives, at least, fighting for or against Milan – it is important to appreciate the pre-eminence of this extensive state, the sinister big brother of the Italian principalities.

For fourteen years the power had been shared by Bernabò and his brother Galeazzo, father of the bride. Galeazzo, reputedly the handsomest man in Italy, who had welcomed the Duke of Clarence with his long golden hair garlanded with a circlet of roses, his favourite headwear, was very much the junior partner in this political collaboration. The two brothers were in striking but not complete contrast, for both had some of the ruthless and deadly characteristics that made the viper so fitting an emblem of their house. But whereas Bernabò was a lusty, ebullient extrovert, Galeazzo was a quiet, reserved intellectual. They had divided their inheritance into spheres of influence. Milan was in theory common ground. In practice, however, Galeazzo preferred to keep his separate court at Pavia, twenty miles to the south, where his palace backed on to the cool-flowing Ticino and the park in which he loved to walk. At Pavia he continued to build up the library started by his uncle, the great archbishop, and to develop the university he had himself founded. It is not an unfair simplification to think of Bernabò as personifying the Middle Ages, Galeazzo the Renaissance.

Bernabò was to play an important part in Hawkwood's career. Galeazzo did not, except inasmuch as he fathered Gian Galeazzo, at the time of the wedding a sixteen-year-old youth, leading his cavalcade of knights in his sister's bridal procession.

Gian Galeazzo deserved a more searching glance than he probably received from Hawkwood on that day. True, he was a well-built, good-looking boy, and his father's sole heir – for Galeazzo, again in contrast with Bernabò, was blessed with only the one son and daughter. True, he was already influentially married, to Isabella of Valois, and bore the title Count of Virtù from one of the remote French possessions this connection had brought him. But for all the brave show he made with his knights jingling behind him, he was reputed to be quiet and timid, uninterested in military affairs, an intellectual like his father. All this was true. It was assumed that he would never count for much, and that one day his uncle

80

64 An allegorical figure of Milan holds the Visconti family emblem, a viper, or dragon, swallowing a man.

or his cousins would eat him for breakfast. This forecast, however, was profoundly mistaken. In time to come the condottieri would find him a man to reckon with.

In the meanwhile the wedding, unshadowed by future events, went off with a smooth splendour. Sixteen courses were served at the banquet, each involving something like a miniature procession, especially since at each course the guests were presented with some gift appropriate to their rank. These included richly ornamented saddles and suits of the finest Milanese armour. There were falcons too, thoughtfully provided with golden chains and velvet hoods. There were pedigree hounds on silken leashes. There were seventy-six of the spirited war-horses for which Lombardy was famed. One must hope that there were also plenty of varlets in attendance, to relieve the diners of any possible embarrassment caused by such presentations in the middle of the meal. Petrarch had a place of honour at the top table. But one suspects that Bernabò, in the classic role of bride's uncle, was really the life and soul of the party.

A long and elaborate programme of festivities followed throughout the summer. Most regrettably they were cut short after little more than four months by the collapse of the debilitated bridegroom and his death on 7 October. But as a diplomatic and political parade, and as a kind of trade fair for Milanese manufactures, Violante's wedding had been worth every penny.

Hawkwood did not stay in Milan for these prolonged junketings. Bernabò had more work for him.

The people of Perugia were at war with their Arezzo neighbours and with the Pope, who was uneasily and temporarily restored to the Eternal City, itself looking anything but eternal after so many years of anarchy and neglect. The pontiff was striving to re-establish the Church's authority in its own territories, a proceeding which inevitably exacerbated the chronic unrest in central Italy.

Perugia appealed to Bernabò for military help. He immediately instructed Hawkwood to provide it. There was one little difficulty: to reach the theatre of operations he would have to pass through territories not involved in the struggle. To get permission might cause embarrassment. To fight his way through would be a wasteful misuse of his forces. The simplest solution was to leak the false information that Bernabò had dismissed him and that he was making his way southwards merely as a captain on his adventures, hoping for employment from the Pope. In such circumstances no government wished to obstruct his passage. Provided his men behaved themselves (and Hawkwood saw that they did) he was welcome to march through, and the quicker his pace the better every one was pleased. Hawkwood had the guidance of Dinolo di Bondo Monaldi, the Perugian envoy to Milan.

In this way he was able to cross the territory of Bologna and travel without impediment through Romagna, and pitch camp in the valley only a mile below the enemy city of Arezzo. Then, whether through exhaustion or over-confidence or the sheer weight of the odds against him, Hawkwood suffered one of his rare defeats. The whole mustered strength of Arezzo fell upon him from that hill-top town. They had the help of papal troops under Simone di Spoleto and of two German mercenary bands under the condottieri Flaxen von Riesach and Johann von Rieten. Even so, Hawkwood and his men gave a good account of themselves. There was a protracted struggle, with no holds barred. In the end Hawkwood was taken prisoner, along with the Perugian emissary and many of his men. Von Rieten distinguished himself on the winning side and was knighted afterwards, 'as was proper to his most excellent valour', the official report assured the Pope.

This seems to have been the only occasion on which Hawkwood was captured, an experience that was almost a routine with some of his professional colleagues. There are no clear records of this brief interlude in his career. He seems to have been out of circulation for about a year. Presumably he was then ransomed. In 1369 he is to be found again in Bernabò's service, in amicable comradeship with the two Germans who had beaten him the previous year. Together they fought against the Florentines, defeating them by a cleverly simulated retreat at Cascina on the banks of the Arno.

Hawkwood continued to serve Bernabò for the next three years. But he seems to have chafed under too much dictatorial interference, and in September 1372, seizing the pretext of delayed payment, he abruptly transferred himself to the new Pope, Gregory XI. Within a few weeks he was actively fighting against Milan, and within a few months he had inflicted decisive defeats upon his late master.

Hawkwood's most unsatisfactory employer was almost certainly the Church.

The Papacy was back in Avignon. For the moment, the attempt to return to Rome and to restore the Pope's political authority in central Italy had met with discouragement. So, from the safety of his distant citadel in Provence, Gregory continued the struggle through his legate, the Cardinal Count Robert of Geneva, and it was from the latter that Hawkwood in practice took his orders.

A few years earlier, another cardinal had performed a similar task with conspicuous success. But the Spaniard Albornoz had been also an experienced military commander and a wise civil administrator. In fourteen years of patient work he had brought order and a popular government to Rome itself, and had tidied up the anarchy of the papal territories. In 1367 he had been able to welcome Urban V to Rome with a wagon full of surrendered keys. But now Cardinal Albornoz was dead, and chaos come again, and the new papal legate was the last man to charm the Italians back to their old allegiance.

A Frenchman, like his master Gregory, Robert of Geneva was monstrously cruel and treacherous. He did not merely believe that the severest measures were justifiable in securing the submission of the various towns, but seems to have derived a perverted satisfaction from using them. He liked to employ the Breton companies, who had a special reputation for savagery, but it was generally conceded that no mercenary, however great a ruffian, could compete seriously with the cardinal himself. The English were no angels: in their first campaigns they had given rise to the saying, *Inglese italianato è un diavolo incarnato* ('An Italianized Englishman is a devil incarnate'), but they were interested mainly in loot and ransom. They might slit your throat if you were obstructive, but they would not do so for amusement, and would regard it as an unprofitable procedure.

65 Cardinal Albornoz was one of those characteristically Renaissance figures – the warrior cardinal. Between 1353 and 1362 he had restored the Pope's authority in the Papal States, receiving the submission (above) of Rimini, Pesaro, Fano, Senigallia and Ancona.

66 A fourteenth-century mounted soldier, from a fresco by Barna da Siena.

Loot and ransoms they must have, for the Church proved the worst of paymasters. Hawkwood complained incessantly. The Pope answered his 'dear son, Giovanni Auguto' with bland expressions of appreciation, promising his 'best favours' to 'your most amiable person, who rests nearest to our heart'. As to actual money, His Holiness was working on the problem. Giovanni Auguto must exercise 'filial patience'.

Hawkwood was still writing a year later. His reminders were carried to Avignon by personal emissaries. His secretary delivered one, Sir John Brise took another. The Pope returned warm verbal assurances, conveyed direct to the general by his own usher, Giovanni de Canis. Aware that Hawkwood might not be able, with the best will in the world, to guarantee the forbearance of his men, the Pope wrote also to individual Englishmen on his staff, Sir John Brise, John Thornbury, Cook, and others who were constables or marshals in the company.

None of these assurances proved very fruitful. Hawkwood was in a difficult position. He soldiered on under the papal banner, partly in the hope of eventual payment and partly, it seems, to show Bernabò Visconti what a mistake he had made in his valuation of the Englishmen. Unfortunately, he did this so effectively that by the summer of 1374 Bernabò was thankful to secure peace, and the Pope at once made a somewhat theoretical economy by terminating Hawkwood's employment. Such was the common price of success in mercenary warfare.

That autumn Hawkwood found himself a true free-lance, holding his band together as best he could, and in every sense living off the country. To this spell of unemployment belongs the famous appeal from a poor nun, Catherine of Siena, who was to become the patron saint of Italy. This devout girl was a prolific correspondent, the more fluent perhaps because, being herself illiterate, she dictated the hundreds of letters with which she exhorted the public men of her day. In a relatively terse communication to Hawkwood she besought him to go on a crusade. 'I pray you sweetly for the sake of Jesus Christ,' she said, 'that since God and also our Holy Father have ordained for us to go against the infidels, you, who so delight in wars and battles, should no longer fight against Christians, because that is an offence against God, but go and oppose the Turks, for it is a great scandal that we who are Christians should persecute one another.' She urged that Hawkwood, 'from being the servant and soldier of the Devil, should become a manly and true knight.'

He would doubtless have been delighted to fight the infidel, subject to terms satisfactory to his company, but about this time the Holy Father offered him a re-engagement, to fight the Florentines, and who was he to dispute God's priorities with His representative on earth?

87

67 The capture of a town: a detail from a painting of c. 1370.

In accepting papal employment again Hawkwood was not as naïve as it might appear. His instructions were to invade Tuscany in May 1375, his forces at full strength and equipped with bombards, the massive wrought-iron siege-guns that – however clumsy – could lob immense stone cannon-balls at the enemy's ramparts with devastating effects. Florence trembled at the news of his approach. Hitherto, her walls had kept out the terrible Englishmen. The bombards posed a new threat.

Hawkwood knew his strength. He was not surprised when Florentine envoys met him on the borders of their territory. And they, shrewd businessmen, well aware of the Pope's record as a bad payer, knew it was worth making an offer. It was now that Hawkwood entered into his first agreement with Florence, the state destined eventually to be his most permanent and appreciative employer. Remembering their rebuff eleven years ago, the Florentines did not affront the rigid Englishman by bribing him to change sides. They merely suggested that, while continuing in the Pope's service, he should promise not to attack Florence. What did he think would be a reasonable consideration for so negative an undertaking? 'A hundred and thirty thousand florins,' said Hawkwood smartly. 'By September.' When the envoys recovered their powers of speech, they said that they must send home for further instructions. The answer came from Florence that they were to achieve an agreement on any terms. The *condotta* was drawn up forthwith and signed on 26 June in Hawkwood's camp, not merely by himself as Captain-General but by two marshals, one constable, and twelve other officers of his company. It provided that 'neither the Company nor any of its men shall for five years injure the commune, the city, the country or district of Florence, nor her dependent towns. . . . The commune pays in recompense 130,000 florins of gold of just weight and of the Florentine mint, of which 40,000 shall be paid in June, 30,000 in July, 30,000 in August, and 30,000 in September.' Thus Hawkwood learned the practical appeal of doing business with a bourgeois society accustomed to honouring its contracts.

Some of the other clauses are interesting. In specified circumstances the company would be permitted to march through Florentine territory, on condition of 'giving four days notice . . . and of marching by reasonable and fit roads, according to their destination, and under guidance of those deputed by the commune for that office; and that they shall pass amicably, paying the price of provisions and doing no damage; nevertheless, they may take wine without payment, poultry, and litter for their horses.' It was further stipulated that during their march 'the knights and men may enter Florence so long as not more than one hundred are within the walls at the same time'.

68, 69, 70 One of Hawkwood's most elaborate expeditions after he had transferred his services from Visconti to the Pope was the invasion of Tuscany in 1375. This time he was furnished for a real assault on a fortified city. He had siege equipment (right) and bombards (below) which could discharge stone cannon-balls with ruinous force against the enemy walls. In the event, the Siege of Florence never took place; Florentine money once more proved stronger than gunpowder.

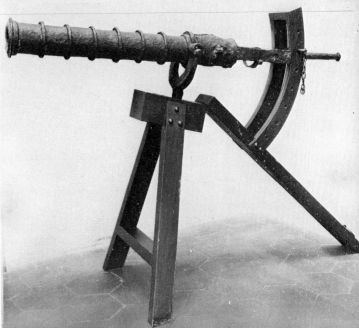

Hawkwood reaped a rich harvest that summer. The original deal with Florence led swiftly to similar bargains with Siena, Arezzo, Pisa, and Lucca. These non-aggression pacts yielded in all a further 95,000 florins. And within two or three weeks of concluding the main bargain with Florence, he negotiated a personal contract with Coluccio Salutati, the new State Chancellor of Florence, whereby the republic undertook to pay 'Capitano Giovanni Haukebbode' an annual stipend of 1200 florins – for the rest of his life.

It seems to have suited both parties not to give undue publicity, for the moment, to the harmonious understanding they had achieved. Hawkwood continued in the Pope's service, nominally at war with Florence, but somehow the opposed forces failed to make any very sanguinary contact, and the city walls remained unbruised by his bombards. In the circumstances it was not surprising that the Pope displayed no more zeal in making up the arrears of army pay. Hawkwood naturally had his own view of this. At Perugia, on New Year's Day 1376, he seized a newly made cardinal and bore him off to Rimini as a living pledge for the money due. To forestall any allegation of pilfering, he had a full inventory made of this prelate's personal baggage, which included not merely such standard items as a mitre and rosary but, less explicably, several women's gowns. Even this strong action produced no cash, but the Pope granted him two estates in Romagna, thus making Hawkwood the first foreign condottiere to hold land in Italy. By the next year, however, the Englishman's patience was wearing thin. If only he had quitted the papal service a few months sooner, he would have avoided the ugliest blot on his reputation, his share in the atrocities at Cesena.

This hapless town, situated on the old Roman highway slanting across to Rimini, was at first occupied by Robert of Geneva and his favourite Bretons. When these mercenaries began looting, and were strongly resisted by the citizens, the Cardinal Legate resorted to a trick. Swearing a solemn oath on his cardinal's hat, he persuaded the people to hand in their weapons. He still further won their confidence by asking for fifty hostages and then immediately releasing them as evidence of his humanity.

He was now nearly ready to take his revenge. He merely lacked sufficient butchers for so large a population. He sent for Hawkwood, who was at the neighbouring city of Faenza, and received him after darkness in the Murata fortress. He required the English, he explained, to join with the Bretons and 'administer justice'. Hawkwood, not fully aware of the latest situation but guessing the Cardinal Legate's intentions, answered that he was quite sure he could persuade the citizens to lay down their arms and return to their obedience. The cardinal retorted that they were already disarmed. By 'justice' he meant 'blood and more blood'. Hawkwood continued to protest, but in the end the professional soldier overcame the man: he was in the Pope's service, despite all those arrears in pay, and he had never yet broken a contract.

So Hawkwood and his company joined the Bretons in the sack of the city and the massacre of its inhabitants which lasted for three ghastly days. The English were as eager for plunder as anyone else – indeed, Hawkwood could scarcely have refused them this chance without losing his position of command – but many of them had no relish for the killing. Wherever possible, they gave the people a chance to escape with their lives, and even a hostile chronicler concedes that Hawkwood himself, 'not to be held entirely infamous, sent about a thousand of the women to Rimini'. The Bretons were more bloodthirsty and carried out their instructions to the letter. The squares of Cesena were heaped with bodies. The moats were full of refugees who drowned because they could not face the dripping swords that barred their escape across the bridges.

71 The fortress of Cesena, scene of Hawkwood's last, and least creditable, action in the service of the Pope (while at the same time receiving money from Florence). In 1377, on the insistence of the papal legate, Cardinal Robert of Geneva, he systematically sacked the town and massacred its inhabitants.

To the nineteenth-century historians Hawkwood's connection with this business, however reluctant it may have been, was a source of great embarrassment. To those of the twentieth century, recording the inhumanities committed in their own era by commanders of many nations pleading the excuse of superior orders, this 'war crime' of a medieval condottiere, while not losing its horror, becomes at least more comprehensible.

It is a relief, none the less, to be able to recall that a month or two later Hawkwood left the papal service.

He was thus spared a conflict of loyalties when, in the following year (1378), Pope Gregory died while in Rome, thereby upsetting all the calculations of the clique entrenched at Avignon and providing their opponents with the opportunity to hold the conclave in its traditional place once more. The resulting election, being dominated by the Roman mob outside, led to the defeat of the French cardinals and the choice of an Italian pontiff again, Urban VI. The dissenting cardinals thereupon withdrew to Fondi, held a conclave of their own, declared the previous election invalid, and felt divinely guided to choose, of all people, Cardinal Robert of Geneva. The butcher of Cesena took the style of Clement VII, under which he is officially listed among the Anti-Popes. The rivals then excommunicated each other (starting the forty-year-long Great Schism) and fought a bitter struggle through mercenaries. Clement's Bretons were trounced by an Italian company led by Alberico da Barbiano, of whom much more was to be heard, and Clement retreated to Avignon, where he eventually outlived Hawkwood by a few months.

72 In 1378 Pope Gregory XI died and the Catholic Church split into two factions, one electing Urban VI, the other Robert of Geneva, who took the name of Clement VII. Right: his coronation. The Great Schism, thus initiated, continued until 1417. Clement's party was eventually disowned by the Church and its leaders branded as 'Anti-Popes'.

The general at home   6

'Last Sunday,' reported Lodovico Gonzaga's ambassador at Milan, in May 1377, 'Sir John Hawkwood conducted a bride with all honours to the house where he was living, the former residence of the late Bishop of Parma.'

This was the general's second marriage. It took place within a few months of the Cesena massacre and a few weeks of his quitting the Pope's service. He had returned to the banner of Bernabò Visconti, and the wedding was another seal upon his contract. The bride was Donnina, one of five illegitimate children born to Visconti by his mistress Porina, herself the daughter of a Milanese nobleman, Leone Porro. It was Bernabò's habit, as already mentioned, to cement the loyalty of his condottieri by marrying them to his bastards, reserving his lawful offspring for the royal beds of Europe. His daughter Elizabeth was given, possibly on this same day in a double ceremony, to Count Lucius Landau, Hawkwood's respected colleague in the mercenary profession. On other occasions Riccarda married Bertrand de la Sale, one of the bloodthirsty Breton captains, and Enrica and Isotta were found equally formidable husbands.

There was never the least embarrassment about the brides' parentage. Regina must have become quite accustomed to her own special status at these weddings. 'The wedding was honoured by the presence of the lady duchess,' went on the ambassador, 'and all the daughters of Signor Bernabò. After the dinner, the said lord Signor Bernabò with his Porina went to Sir John's house, where jousting was in progress all day. They tell me that after dinner the lady Regina made a present to the bride of a thousand gold ducats in a vase.' The Signor Marco and the Signor Luigi, he continued, each gave pearls to the value of 300 ducats. These young men were the bride's legitimate half-brothers: manifestly, Bernabò's family was not only varied and numerous but also united. But, the ambassador concluded, 'they had no dancing, out of respect for the late lady Taddea'. Taddea's identity is uncertain, but it is noteworthy that some at least of the conventions were maintained.

Donnina herself took pride in her illustrious if irregular parentage. She described herself thereafter as 'Donnina Visconti of Milan, consort of Sir John Hawkwood'. The latter, with the complacence of his class and nation, was usually content to subscribe himself *miles anglicus* ('English knight'). Since Crécy and Poitiers, he may have reasoned, who could go higher than that?

The honeymoon was spent at Cremona. That city happened to be convenient for the military preparations involved in his next assignment. This was part of the general campaign against his last employer, the Pope, a campaign in which Milan was allied with Florence and a number of other cities, many of them paying their own contributions into Hawkwood's purse. He was recognized now as the foremost commander in Italy. His gross income was 250,000 florins per year.

He still held the estates the Pope had granted him in lieu of cash, and these provided him with a permanent home, where Donnina could quite literally 'hold the fort' during his absence and bring up the children as they arrived, first Janet, then Catherine, Anna, and John.

These possessions lay in the flat country that stretches from the die-straight Via Emilia and the Apennines across to the melancholy marshes and lagoons bordering the sea round Ravenna. One estate was at Bagnacavallo, where centuries later Byron's Allegra was to die of fever at her convent-school. The other was a few miles distant at Cotignola. Here, a year before his marriage, Hawkwood had taken over a dilapidated little town and refortified it, adding new walls and a deep moat to enclose five times as large an area, and constructing a positive stronghold, complete with dungeons, for his personal safety. The boundary-extension necessitated his taking over some land from a neighbour and duly compensating him. This man's family was destined to figure frequently in the chronicles of the condottieri under the name which was adopted by his son, Sforza.

That son was Muzio, the accommodating neighbour himself was Giovanni Attendolo. Muzio – one day to have a still more famous son, Francesco, the first of the Sforza dukes – was born on 10 June 1369, and was therefore a child when the illustrious Englishman came to Cotignola and put those impressive alterations in hand. Enemies in after-years, keen to belittle the family, sneered at the Attendoli as humble peasants. They were undoubtedly rough folk, but Giovanni must have been a man of some substance or there would have been no transfer of land to Hawkwood.

94

73 The first of the Sforzas: Muzio Attendolo (right) took the name of Sforza ('force') when he became a mercenary captain.

FVLMEN · BELLI

IN · MEMORIA · ETERNA · ERIT · IVSTVS

SFORTIA · ATENDOLVS ·
ITALICORÛ · DVCVM
CLARISSIMVS ·

The impoverished country of Romagna was a seed-bed for condottieri. Another near neighbour was Count Giovanni da Barbiano, who held the castle of Cunio. His more celebrated brother, Alberico, was in the end to have a greater influence even than Hawkwood upon the development of Italian warfare over the next century. Alberico had already won recognition: he too had received letters of well-meaning but foredoomed admonition from Catherine of Siena. He had taken part, with his two hundred lances, in the massacre at Cesena. A year later he had changed sides, like Hawkwood, and was under contract to Bernabò, fighting against Bernabò's in-laws, the Scaligers of Verona, a conflict in which the militant lady Regina gave her husband every encouragement against her own kin. Alberico da Barbiano was sometimes Hawkwood's comrade-in-arms, sometimes his opponent. This would not have precluded their being good neighbours at home in Romagna, or even warm friends, but it is not unlikely that between these particular condottieri there was, at least on da Barbiano's side, a basic lack of sympathy. Alberico was an Italian knight, poor in means but proud of the tradition to which he belonged. He neither liked nor understood Hawkwood's passion for dismounting his troops before battle. It was ungentlemanly, it undermined the status of the warrior caste. No less did he resent the domination of the country by foreign adventurers. In 1379, heading his own newly formed and all-Italian Compagnia di San Giorgio, he won a notable victory over Anti-Pope Clement's favourite Bretons, which so pleased Pope Urban that he presented Alberico with a banner optimistically inscribed *Italy Freed from the Foreigners*. One way and another, it seems improbable that Hawkwood and Alberico saw eye to eye on the issues most affecting them.

With such neighbours on his doorstep, and with a similar condottiere family evolving in almost every town in that region – a Malatesta in Rimini, a da Polenta in Ravenna, an Ordelaffi at Forlì – Hawkwood wisely took precautions to safeguard his estates, particularly now that he was no longer serving the Papacy from which he had received them. He garrisoned them with trusted Englishmen from his company, and saw that they were well supplied. Soon after his wedding, he dispatched a consignment of arms to Bagnacavallo, including battle-axes and crossbows. He knew the value of the latter weapon in its right context. In the following year he requested a safe-conduct for a flotilla of six boats that were going down the Po to Ferrara, loaded with additional arms, tools, corn, timber, and other cargo intended for his estates. Bagnacavallo and Cotignola would not in themselves produce great revenues. They would supply him with wine, provisions, and local labour – they were the equivalent of a couple of manors held by an English lord – but they would

97

74 Ostasio da Polenta, lord of Ravenna between 1390 and his death in 1396. His tomb shows him in the pious habit of a Franciscan friar.

75, 76, 77 Hawkwood's neighbours included the condottiere families of Ordelaffi and Malatesta, then establishing themselves in castles at Forlì (above) and Rimini (below left). The defence of his own estates was not neglected; he built the tower (below right) at Cotignola.

78 Rural pursuits: cleaning out the wine-barrels, from an Italian manuscript.

not maintain him in any luxury. That was why similar native landlords turned condottiere. To possess two homes within a few miles might seem odd to us today, but, apart from doubling his local supplies, they provided certain practical advantages, notably for the thorough cleaning of one house while the family were occupying another. Even in the cooler climate of England, the medieval sanitary arrangements made it desirable to own more than one castle, if only to offer a change of air.

Hawkwood's period as a Romagnol lord lasted only a few years. His relationship with Bernabò, renewed so auspiciously at the time of his marriage, seems never to have been an easy one. Hawkwood turned more and more towards Florence. It was while he was at home with Donnina at Bagnacavallo, in the autumn of 1379, that a singular incident occurred, the full facts of which are unlikely to be discoverable now.

Hawkwood, it seems, wrote confidentially to the Signoria, warning them of 'great conspiracies afoot in Florence', a suggestion which must have alarmed, but hardly surprised, the government, since the city had been bubbling like a volcano for some time. It will be noticed that this was the year following the suppression of the historic revolt by the *ciompi*, or wool-carders, against the domination of the wealthier merchant class, an event marked by mob violence and every sort of political reprisal that accompanies an outbreak of class war. When, therefore, Hawkwood informed the city councillors that the opposition faction were plotting with their exiled comrades in Bologna to produce a revolution supported by the *ciompi*, there was no disposition to make light of his warning.

He had the whole story, he assured them, from a most reliable informant who must remain nameless. This too was plausible enough. Hawkwood's mobile life gave him contacts everywhere. His detachment from the ordinary quarrels of Italy made him an impartial listener. His own taciturn and discreet habit encouraged men to trust him with confidences. As a military commander, he set a high value on information, on which many of his brilliant forced marches and other manoeuvres depended for their success. Some years after this, Giovanni Cavalcanti mentions in his history of Florence the well-organized spy service that Hawkwood had built up, and it is recorded that in 1388 this enabled him to save the life of Bernabò's son, Carlo Visconti, from the poison put into his breakfast figs by his doctor at the instigation of a cousin.

On the present occasion Hawkwood offered to sell the whole story of the conspiracy for 50,000 florins and an amnesty for any six individuals he chose to name. Alternatively, there could be an economy package: a general outline of the plot, without a full list of the plotters, for 20,000 florins. In either case the Signoria of Florence must dispatch their own plenipotentiary to Bagnacavallo for the anonymous informer to reveal all – or rather all that was paid for. For reasons not hard to imagine, he preferred not to appear in the city itself.

Guccio Gucci, a rich and reliable citizen, was deputed to handle this delicate transaction. He duly arrived at Hawkwood's Romagnol home, and, had the affair lent itself to a public communiqué, it would no doubt have been announced that talks had opened 'in a frank and friendly atmosphere'. They went slowly, however, as such negotiations are apt to do. Though keen to save his country from disaster, Gucci had instructions to save it as cheaply as possible. The two parties groped towards each other like modern trade unions and employers, both aware that an agreement was eventually certain, but both continually repeating that they had said their last word. The talks dragged on so long that the nervous Signoria were sending daily messengers to inquire about their progress. Hawkwood came down to 20,000 florins for the full dossier, 12,000 for the economy version. Gucci settled for the cheap rate.

The informer was to tell his story, 'back to the camera', as it were, in Hawkwood's room which would be lit only by a charcoal brazier. There was a brief period when the mounting suspense of this cloak-and-dagger drama threatened to dissolve in bathos, for Hawkwood was unable immediately to lay hands upon him. It must have been difficult to keep the man always ready in the wings as one day had given place to another without a settlement. However, the informer turned up in time and the plot was duly revealed in the dark room at Bagnacavallo. It would seem that this story was well based, and that the Signoria took the counter-measures needed to forestall a flare-up of the previous year's rebellion. If they had felt that Hawkwood had tricked them, or even felt partly dissatisfied with their bargain, they would not have shown the confidence in him that they displayed so markedly in the years that followed.

There was an outstanding demonstration of this in January 1382, and again two months later. A rebellion had then actually broken out in Florence. The Captain of the People, the official guardian of the public peace, took the unusual course of appealing to Hawkwood for help: it was no part of a condottiere's normal duties to intervene in civil disorders. The Piazza della Signoria was packed with a tumultuous crowd. The appearance of Hawkwood with ninety lances was enough to restore calm. But during the night trouble broke out again, and the return of daylight found the piazza once more a scene of violence, so much so that the Captain of the People threw down his baton and resigned on the spot. This kind of desperate situation might have been made for the veteran English commander. Calmly and firmly he and his men cleared the piazza and paraded through the city, damping down the fiery spirits of the demonstrators. As a result of this, and of a similarly successful operation in the following March, the Signoria made a remarkable if not unique agreement for the use of the mercenaries in preserving internal order.

By the end of that year Hawkwood's connection with Florence had become so close and permanent that it no longer made sense to maintain his own home in Romagna. His contract in 1381 debarred him from travelling more than eighty miles from Florence without leave of the Signoria. By October of the following year he was seeking to establish his family in the city. In fact, he never acquired a home within the urban boundaries, and usually, if he required to stay in Florence overnight, lodged at the big convent of Sant'Antonio, just inside the Faenza Gate. In January 1383, he bought an estate at La Rocchetta, in the Val d'Elsa near Poggibonsi, nearly thirty miles to the south of the city.

79 The convent of S. Antonio, Florence, where Hawkwood lodged in the early days of his service with the Florentine republic.

+ Santo · antonio + ispedali · disanto anto

101

The Romagnol estates he managed to sell for 60,000 florins. At various times he acquired other properties. For about ten years he was lord of Montecchio Vesponsi, a hill-top castle near Cortona which is still pointed out as a former home of the great condottiere, though it is questionable how much time he actually spent there. It brought in a useful income in tolls and dues, as did one or two other little strongholds that he came to own in the Arezzo region. Eventually, however, he disposed of them to the Florentine government for cash. It is clear that Hawkwood, unlike so many other commanders, was never bitten by the bug of territorial ambition, and that, for all the vast sums of money that passed through his hands, little of it stuck to his fingers. Certainly he paid his men punctually and looked after their interests. But with his absence of extravagance, with a family life that has been described as bourgeois, he should never have been – as he certainly was – embarrassed by a lack of ready money. Fritz Gaupp suggests that 'the clever Florentines had understood how to bring back into their coffers through their pitiless taxation machine what they had had to pay out to the Englishman'. If so, they were anticipating (as in so many other ways they anticipated) the ingenious devices of twentieth-century government.

Hawkwood made his real home not at La Rocchetta, which was inconveniently far from the city (Cavalcanti tells us that 'this excellent man went most mornings to consult with the Ten of War', or defence committee) but at San Donato in Polverosa, only a little way from Florence. Here he had a modest estate of the sort that many well-to-do Florentines liked to possess as an alternative to their town-houses. At San Donato he had a residence for his family, staff cottages, and the owner-ship of several surrounding farms or *poderi*, whose cultivators either paid rent or operated the spreading Tuscan system of *mezzadria* or profit-sharing, and in any case must have kept the Hawkwood table well supplied with food.

It is easy to picture the ageing soldier's life at San Donato, surrounded by the growing children of his second family. To say 'ageing' is merely to recognize a biological fact. Hawkwood never retired, and the old war-horse, as will be seen, could astonish the enemy with his dash and speed even to the end. But at times when the trumpets did not call he was enjoying longer placid periods at home, and again it is possible to see in him the prototype of the figure familiar in later centuries, the British general congenially transformed into a country squire.

The Tuscan landscape of those days is preserved for us in contemporary paintings and the writings of men like Leone Battista Alberti, who was lyrical about the crystal-clear air, the bird-song, the new-born lambs, the

80 At various times Hawkwood owned several estates in Italy, finally settling down at San Donato in Polverosa, not far from Florence, in countryside similar to that shown in the Lorenzettis' fresco of Good Government.

faithful sheepdogs, and the pure hill-streams 'leaping down or hiding beneath tunnels of overhanging foliage'. As for the houses – and Hawkwood's was typical of hundreds – Alberti was equally enthusiastic. 'Blessed villa,' he wrote, 'sure home of good cheer, conferring endless benefits: springtime verdure and autumn fruit, a rendezvous for good folk, a delightful retreat.'

Against this pastoral background moves the grizzled condottiere, the scenery and way of life so different from the Essex manor where he was bred, but now after so many years in Italy much more familiar. The almond trees spread their pink clouds of blossom, the olive trees shimmer silvery green, the peasants in their grey homespun tunics prune vines along the stone-walled terraces, and it is olives, not English cider apples, that are being crushed in the press. Hawkwood would not be Hawkwood if he did not inspect his property – strolling out of the loggia, through the courtyards to his walled stables, round the garden and orchard, before taking horse to look at the farms. He can by now talk fluently and firmly to these people in their own language. Whether or not he can dispute with them the finer points of Italian agricultural practice is quite another matter. In this respect he is at no worse disadvantage than any of the Florentine businessmen who have bought similar estates outside the city, and who (if contemporary writers may be trusted) carry on a ceaseless and foredoomed struggle with the cunning rustics supposed to be their inferiors. 'Ask no service of them without pay,' warns Giovanni Morelli cynically, 'unless you want to pay the cost three times over. Above all, trust none of them, and if you do thus, you will be the more loved and respected, and whatever good there is in them you will bring out.'

Perhaps that regular daily meeting with the defence committee made an agreeable interlude, for at least it meant that Hawkwood was back on his own ground. 'More often than not,' says Cavalcanti, 'it happened that the said commander gave advice to the Ten, instead of the Ten giving instructions to him. His attendance at these meetings indicated that he was especially anxious for the welfare of the city.' Not all professional soldiers would have been happy in this day-to-day discussion with civilians from whom, in the last resort, they had to take their orders, but Hawkwood had a diplomatic way with them. It was rare indeed for his impatience to flash out, as once it did when he was arguing with Andrea Vettori. For a moment the authentic voice of Hawkwood comes through to us, ringing down the centuries.

'You go and weave your cloth', he said, 'and leave me to lead the troops.'

Hawkwood had found himself a congenial niche at Florence and it is unlikely that he would ever have wished to return to the most obvious of his alternative employers, Milan. In any case, something happened in 1385 which would have made it impossible for a man of his temper to do so.

This event serves to bring upon the stage what E. R. Chamberlin has called 'the shadowy but noble figure of Jacopo dal Verme'. 'Shadowy', because apart from his military record not much is known about this condottiere. 'Noble', because he served the same master loyally throughout his reign, and that master's appalling heir as long as it was possible to do so, and because his own honour was never impeached.

Jacopo dal Verme, indeed, may be compared with Hawkwood for his discretion, his reliability, and his freedom from political ambition. The two men were destined to be regular opponents in the last campaigns of Hawkwood's career.

Dal Verme came of a Veronese soldiering family and at least one brother served at his side. He first achieved prominence in 1378, when Galeazzo Visconti died and was succeeded by young Gian Galeazzo. The new ruler of Pavia promptly made dal Verme his Captain-General. He was to hold that title for the next quarter of a century, although, to the confusion of historians, he sometimes shared it with other commanders. It was perhaps rather a rank than a command. Condottieri of a certain standing disliked accepting a subordinate status. When a major war was pending, a rich power like Milan tried to build up the strongest possible team of such generals, even engaging more than were needed, to prevent their being signed up by the enemy.

Gian Galeazzo, whom we first noticed as a studious sixteen-year-old, uncongenially arrayed as an armoured knight at his sister's wedding, found himself at twenty-six in uneasy partnership with his uncle, Bernabò. His prospects were poor, indeed to the superficial observer almost non-existent. It says much for dal Verme that he discerned the potentialities of the young man and was prepared to back an outside chance – and indeed, when the day of crisis came, to take a terrifying risk. Gian Galeazzo, in his turn, no soldier himself but a man who needed soldiers as instruments of policy, showed no less discernment in picking the right general at the very outset of his reign.

The young Visconti had grown up in the atmosphere of the Renaissance at his father's court in Pavia. He never ceased to love the great fortress-palace which his father had built into the north wall of the city, and here dal Verme, as one of his trusted inner circle, his principal military adviser, spent much of his time when not absent in the field.

The Castello was of brick, a perfect square, with two storeys each containing forty rooms looking inwards upon a magnificent arcaded courtyard, the setting for tournaments and other spectacles which could be watched from the loggias above. Another loggia opened out of the great hall and faced the gardens at the rear: this was where the family loved to dine on warm evenings. Grim battlements and a deep moat confronted the outside world, but it was characteristic that, while one of the corner turrets housed a very necessary armoury, others were filled with the books and art treasures in which both father and son found their deepest satisfaction. This is not the place to discuss Gian Galeazzo's contribution to the history of Italian art and scholarship through the patronage he exercised in Pavia and Milan, but the doings of dal Verme, and of the other notable condottieri he employed, have little meaning without a full understanding of the remarkable character whose designs they executed.

81 The Castello of Pavia, begun by Galeazzo Visconti (Bernabò's brother), and the early background of his celebrated son Gian Galeazzo.

He was a thoughtful young man. From his earliest years he had plenty to think about. 'He was accustomed', his biographer, Paolo Giovio, tells us, 'to devote himself to meditation during walks by himself.' Like his father, he loved the quiet gardens of the Castello, and the wooded park that stretched away on the other side of the Ticino. But, while he could be reserved and even secretive, he knew how to use advisers and when to delegate. It was his habit, Giovio continues, 'to confer with those most experienced in each department of affairs', and as he had no military ambitions of his own he must have leaned heavily on his Captain-General.

His family life had been tragically unfortunate. At twenty-six he was already a widower. He had lost not only his French princess, Isabella of Valois, but also their three sons. It was small wonder that he adored their surviving daughter, Valentina, who grew up to love the Castello as much as he did. But men of his rank could not nurse private griefs for ever – especially when the lack of a male heir constituted such a temptation to ambitious rivals. One of Gian Galeazzo's first acts on succeeding to his father's share in the government of Milan was to negotiate a secret betrothal to the Sicilian princess, a diplomatic alliance that would have done much to bolster his position against his uncle. Bernabò, however, heard of the scheme and of a vital clause in the agreement: if the marriage was not consummated within twelve months, the deal was off. Exerting all the influence at his disposal, Bernabò effectively ensured that the wedding did not take place. His nephew was at this stage completely at his mercy. After

82 The young Gian Galeazzo, in an idealized relief, leads troops on a military expedition.

83 The courtyard of the Castello of Pavia.

accepting his uncle's advice on various other matters, always to Bernabò's advantage, Gian Galeazzo was compelled in 1380 to accept one of Bernabò's legitimate daughters, Caterina, as his second wife. When, after several years, this marriage had still produced no heir, Gian Galeazzo might have been forgiven for crediting his uncle with an almost diabolical ingenuity in seeing that all the Milanese dominions should soon be reunited under one branch of the family.

He lay low until 1385. We may imagine his long soul-searchings as he paced the gardens of Pavia, contemplated the velvet grace of his caged leopards, leaned with unseeing eyes over the open pages of some treasured book. Ancient history was full of parallels . . . tyrants overthrown by bold coups . . . dramatic reversals of fortune for complacent rulers who deemed themselves untouchable. . . . He loved classical, bookish parallels. Sometimes, it may be, he irritated the less scholarly of his advisers by seeming to assume that, if such-and-such a thing had happened to some long-dead Greek or Roman, a similar result could be produced again. But, for all his taste for quotations and historical analogies (a fashionable failing in Renaissance Italy), Gian Galeazzo never really let them warp his judgment. He remembered the hard facts. He had few resources of his own, since any attempt to build them up would have blazed like a beacon to warn his uncle. He was up against Bernabò and his five sons, all as lethal as the viper they bore as emblem. He himself was cursed with a timidity, a distaste for the martial exercises, that put him at a permanent disadvantage when dealing with these aggressive relatives. Yet act he must, and not merely in self-defence, striking out like a desperate animal at bay. He must act because he had his own dream, his own steel-hard purpose, veiled by his deceptively innocuous appearance. To fulfil that purpose he too required the undivided resources of all Milan.

He consulted dal Verme and took the soldier into his confidence. That much is self-evident from the sequel. Dal Verme's contribution was crucial. If the condottiere had not been fully prepared – if he had hesitated for one instant when his cue came, or if he had prudently switched his allegiance as many would have done – Gian Galeazzo would have been doomed. For dal Verme, when the idea was put to him, it must have been a fearful decision to make. He agreed, and the plan went forward. Gian Galeazzo consulted the stars as well. He was a great believer in astrology.

On 5 May he announced that he was going on a pilgrimage to the shrine of the Madonna del Monte at Varese, between Como and Maggiore. This news surprised nobody. His devotion to the cult of the Virgin was widely known, and was probably the subject of irreverent witticisms in his uncle's robust circle. Nor was undue comment aroused by the devout

84, 85 Gian Galeazzo Visconti and his wife, his cousin Caterina. With the aid of the condottiere Jacopo dal Verme, Gian Galeazzo was able to depose his uncle Bernabò and assume sole rule of Milan.

young man's taking Jacopo dal Verme and four hundred men-at-arms upon this religious exercise. Was not his timidity proverbial? No doubt the godless soldiers would be all the better for sharing in it.

The road from Pavia to Varese lay through Milan. The pilgrims made their first overnight halt at the castle of Binasco, about ten miles south of Bernabò's capital. A message was sent proffering Gian Galeazzo's excuses for not entering the city. He proposed, however, to make a brief wayside halt as he skirted the walls and came opposite the Porta Giovia. There he would be delighted to pay his respects to his uncle and cousins, if they cared to ride out and greet him. Bernabò is said to have been much amused. It was so pitifully obvious that this lily-livered nephew was too scared to enter the spider's parlour. Very well, the spider resolved good-humouredly, he would go out and have a word with him. He sent the two sons who were at home to ride out ahead of him, and, mounting his own horse, followed them through the gates with no more than a handful of attendants.

The initial greetings were exchanged. Gian Galeazzo then nodded to dal Verme. The soldier clapped a hand smartly on Bernabò's shoulder, and the bodyguard swirled round the little party. Bernabò and his two sons were quickly hustled into the convenient dungeons of the castle of Porta Giovia. Gian Galeazzo made a triumphal entry into the city, the inhabitants turning out and shouting with suspicious unanimity, 'Long live the Count of Virtù! Down with the taxes!' The coup must have been extremely well prepared, for the Pisan government voted its congratulations to Gian Galeazzo on that very same day: Pisa is about a hundred and forty miles to the south.

Gian Galeazzo had made his calculations well. Give the Milanese their heads, and they would gladly welcome him as their liberator. There was some temporary disorder, natural and healthy enough. The houses of Bernabò and his sons were looted and fired. There was a judicious hand-out from the tyrant's treasury, there were promises of tax-reduction and a more lenient régime. A general assembly of citizens was convened and unanimously voted that the sole and absolute lordship of Milan should be conferred on the Count of Virtù. The title, 'Duke of Milan', was an extra honour that had to be obtained from the nominally superior authority of the Emperor. Gian Galeazzo bought it later from the incompetent Wenceslas IV.

Meanwhile, from the moment dal Verme arrested Bernabò outside the Porta Giovia, Gian Galeazzo remained the unchallenged master of Milan, free to embark on the grand design that extended his power across northern Italy from Piedmont to the Adriatic. In the next seventeen years he was to

86, 87 Divine approval of the Visconti, whose lives for the most part had no conspicuous claims to sanctity, is hopefully anticipated in these two eulogistic miniatures stemming from the Milanese court. In the first the Christ Child crowns Gian Galeazzo. In the second God the Father blesses the Visconti lands. Note the heraldic vipers.

swallow Genoa, Pisa, Perugia, Siena, and Bologna, and to threaten even Florence. Always he was the astute statesman, never the infatuated conqueror. His subsequent operations were planned as skilfully as the first. It was said that he never undertook a campaign if it was avoidable, and that if his troops were compelled to move against a city it was often with the private assurance that the gates would be opened to them by a dissident faction inside. He had learned something from at least one classical model, Philip of Macedon. His debt to dal Verme, however, must have been great. Dal Verme was no hothead, he had no wish to fight unnecessary battles, he knew when to preserve his forces intact. He and his master were well suited.

Gian Galeazzo rather liked to play the peace-maker. He hated the mercenary companies, especially the foreigners, and constantly took the initiative in attempts to secure agreement between the various Italian states to combine against the common menace. As many people, the Florentines especially, were even more suspicious of Milan than of the mercenaries, his efforts in this direction were no more successful than the disarmament proposals of our own century.

Bernabò lived as a prisoner for some time. Inevitably it was said, and widely believed, that his death was due to poison. It is too late now for a post-mortem. Presumably that century had its normal quota of sudden and painful deaths more easily explained by poison than by the various internal conditions then unknown to the doctors and in any case quite inoperable at the time. Gian Galeazzo, we may be sure, would not have hesitated to liquidate his uncle if it had been necessary, except in so far as he might not have wished to upset Caterina, who seems to have accepted her husband's political line without voicing any open protest. Perhaps he hastened her father's end, perhaps he did not need to.

Her brothers – those at least who were at liberty – did all they could to avenge their father's downfall, but they could not do much. Carlo Visconti, for example, came hastening back from Germany and enlisted with Hawkwood, rightly guessing that this would give him the best opportunity of campaigning against his cousin. This was the Carlo whom Hawkwood warned against the poisoned figs. The men seem to have been good friends, as well as half-brothers-in-law, through Donnina.

Bernabò might have been a brute, and Gian Galeazzo – to our modern taste at least – a more attractive man to know. Hawkwood, however, had his own code. There could be no question now of serving this duke, who had deposed and probably murdered Hawkwood's father-in-law and the father of his friend. Inescapably, Hawkwood and dal Verme were to be pitted against each other on the plains of Lombardy.

Castagnaro: the classic victory 8

Any study of the condottieri would be unreadable if it dealt in detail with their military operations. The tactics are too elementary, the strategy non-existent, the political results so transitory. The set battles are far out-numbered by the raids and skirmishes, yet it was often through these smaller actions that the condottieri justified their pay. In the ceaseless warfare of the Italian states irritation and deterrence were more often the aim than a knock-out victory.

Such victories did occur, however, from time to time. It was not all shadow-boxing, by any means, or decisions on points. Castagnaro was such an engagement, and is worth singling out for examination. 'Hawk-wood's greatest battle, a triumph of his old age,' was the verdict of Sir Charles Oman in *A History of the Art of War in the Middle Ages*.

It was fought on 11 March 1387, nominally between Padua and Verona, the latter being supported by Venice. Neither Milan nor Florence was officially involved. Gian Galeazzo, only newly come to power, was watching keenly from the side-lines, letting the combatants exhaust themselves: within a year or two he had absorbed them both. Florence, not requiring Hawkwood for the moment, released him to Francesco Carrara the Elder, who had been lord of Padua for more than thirty years, an inveterate enemy of the Venetians, and a man with inflated ideas of what was politically possible for his state. He was engaging all the mer-cenaries he could afford. Hawkwood went to him with five hundred men-at-arms and six hundred of his mounted English bowmen. It was understood that Hawkwood should be in effective command of the whole army, though for form's sake he deferred to his employer's son, Francesco Carrara the Younger, usually referred to as 'Francesco Novello'. His subsequent career shows this young prince as a soldier of great courage and resource: it is sad to record that after nearly twenty years of escapes and other romantic adventures he was to end his days wretchedly, strangled by his Venetian jailers. But in the spring of 1387 he was a gay cavalier, taking his cue from the elderly Englishman who was riding at his side.

During February they had been blockading Verona, then ruled by Antonio della Scala, the unlovable character in whom that proud dynasty came to its inglorious end. He had seized power five years earlier, by murdering his elder brother and co-ruler and then falsely accusing two other men, who were tortured to death, along with the equally innocent daughter of one of them. Then, with that blending of the aesthetic and the bestial which characterized so many Italian princes of the Renaissance, he distracted public attention from the scandal by the additional splendour of his own wedding festivities that followed shortly afterwards. A whole month of shows and spectacles included tournaments in the ancient Roman amphitheatre, with a 'Castle of Love' set up in the centre of the arena, garrisoned by beautiful girls who bombarded the attacking knights with flowers, sweets, and jets of scented water.

These, then, were the opposing despots, Antonio della Scala and the two Carraras, whose forces were arrayed against each other in the more serious warfare that led up to Castagnaro. Under their banners were ranged, on both sides, some of the best condottieri then in practice.

The Veronese forces were originally led by della Scala's brother-in-law, Serego, but he was taken prisoner at an early stage and had to be replaced with Giovanni dei Ordelaffi, one of the family that dominated Forlì for over a century, combining their petty lordship with mercenary service. Ordelaffi's second-in-command was Ostasio da Polenta, who brought a contingent from Ravenna where his family operated on a similar basis. It was Samaritana da Polenta whose wedding to Antonio della Scala had been so memorably celebrated a few years before and whose excessive extravagance had since infuriated the Veronese, contributing in the end to her husband's downfall.

These two Romagnol war-lords were assisted by a number of other captains. There was Facino Cane, that Piedmontese ruffian who was to carve himself so profitable a career under the Visconti. There were two dal Verme brothers, Ugolino and Taddeo. It was a well-known Veronese family. Jacopo seems not to have been involved. It is unlikely that Gian Galeazzo would have lent his right-hand man to either army. Although it was to be Jacopo who would seize Padua for Milan in the following year, Gian Galeazzo at this moment gave the impression of inclining, if anything, to the Paduan side, deceiving the Carraras with the hint that he might help them against Verona. So, had the great dal Verme been present at all, he would probably have been with Hawkwood.

88 A 'Castle of Love' was part of the medieval pageantry with which Antonio della Scala of Verona distracted his subjects from his own crimes shortly before the Battle of Castagnaro.

89, 90 The two contestants at Castagnaro were Padua and Verona, both of them nearing the end of their independent existence. Antonio della Scala was the last of his illustrious family; Verona was destined to lose the war against Padua and then to be absorbed by Milan. Left: the seal of Verona. Below: part of the castle and fortified bridge of the Scaligers.

The Englishman had no lack of military talent to aid him. For second-in-command he had Giovanni d'Azzo degli Ubaldini, an exiled Florentine nobleman variously and confusingly referred to by historians as 'Giovanni d'Azzo' and as 'Ubaldini'. A few months previously, Gian Galeazzo had advanced him money with which to form his own company, and for the rest of his short life Ubaldini (with what the Renaissance would have regarded as commendable loyalty) served the interests of Milan against his native city. He seems to have been an able soldier and a pleasant fellow, who got on well with Hawkwood and made no difficulties about accepting a subordinate position. Hawkwood in turn admired and respected him. The fact that Ubaldini was a Florentine exile, an official 'traitor' in the eyes of the government who were Hawkwood's permanent employers, created no personal awkwardness between them.

Other captains on the Paduan side were Giovanni di Pietramala, Ugolotto Biancardo, Cecchino Broglia and his inseparable comrade-in-arms Brandolino, Filippo da Pisa, and others eminent in their day but whose sonorous names convey little to the modern reader.

In all, Hawkwood had close on seven thousand men-at-arms at his disposal, plus the six hundred English archers and about a thousand other infantry.

The provisioning of such a force, at the end of the winter, presented its own problems. Hawkwood's communications with Padua were stretched to their utmost and were cut from time to time by enemy raids. Always a prudent commander, he had to explain to Francesco Novello the futility and danger of continuing the blockade. They agreed to withdraw south-eastwards down the River Adige, which flowed beneath the ramparts of Verona, until they reached Castelbaldo, where a big accumulation of supplies awaited them.

The retreat proceeded in orderly fashion. Hawkwood was a master of the strategic withdrawal. The discipline of his own men, and his tremendous general reputation, prevented that snapping of confidence which might have turned retreat into disintegration under a lesser commander. On the night of 10 March he halted near Castagnaro on the west bank of the river, still a few miles short of his destination. The Veronese were on his heels. They had come out in gleeful pursuit, gathering extra forces as they came. Ordelaffi by this time commanded nine thousand men-at-arms, two thousand six hundred crossbowmen and pikemen, and an uncounted multitude of hastily mustered citizens and peasants.

As if this last embarrassment was not enough, he had, in addition to more than twenty bombards, three fantastic and quite useless weapons devised by Antonio della Scala's over-ingenious brain. Had they been the child of anyone else's fancy, it is unlikely that Ordelaffi would have troubled to bring them along. These *ribauds*, as they were called, seem to have been a premature essay in the field of the machine-gun. Each was constructed with twelve dozen individual tubes, loaded with shot. Twelve could be fired simultaneously. It was a pleasing conception, but in the then-rudimentary state of artillery design the necessary complex of gun-barrels involved a structure some twenty feet high. Fortunately for the adventurous gunners responsible for manning these monstrosities in battle, each required four powerful horses to draw it, and in the annals of Castagnaro there is no word to suggest that the *ribauds* ever got into position in time to fire a single volley.

Ordelaffi, like Hawkwood's own captains, confidently expected that he would cross the river and draw his forces snugly into Castelbaldo where his supplies awaited him, rather like a snake gliding into a hole. In the failing light of that March day, however, Hawkwood's practised eye had taken in the lie of the land and judged it admirable for one of those defensive battles in which his old master, the Black Prince, had excelled. It was a pity that there were no slopes to help him, such as he remembered from Poitiers, and that he had not more English bowmen at his disposal. But there was one of those Lombard canals, there was an irrigation drain, and the fields in general were heavy and water-logged at this season – everything favoured the English style of fighting on foot rather than the Italian cavalry charge. The sage old man (he must have been in his middle or late sixties by then, and today would have been drawing his pension) decided that the setting would do very well. His confidence is impressive. There seems no reason why he should not have withdrawn without loss into Castelbaldo. Clearly, since he was never one to take foolish risks, he felt that he knew exactly what he was doing.

Hawkwood camped where he was. In the morning Ordelaffi was surprised to learn that there was no sign of the Paduan army resuming their march. Rather, it seemed, they had turned at bay and proposed to offer battle. He had not bargained for this and he was not ready for immediate acceptance.

Hawkwood was about early, mounted on a Thessalian charger, riding through the ranks and pausing to chat with his men. He wanted to know if they had had their breakfast. There would be some heavy work today. He knighted some of his own company. It was not for him to confer honours on the men of Padua, but in their case he presented the golden spurs and young Francesco Carrara bestowed the accolade. There was something to be said for distributing the honours before, rather than after, the battle. The gratified recipients were then sure of them, whatever happened, and

91 Francesco Carrara (right) ruled Padua at the time of Castagnaro. Hawkwood, officially in the service of Florence, had been 'lent' to him for the occasion.

92 Francesco Carrara the Younger (left) took part in the Battle of Castagnaro at Hawkwood's side. In 1387 his father abdicated in his favour, but it was too late to save Padua from the coils of 'the Great Serpent', Gian Galeazzo Visconti.

were put on their mettle. It might also occur to them that now, if they surrendered, their ransoms would be assessed at a higher figure.

The army was drawn up so as to exploit the features of the terrain as Hawkwood had noted them the evening before. The irrigation channel offered a convenient line along his front. The enemy would bridge it, of course, or fill it up with long bundles of faggots in the usual way, but it was sure to break the impact of their charge, already slowed by the softness of the sodden fields. His right flank was covered by the canal, his left by a swamp. The river lay behind him, a bad situation for faint-hearts but good for resolute men who had no intention of running away.

He had surveyed the ground with Ubaldini and Biancardo and the dispositions had been agreed. The main body of men-at-arms, all dismounted, were formed up in six groups or 'battles' under their several commanders. There were two lines of three 'battles' each. Having a clear notion of how he intended the fight to go, Hawkwood kept a seventh group in reserve. It formed a third line, together with his personal company, and both these units were ordered to remain in the saddle, not to send their pages and horses to the rear like the others. In Hawkwood's plan they were not an emergency reserve but a striking force to be used at the right moment.

In the centre of this third line, between these two groups of armoured riders, stood the great *carroccio* of Padua, that curious symbolic object which served the Italian states as a standard and as something more. It has been described as a sacred war-chariot. More correctly, it was a flat rectangular cart or dray, brightly painted and carrying not only the civic banner but an altar at which Mass could be celebrated. It was usually hauled by oxen. In the heat of the conflict it afforded a convenient platform from which trumpeters could transmit orders to the various commanders. Combining as it did the sentimental associations of the regimental colours with the practical importance of a battle headquarters, the *carroccio* was always stoutly defended. In the famous Battle of Legnano, two centuries earlier, Barbarossa and his German knights had made herculean efforts to cut their way through to the *carroccio* of Milan, but they had been driven back by the two special groups of young volunteers entrusted with its defence, the Company of the Carroccio and the Company of Death.

Hawkwood must have sighed for the myriad longbows of his French campaigns. His English archers were all too few. He could not deploy them along his front and he seems not even to have sent them to the right flank with his arbalesters or crossbowmen. The latter, together with his few gunners and their bombards, he sent to line the canal-bank. His own archers he kept, for the time being, along with his lances at the rear, and

93 The *carroccio* was both a mobile headquarters and a symbol of loyalty.

like the men-at-arms still mounted and mobile. It is another pointer to the manœuvre he had in mind.

It took Ordelaffi an inordinate time to array his own forces for the attack. There are several possible reasons why the battle did not begin until quite late in the day. The drain could not be crossed without a vast quantity of fascines: the mere assembly of these, if the need for them had not been anticipated, could have occupied some hours. Then there were those fantastic *ribauds*, lumbering up the road behind: perhaps Antonio della Scala would be mortified if his invention was not tried out. Not the least plausible explanation of the delay is that Ordelaffi and his captains argued about the wisdom of a frontal attack on the fearsome Hawkwood standing at bay on ground of his own choice.

However that may be, the Veronese army got into position at last. It is noteworthy that Ordelaffi dismounted his men and prepared to fight in the English fashion. He ranged them in two long lines across the fields. He too kept the *carroccio* in the rear, with a picked company of three hundred lances to defend it. He held another large force of cavalry in reserve, and in the extreme rear, behind even the precious *carroccio*, he massed the town and country levies, praying no doubt that he would have no need of their unpredictable services.

The fight began. With loud yells of 'Scala! Scala!' the Veronese front line advanced to the edge of the ditch and began hurling in the fascines, until there were many points at which it was filled in and they could push their way across. The Paduan troops retorted with the Carrara family war-cry, 'Carro! Carro!' Hawkwood left his own company in the charge of Pietramala and galloped forward with his page to direct the battle himself. Over the sea of helmets, undulating as the two lines of lances pushed and strained, he could see Ordelaffi, a lonely mounted figure on the other side, thundering to and fro as he rallied his men and threw fresh detachments into the mêlée.

At the outset the Veronese troops could win no foothold on the other side of the ditch. As fast as they scrambled and stumbled across the improvised bridge of faggots, the Paduan forces poked them back with their bristling lance-points. Then, as the attackers persisted, they managed here and there to dent the straightness of the line opposing them. Where they established themselves, Ordelaffi reinforced them from his groups behind. Hawkwood saw that it was only a matter of time before his own front gave way under the pressure. He brought forward his next three battles. The conflict grew more and more intense. One would imagine heaps of corpses, the irrigation channel red with blood, but the ultimate casualty figures suggest otherwise. At this stage it was very much of a shoving match, and, with every one so well protected, not noticeably more fatal than a robust riot between modern civilians. Ordelaffi committed the whole of his second line and even called up some of his infantry. Outnumbered, the Paduan men-at-arms began to yield ground in places, but doggedly, yard by yard.

Hawkwood knew it was now or never. With superb timing and nerve, he had waited until almost all Ordelaffi's effective strength was engaged. He left the direction of the struggle to Ubaldini. There was a clear understanding between them. When Ubaldini saw that Hawkwood had struck his master-blow, he was to rouse the tired men to one final effort and lead them in a counter-attack.

Hawkwood's plan was to make a surprise attack from flank and rear, modelled on the one launched so successfully at Poitiers by the Black Prince's Gascon commander, Captal de Buch.

Resuming his position at the head of his own company he led them, men-at-arms and archers, all still mounted, across to the right of the position, where the crossbowmen and bombardiers were still strung along the other water-cut, presumably peppering the enemy with irritating missiles as opportunity allowed. As he rode past them, Hawkwood gestured with a sweep of his baton, gathering them up into a useful light

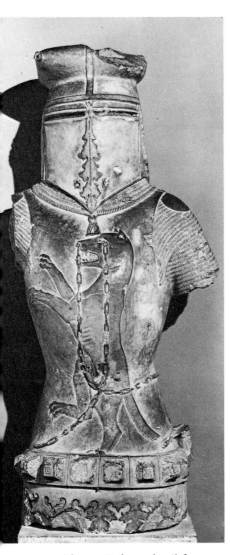

94, 95 Above: Padua – detail from a
knight's tomb in the Oratorio di S. Giorgio.
Right: Verona – part of a votive
fresco of the Cavalli family in S. Anastasia.
Enemies at Castagnaro, the two cities
were soon to share the same fate,
domination by Milan.

infantry detachment racing at his heels. For at this moment he wanted every man. But perhaps his most serious worry was young Carrara's insistence on taking part in the attack. It would never do for his employer's son to perish by misadventure and spoil the triumph. At least he had managed, just before moving off, to switch Francesco and his knights to the less exposed side of the formation, where if things went wrong he would have the best chance to escape.

We do not know the width or depth of this other water obstacle on the flank, or just how the English crossed it. Obviously Hawkwood had reconnoitred it thoroughly and knew what he was going to do. Otherwise his whole plan would have collapsed into tragic farce. This much seems certain: the crossing was swift, unexpected, and unopposed. Ordelaffi's men, confident that they were on the brink of victory, knew nothing until they received a shower of arrows and bolts from behind them. And, as they turned aghast, grim Hawkwood and his horsemen were upon them.

Hawkwood tossed his commander's baton into the throng of enemy, confident of its recovery. Then the old man drew his sword and spurred into their midst. He was never one to go in for personal heroics – he was essentially a commander, not a paladin of romance – but incidents such as this indicate that he did not lack physical courage.

'Carne!' he is said to have shouted. 'Carne!' Thus, with a gruesome pun, he changed the Carrara war-cry to one that meant 'Flesh! Flesh!'

The nearest Veronese were ridden over at the first onset. It could not have been easy for pairs of men, sharing a long and heavy lance in the midst of a struggling crowd, to turn quickly and point it in the opposite direction. The unfortunate Veronese dissolved into confusion. Ubaldini, seeing the moment had come, ordered the main Paduan line to counter-attack – and the breathless men found it easier to obey than they would have dreamed possible, for the enemy who had been driving them back a minute ago were now melting away in disorder. Meanwhile the English archers showered in their arrows, so long as it was possible to distinguish friend from foe. Then they whipped out their short swords and joined in the fray.

It cannot have lasted long after this. The Veronese ranks disintegrated. Men-at-arms stumbled across the muddy fields, calling to their pages to bring forward their horses. Ordelaffi and Ostasio da Polenta attempted a counter-attack of their own, charging with the reserve cavalry, but they struggled in vain against the stream of their own fugitives. Hawkwood, having smashed the Veronese left wing, relied on Ubaldini to roll up the remnants of the enemy line. He wheeled his own column against the

96 A lively camp scene by an artist of Verona about the time of Hawkwood's victory.

carroccio in the rear and the dumbfounded civic levies massed behind it. The *carroccio* was captured and even its guards surrendered. The civic levies fled. Only one detachment of hapless peasants, part of an infantry company commanded by Giovanni da Isola, took literally the rhetorical instruction to fight to the death: not knowing how to behave like professionals, they refused to surrender and died where they stood. Ordelaffi himself put up a resolute resistance with about two hundred men, but having saved his honour saved his life as well and was taken prisoner. Ubaldini was tireless in exploiting Hawkwood's success. Riding forward with the mounted reserve, quickly reinforced by every other man-at-arms who could get to horse in time, he swept across the chaotic battlefield and harried the fugitives until darkness came down.

The Paduan triumph was complete. Besides Ordelaffi, the prisoners included Ostasio da Polenta, Facino Cane, the dal Verme brothers, and most of the other condottieri on that side, together with some four thousand six hundred men-at-arms and eight hundred foot-soldiers of negligible ransom value. For a few minutes there had been really bloody fighting. The total casualties are recorded as seven hundred and sixteen dead, eight hundred and forty-six wounded. Only about a hundred of these dead were on Hawkwood's side, and this is a credible proportion, not to be discounted as a victor's boasting. The Veronese were at a disadvantage during the worst part of the battle and they suffered the extra scourge of the English longbow. The total figure of their dead was inflated also by the heroic but useless defiance of their peasant levies. Castagnaro shows that condottiere battles were by no means the bloodless charades that Machiavelli liked to suggest. On the other hand, the slaughter did not compare with the fifteen hundred knights and ten thousand common soldiers killed at Crécy, let alone the exceptional casualties at Towton in the Wars of the Roses, where, suggests Lieutenant-Colonel A. H. Burne in *The Battlefields of England*, 'over 26,000 combatants were killed'.

The material booty was as impressive as the number of prisoners. Hawkwood held not only the sacred *carroccio* of Verona but the entire enemy camp and supply-train, with twenty-four bombards, forty munition-carts, and the three *ribauds*.

It was no wonder that young Carrara could not wait to acquaint his father with the good news. Sitting down in the torch-light he began his exultant dispatch: 'From Castagnaro, in my fortunate army, on 11 March, an hour after sunset . . .'

It was a wasted victory. Within a year or two Hawkwood was to see, as innumerable brilliant specialists in every field of human endeavour have seen since, all his efforts nullified by subsequent mistakes of his employer.

Gian Galeazzo walked in his Pavia garden, beautiful and terrible as his own pet leopards. His short pointed beard had the reddish fleck that often showed in the hair of the Visconti family, and gave him a slight but appropriate foxiness. When he hunted – and he had a moderate taste for the traditional country sports of the aristocrat, though no liking for their indoor amusements, whether dice, buffoonery, or seduction – he rode informally and unannounced through the countryside, his route and plans in this, as in other matters, undisclosed. He would halt and give audience in a forest glade, a pleasant Shakespearean touch – but after all this Italy was the Italy that Shakespeare was to transmute at third hand, two centuries later, into what seem to us now unreal, if colourful, fables. In Gian Galeazzo's time the plots were real enough, almost everyday occurrences. Brothers did murder or exile each other to seize dukedoms. Cities were split by factions as in Juliet's Verona, and what was Othello, if not a condottiere in the Venetian service who married the daughter of one of his employers?

Alone with his thoughts, or consulting with his inner cabinet in the bright big-windowed apartments of the Castello, Gian Galeazzo reviewed the state of Italy and planned the downfall, *inter alia*, of both sides in the recent battle at Castagnaro. Owing to the strong influence of hostile Florentine writers, Gian Galeazzo was usually portrayed to posterity as an arch-villain. Yet if Italy had been ready for the measure of unification he tried to force on her, if he could really have created in the northern half of the peninsula a single state fit to stand with France and England, would not his deceptions be now forgotten or forgiven and his memory revered as a political genius? Like his father, he was not given to wanton cruelty. For ruthlessness and treachery he was matched, and often surpassed, by his victims: they were merely less effective. And at least Gian Galeazzo was driven not by caprice or petty vanity but by a grand design.

Verona fell quickly into his hands. On the night of 18 November 1387, just eight months after the Castagnaro débâcle, Antonio della Scala fled to Venice, and Verona was immediately declared part of the Milanese dominions. In exile Antonio turned for help to Carlo Visconti, who was still actively pursuing the vendetta against his cousin, but before these intrigues could produce any hope of a restoration Antonio died, leaving his wife and family to the charity of the Venetian republic.

Padua went the same way. At first old Carrara had believed Gian Galeazzo his friend. There had been an understanding that, if he helped Milan to get Verona, the neighbouring city of Vicenza would be given to him as the jackal's share. When the moment came, Carrara was outwitted. Gian Galeazzo's agents made sure that the people of Vicenza too would declare their preference for the overlordship of Milan. This failure in external policies increased Carrara's unpopularity with his own subjects. The old man abdicated in favour of his son, but that move was too belated. A mass movement gathered strength, encouraged alike by Gian Galeazzo's propagandists and by his troop movements, directed by Jacopo dal Verme. The upshot was that the commune of Padua 'voluntarily' offered its over-lordship to Gian Galeazzo, the Carraras became political prisoners, and the city declined into a satellite of Milan. It was an all too sad foreshadowing of the twentieth century.

Gian Galeazzo's expansionist policy was going well. Venice, seeing his triumph over Verona, Vicenza, and Padua, withdrew into her shell: she had yet to decide finally on the wisdom of mainland adventures, and the Visconti successes were an argument in favour of concentrating on her eastern Mediterranean interests. The only Italian state capable of standing up to Milan was Florence, and she did.

To begin with, Gian Galeazzo probed and nibbled. Characteristically he preferred to weaken his enemy by blocking trade routes and using other economic irritations, confining military action to indirect and devious 'measures short of war', another anticipation of methods favoured by some modern dictators. He made much use of Hawkwood's colleague at Castagnaro, the exiled Florentine, Ubaldini. After the fall of Verona, Ubaldini wandered through Romagna with his band, causing consider-able alarm in his native city, since at that time it was unknown for certain whether he was in Gian Galeazzo's pay or not. This ambiguous arrange-ment suited the Milanese ruler: he could keep his enemies guessing and always, when it suited him, disclaim responsibility. In August 1389, when Milanese-Florentine relations were near breaking-point, he sent

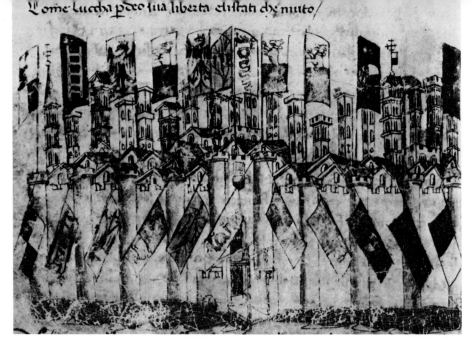

99 Lucca, the city to the west of Florence which Ubaldini hoped to draw away from the Florentine and into the Milanese sphere.

Ubaldini to Parma, which was a key point controlling the road to Bologna. Here the condottiere engaged in a plot to provoke a revolt in Bologna, planned the simultaneous capture of the valley roads leading over into Tuscany, tried to detach Lucca from her support of Florence, and enlisted more troops for the war that would follow these intrigues.

Another of the condottieri who had fought at Castagnaro, Ugolotto Biancardo, was also threatening the Florentine territories. Gian Galeazzo sent him into Romagna and the Marches, giving him more than 20,000 florins and authority to enlist up to two thousand lances.

When the war came, Ubaldini made a surprise appearance in Umbria with the object of harassing the Florentines in every possible way. First he had to reassure the nervous Perugians that he had come to protect rather than to molest them. Then he began a series of damaging raids into the Valdichiana, capturing a number of small places. This campaign was cut short by his sudden death at midsummer. Gian Galeazzo had sent him, as reinforcements, two hundred lances under Paolo Savelli, a Roman nobleman very much in the inner circle at Pavia, but this haughty gentleman was less successful as a mercenary leader than the good-natured Ubaldini had been. The Tuscan operations petered out.

The real war, in any case, was between Jacopo dal Verme and Hawkwood.

131

98 Paolo Savelli, commander of the Milanese forces against Florence after the death of Ubaldini in 1389.

Hawkwood had in no sense been vegetating since his Castagnaro triumph.

His life-contract with Florence left him free to undertake other work, and in 1389 he was away in the south, occupied in the dynastic conflicts of Naples, a subject best reserved for separate treatment in a later chapter.

Conscious of the threats building up against her from Milan, Florence sent him urgent notice of recall. Hawkwood responded with his usual dependability, and, though he was by then approaching seventy, made one of his celebrated forced marches. When he reached Rome, he had reason to fear that his northward journey might be obstructed by the Sienese or other powers anxious to please Gian Galeazzo. The system of safe-conducts through neutral territory assisted him to set up a smoke-screen of uncertain intentions. He sent forward emissaries to various places, applying for permissions he never meant to use. Having thus established a completely false picture of the route he planned to follow, he set off through the Maremma, the Tuscan coastal region normally avoided because of its malarial swamps. It was a bad road for an army, and he lost a number of horses, as well as exhausting his men. But to everybody's amazement the indefatigable old man turned up safely in Volterra and thence rode triumphantly into Florence, where he was received with joy and immense relief.

The republic had meanwhile taken the precaution of approaching Alberico da Barbiano. It had occurred to those shrewd councillors that Hawkwood was not immortal. Also, though they had complete confidence in Hawkwood while they had him, and did not feel that he required re-inforcing with Alberico, they did not want the Italian to be snapped up by

100 It was one of the aims of Gian Galeazzo's diplomacy to surround Florence with cities in alliance with himself. This miniature of 1400 represents one of his successes. The Visconti viper hovers over the cathedral and Palazzo Pubblico of Siena.

the other side. So they sent a representative to him at Ravenna, empowered to offer him a six-month contract, renewable for another six months, at the same rate of pay as Hawkwood. The official instructions to this representative ran: 'In conclusion request Barbiano that it may please him to be our captain-general together with Sir John Hawkwood, not because we wish to keep them together, but in different camps, each with an honourable brigade of Bolognese and our own troops. . . . If he is not satisfied, and wants a better offer, do not break off negotiations with him, but hold out good prospects without committing yourself.' Various other condottieri were recruited for the Florentine service at this time, including Conrad Landau with two hundred lances. Dal Verme, on the other side, had the assistance of Facino Cane and several equally well-known captains.

In the early summer of 1390 dal Verme had established himself in a well-fortified position at Crevalcore, north-west of Bologna. Six miles on the southward road to that city, Alberico's brother, Giovanni da Barbiano, faced him with twelve hundred lances and two thousand infantry. When Hawkwood arrived there, with no more than a personal escort of fifteen lances, the Milanese withdrew from their position, strong though it was, and for a while Hawkwood's men were free to go raiding into the adjacent lands of Modena and Reggio, rounding up cattle and prisoners. Then, in June, dal Verme moved forward again, and Hawkwood had to concentrate his forces to defend Bologna itself. He fell back almost to the city suburbs, occupying Casalecchio and the bridge by which the Via Emilia crosses the River Reno and enters Bologna from the west. Dal Verme threw up entrenchments facing him. Neither general was of the foolhardy kind.

Hawkwood, none the less, felt sufficiently confident of his strength to seek battle. He therefore sent his trumpeter, Zuzzo, to challenge his opponent by delivering a blood-stained glove, an offer which the Milanese commander-in-chief declined with thanks. Zuzzo was sent again. This time his welcome was less cordial. Dal Verme sent him about his business with abuse. Hawkwood felt sure by now that the advantage was on his side. Once more the willing Zuzzo was sent across the river with the glove. On this occasion dal Verme detained him at his headquarters for the night. The Milanese army is thought to have been short of food – its supply-line was fully stretched, whereas Hawkwood had a friendly Bologna immediately at his back, a city of such proverbial good living that its defenders would scarcely have been allowed to go hungry. Whether because of his commissariat problem, or a lack of confidence in his powers to defeat Hawkwood at that place and time, dal Verme determined on a stealthy withdrawal and used the unfinished parley with Zuzzo to disguise his

101 Before the walls of Bologna, Hawkwood fought one of his last battles, against the Milanese condottiere Jacopo dal Verme, on Midsummer Day, 1390. This detail shows the city, with its leaning towers, as a model presented to the Virgin.

intentions. That night, and unluckily for him it was Midsummer Night with only a few hours of darkness, dal Verme began his retreat. Hawkwood discovered what had happened and started in pursuit. So prompt and energetic was this move that he soon overtook the Milanese column and compelled dal Verme to stand at bay. A charge from the flank, led by Giovanni da Barbiano, decided the battle within an hour or two. Dal Verme's orderly withdrawal turned to hasty flight. Hawkwood captured fifty men-at-arms, including Facino Cane – his prisoner for the second time in three years – and another captain of repute, Anghelino da Padula. He also took two hundred and twenty horses. It was not a massive victory, but it was a smart rap on the knuckles for Gian Galeazzo, who must have been strengthened in his preference for diplomacy and subversion rather than a military conflict with an incorruptible opponent. It does not seem to have lessened his faith in dal Verme, however, for in that year the condottiere was honoured with the citizenship of Milan. He was a citizen also of Piacenza and, as a more material sign of Gian Galeazzo's favour, holder of various fiefs. His master knew when he had the loyalty of a sound general, and dal Verme was sound enough.

That season ended well for Hawkwood. His success in front of Bologna was not unnoticed in Ferrara, immediately to the north-east, where the unpopular marquis had increased his unpopularity by changing his city's traditional alignment and cultivating the friendship of Milan. Now he executed a quick volte-face, made a separate peace, and in October accepted a treaty of alliance with Florence. Padua, too, had briefly thrown off the domination of Milan: young Carrara had escaped from captivity, and with help from various anti-Visconti sources, Florentine, Bolognese, and Venetian money, and a force of German men-at-arms, had been joyously restored to the city. It looked as though Gian Galeazzo's advance towards the Adriatic had been checked.

There was to be more work for Hawkwood in the following year. But before the campaigning season opened in earnest Florence decided to give him the same honour that Milan had conferred on his adversary. On 8 April 1391, the Englishman was made an honorary citizen, the same privilege to be extended to his male descendants. It is worth noting that he was, however, specifically disqualified from holding any office in the civil administration. The Florentine merchants were not letting foreign soldiers set foot within the corridors of power.

In 1391 there was, for once, something approaching a strategic plan. Milan was to be assailed in a grand pincer movement. Hawkwood had the task of advancing across the Lombard plain from the east, while a French army under the Count d'Armagnac descended from the Alpine passes in the west. Dal Verme was well aware of this double threat. That awareness makes comprehensible – and in the end entirely justifiable – the caution he showed in his manœuvres against Hawkwood.

The Englishman opened his campaign by crossing the Adige on 15 May. Dal Verme made no attempt to stop him. He dared not commit major forces so far from Milan when no one knew how soon d'Armagnac's advance guard would be sighted on the Alpine foothills. He let Hawkwood push on. Hawkwood crossed, one after another, the succession of rivers that run across the vast plain to join the Po. Still dal Verme held his hand. Every day lengthened the Florentine supply-line, and he himself had learned in the previous year how decisively that could inhibit a commander's freedom of choice.

102 One of the rewards of the successful condottiere was the right of citizenship.
Hawkwood became a citizen of both Florence and Lucca. Above: the Lucchese
grant, of 1375.

Valfe el c° della lana' aᵱs contanti 26 ꝑ 13 β 4 ᵭᵱ di ꝑꝯ

103, 104, 105 Florence, Hawkwood's last and most generous employer, was a republic of businessmen. These illustrations show a wool merchant (above), a dyer (below left), and goldsmiths.

106 A gonfaloniere holding the banner of the people of Florence; from a chronicle of Florentine history.

Hawkwood also knew what he was doing. He had a well-disciplined army, his handling of which still amazed most of his contemporaries. All he did not know, any more than dal Verme, was the date on which his French allies would appear in Italy. He had reckoned on their arriving soon, but there was still no sign of them. Nevertheless, he was quite ready to take on the Milanese single-handed. But it must be soon. Even he could not guarantee to supply his army much longer, so far from its base.

He advanced to within thirty miles of Milan itself. There was alarm in the city. Gian Galeazzo organized processions and services of intercession: in the fashion of his age he found it possible to combine Catholic piety with a reverence for the ancient pagans, political realism with a respect for astrological indications. But in this particular instance he probably calculated that these religious demonstrations would help to make his subjects realize the gravity of the crisis, while at the same time heartening any with a tendency to panic. For his own part, as always, he trusted dal Verme and did not interfere on the military side.

Still the Milanese commander bided his time. Hawkwood shrugged his shoulders and ordered retreat. He could wait no longer. Nor could he press forward to the gates of Milan, with dal Verme poised to leap upon him at the most awkward moment, with the Milanese citizenry ready to do battle in defence of their own homes, and with no news still of d'Armagnac's arrival in Italy. Even so, Hawkwood had no reason to be dissatisfied with his achievement. He had traversed the Visconti dominions unopposed and carried the banner of Florence almost to the enemy capital. He had scored a moral victory that would not be lost upon the neutral or hesitant states, and he had, at least for that season, saved the Florentine and allied territories from aggression. All this had been done without expensive casualties. It was war as the businessmen liked their condottieri to wage it.

138

107 Paolo Uccello's painted monument to Sir John Hawkwood ('Johannes Acutus'), in Florence Cathedral, completed long after his death.

IOANNES·ACVTVS·EQVES·BRITANNICVS·DVX·AETATIS·
VAE·CAVTISSIMVS·ET·REI·MILITARIS·PERITISSIMVS·HABITVS·EST

·PAVLI·VGIELLI·OPVS·

Now, at last, dal Verme moved. A retreating army, both psychologically and in other respects, should be less formidable. He sent Gian Galeazzo a confident dispatch: 'Write and tell me how you wish me to settle them.' Gian Galeazzo left it to him, as dal Verme knew he would.

The rival commanders also exchanged courteous messages. It may seem odd to the modern reader, but such exchanges were not merely determined by the gentlemanly conventions of warfare, they were bound up with the practical conditions under which that warfare was carried on. A real decision usually demanded a set battle and a set battle implied a willingness on both sides to deploy their forces on a piece of ground suitable for the purpose. Hence, as occurs so often in Shakespeare, the constant passage to and fro of heralds trying to arrange the match.

So, Hawkwood drew back in good order, and dal Verme rode after him, cautious as ever. He sent the Englishman a caged fox as a taunt. Hawkwood studied it gravely. Then he remarked to the Milanese messenger: 'I can see that the creature is not stupid – he will find a way out.' He snapped one of the bars and in a moment the fox had squirmed through to freedom.

On another occasion he sent dal Verme a challenge to battle, once more the symbolic blood-stained glove. This time dal Verme picked up the glove and agreed to fight on the following day. But Hawkwood had not forgotten dal Verme's behaviour the previous summer. Now it was his own turn, he decided, to fool the enemy with a midnight vanishing trick. He left banners flying from trees, trumpeters to sound reveille to the empty camp before they mounted and galloped after him, and spare transport animals as booty to distract his pursuers. Then silently he took to the road with his army.

History continued to repeat itself – but with those significant variations that can be the downfall of the careless student. Twelve months before, Hawkwood and Giovanni da Barbiano had galloped headlong after the men who had deceived them. Now Facino Cane and a strong body of Milanese cavalry went in hot pursuit of the sly Englishman. This was exactly what Hawkwood and da Barbiano had expected. They laid an ambush and the Milanese fell into it. For the third time Facino Cane became Hawkwood's prisoner, and one begins to wonder on what basis this man's reputation as a condottiere rests.

Dal Verme, however, had preserved his main forces intact, and it was now that he displayed his great ability. The threat from Hawkwood was past. Too late to co-operate with the Florentines, the French under d'Armagnac were at last debouching from the Alpine valleys. With a speed and efficiency worthy of Hawkwood himself, dal Verme wheeled

108 A military camp, from a *cassone* painted a few years after Hawkwood's death.

his army and made a forced march from Lodi across to Alessandria, the strategic Piedmontese city commanding the western invasion routes into the north of Italy. Under the walls of this city, on 25 July, he completely smashed the French army. There were none of the professional courtesies of condottiere warfare. D'Armagnac perished with the finest of his knights. The survivors fled back into the mountains, where many were waylaid and hunted down by the peasants. Only the tattered remnants of the leaderless army managed to reach safety in Provence.

That was the end of the main operations, and they left the rivals with honours even. Hawkwood had executed a masterly advance and retreat which, says Fritz Gaupp, 'won him even more fame than his greatest victories'. Dal Verme, on the other hand, *had* won a great victory, but not over Hawkwood.

The rivals had not quite finished with each other. As soon as he had recovered his breath, dal Verme opened a new front in Tuscany. Quick as lightning, Hawkwood slid across the board to check him. The comparison with chess is unavoidable. From late September until the arrival of winter the two generals marched and counter-marched in the Val d'Arno without decisive action. There was one stiffish engagement in the Val di Nievole, when Taddeo dal Verme, commanding the rearguard for his brother, was captured by Hawkwood. But essentially it was a drawn match. The Milanese troops withdrew, and peace was signed in Genoa on 26 January 1392. There was great rejoicing in Florence, where it was felt that Gian Galeazzo's aggressive plans had been defeated and that once more the English captain had splendidly repaid the city's confidence.

He had fought his last battle – not because he was past fighting another, had need arisen, but because, so long as he lived, no further attack was mounted against the city of his adoption.

Hawkwood's last years were not without care. He had financial worries, he was an old man with young daughters to marry off, and his iron constitution was beginning at last to crack.

In 1390 his tax-payments were heavily in arrears. But he had just conducted his successful campaign in defence of Bologna and the Florentines were not ungrateful. That November they wiped the slate clean. In the following April, when they granted him the freedom of their city, they coupled with that honour some substantial benefits: he was to enjoy certain tax-exemptions, which would be passed on to his male heirs, he was voted an immediate grant of 2000 florins, over and above his normal pay for life, Donnina was guaranteed a widow's pension of 1000 florins, and each daughter would receive a dowry from the state of 2000 florins.

This last provision must have relieved both parents of considerable anxiety, for Janet had reached the accepted marriageable age of fourteen, and soon there would be Catherine to think of as well. Weddings in Florence were expensive, ostentatious affairs, and Hawkwood's family had to comply with the bourgeois standards of the society he served – though the old man himself, like many fathers subsequently, seems to have rebelled to some extent and to have shifted the responsibility to his wife.

Janet's wedding took place in September 1392, when there was peace with Milan and no other campaign to take the general away from home. The bridegroom was Brezaglia, son of Count Lodovico from the Lombard duchy of Friuli in the north-east. This nobleman had, according to the custom of the Italian states, held various offices as an impartial outsider, first in Ferrara as *podestà*, then as Captain of the People in Florence, when he must have been well acquainted with the city's Captain-General.

The preparations may be imagined. It was common for a tailor to move into the house some weeks beforehand, accompanied by one or two of his

work-people, and make clothes for the entire household. Hawkwood was not alone in quailing at the thought of such expenses. Other fathers shared his feelings, and sumptuary laws were continually being passed in a vain attempt to keep wedding costs within bounds. Never was it truer to say that 'the laws are made by the men', but in this instance it was certainly the women who took the lead in getting round them. There was, for instance, a Florentine restriction on the most expensive fur of all, ermine, which was reserved for knights and their ladies. We may be sure that Donnina pointed to this and insisted that Sir John and Lady Hawkwood could wear nothing less. We may be equally sure that he retorted by reminding her that nobody observed the distinction, and in fact everyone who could afford ermine (and many who could not) wore it in defiance of the regulation. This fact could hardly have escaped – or pleased – the lady

109, 110 The weddings of Hawkwood's two eldest daughters, Janet to an Italian count in 1392 and Catherine to a German condottiere the following year, were happy events of his old age. They were occasions for lavish festivity and display. Left: a lady visiting her tailor, from a manuscript of this period. Right: an illustration from the so-called 'sumptuary laws' of Siena, 1421, forbidding excessive extravagance in dress.

prouifiom contra (cominc vcliportarc ueftmen
fi vifctaja; c .ucllun. orippi. p̄m̄ nach anah o
ucramente profilatn vo:o ovameuto :⟩

'Donnina Visconti of Milan, consort of Sir John Hawkwood'. It was regrettable, it was monstrous, but it was no reason why those whose rank entitled them to ermine should content themselves with squirrel, fox, marten, cat, dormouse, or any of the other less impressive furs.

So too with the materials for the clothes, not forgetting the opulent linings to be so discreetly revealed. A bride's home would be strewn with samite and other fine silks, white damask and crimson velvet and scarlet taffeta. Belts were a major item, buttons a topic for exhaustive discussion. Old laws said that a silver belt must not weigh above five ounces, that the row of buttons on a sleeve must not rise beyond the elbow – but who took any notice? The bride must wear a splendid head-dress on the day, but she might need another half-dozen for her trousseau. Hawkwood may well have anticipated the cry of St Bernardino of Siena,

145

111 Wedding scene from a Florentine *cassone*. Note the jewellery, the expensive cloth an[...]

112, 113 Ladies' fashions from frescoes at Monza showing a wedding (below left) and in Piedmont showing characters from a romance.

urs, which the Signoria vainly attempted to curtail.

who was only a boy of twelve at this time. 'I know some women', the Franciscan was to declare a few years later, 'who have more heads than the Devil. Every day they put on some new headgear. I see some wearing them shaped like tripe, some like a pancake, some like a dish. . . . If you could only see yourselves, you look like a lot of owls and hawks! You women have made gods of your heads.'

So it was with everything, from the bride's silk-covered prayer-book to her thimble. The marriage-chests, or *cassoni*, that survive today in our museums as works of art, are just the symbols, the only extant reminders, of all that daunting expenditure.

Janet was married at San Donato, and the festivities may be imagined. The Hawkwoods might not be able to rival the splendours of that day in Milan when Bernabò had put on so lavish a show for his daughter, but Donnina, remembering that occasion, did her best for her own eldest girl. Regulations set a limit on the number of guests, the menu, and even

147

the dress of the maid-servants. The law said that these girls must wear simple kerchiefs, not silk head-dresses, and that they must clatter about in clogs, not trip daintily in high-heeled shoes or slippers. If they disobeyed, they might be fined or even birched naked through the town. Who worried about such rules out at San Donato? And what wedding ever kept within its original budget? Says Capulet, fixing Juliet's marriage-day with Paris:

> *Therefore, we'll have some half a dozen friends,*
> *And there's an end . . .*

A few pages later in the play, he is bidding a servant:

> *Sirrah, go hire me twenty cunning cooks . . .*

and then instructing the Nurse:

> *Look to the bak'd meats, good Angelica.*
> *Spare not for cost.*

When the time came, Hawkwood was probably like any bride's father.

All too soon, it was young Catherine's turn. Within two months of her sister's wedding, she was betrothed to a German condottiere, Conrad Prospergh.

Conrad was at least a bridegroom after the old man's heart. In the recent war against Milan he had been hired with his two hundred lances by the Florentines and had served under Hawkwood in the famous retreat across Lombardy. He evidently acquitted himself well, for he was awarded his gold spurs by his future father-in-law. In the final phases of the war, while Hawkwood and dal Verme were marching up and down in Tuscany, the young German had been given a *condotta* for six hundred lances by the allied government of Bologna. He had operated in the Reggio area and again distinguished himself by luring the Milanese forces into an ambush, capturing a number of men-at-arms, foot-soldiers, and horses.

Once peace was signed, he was prominent in the tournaments that formed a part of the celebrations. There was one in the main square of Bologna in February 1392, when he led a team of knights. On 12 May there was another at Florence in the Piazza Santa Croce. It is extremely likely that Hawkwood and his family were present, and that the girls were thrilled by the triumph of the young German whom their own father had dubbed knight the previous year. Conrad carried off the honours of the day. He led the Red Company of forty knights against the White Company commanded by Count Antonio Guidi and was awarded the trophy, a small lion covered with pearls.

148

In the following November he gained the hand of Catherine Hawkwood. They were to be married early in the New Year, but her father was either unwilling or unable to foot the bill. The state dowry of 2000 florins was of only slight help. It was paid straight over to the bridegroom, so, while it saved the bride's father from the necessity of finding the cash, it did not help him with the wedding expenses. Conrad was away in Bologna. Donnina had taken over the problem from her husband and was attacking it with matronly determination. She wrote to her prospective son-in-law, and he in turn wrote from Bologna on 9 January to the Florentine authorities, appealing for the advance of 1000 florins due to him in pay, so that 'Madonna Donnina may dress my wife for the wedding . . . Madonna Donnina writes that nothing is lacking but the money to dress her. I have told them to put on great festivities, but they have delayed so long in buying gowns for the young lady.'

The Signoria of Florence were sympathetic. At all events, the second Hawkwood wedding was duly celebrated eleven days after the writing of this letter.

114 Jousting in the Piazza S. Croce, Florence, c. 1450. It was at such a tournament that Catherine Hawkwood saw her future bridegroom.

The general knew by now that his soldiering days were over. Even if Florence were to need his services again, he was too old to ride forth, baton in hand, to save the republic.

His thoughts turned to the native country he had not visited for so long. He conceived a desire to end his days in England. It was no mere sentimental impulse of senility. Never for one moment had he ceased to think of himself as an Englishman. In his contracts he always insisted on a clause excusing him from participation in a war against the King of England. That king was now young Richard II, son of his one-time commander, the Black Prince, a sufficient reason for Hawkwood's continuing loyalty. And though the general had not been out of Italy, much less crossed the Channel, for more than thirty years, he had by no means lost all contact with England. There were important economic links between that country and Florence, notably the wool trade, and his value had been recognized as a thoroughly dependable Englishman domiciled in Florence, *persona grata* with the government there, and fluent in the language. Evidence of this is the deed of attorney executed at Westminster on 6 February 1385, empowering three Englishmen to sign commercial agreements with Florence and other Italian cities. The knight, 'Johannes Haukewood', was named first, followed by 'our Secretary, John Bacon, deacon, of St Martin's the Great, London', and Sir Nicholas Dagworth, 'of our Council'. Hawkwood must have acted as spokesman, receiving the other two when they came out to Italy, and generally facilitating the course of their negotiations. Had he fulfilled his desire to return to England, nine years after this service to the country, he would obviously not have found himself friendless or unknown.

First, though, he had to arrange his affairs, dispose of his Italian properties and come to an arrangement with the Signoria of Florence, so that he was assured of a livelihood in his retirement. Early in 1394 he sold his estate at Poggibonsi and began negotiations with Florence for the transfer of Montecchio and the other small places he owned, and had fortified, in the region of Arezzo. The house at San Donato he retained until the end. The outstanding problem was his life-pension: what would happen to that, when he had left not only Florence but Italy? Lengthy official discussions began.

He was far from well by now. Much of his time he was in bed or lay upon a couch. Only a man of his indomitable spirit would have held to a dream that involved the crossing of a continent under the hard travelling conditions of the fourteenth century. Yet still he talked of England. Donnina listened, privately doubtful whether he would ever start on the journey, let alone complete it. He must have talked persuasively, or the

Milanese woman would scarcely have entertained the idea (as she certainly did) of travelling to the unknown island with her younger children even after his death.

In March of that year, after much debate, the full Council of Florence passed a resolution by a hundred and eighty-one votes to twenty-four, commuting his pension as he had requested. The resolution began: 'Considering that Hawkwood, weary by reason of his great age, and, as he states, incapacitated by infirmity, desires to retire to his old country and to convert his annuity . . .' The permission, however, had come too late.

Five days after the Council's resolution Hawkwood had a stroke and died, probably during the night of 16 March. Death seems, at the end, to have taken him by surprise. There was no will made, as wills commonly were, during those last declining days, though he had given power of attorney to Giovanni di Jacopo Orlandini in the interests of his children.

When the news of his death reached the city next morning a public committee was at once set up to arrange his funeral without any stinting of the cost. It is the best tribute to Hawkwood's loyalty and the affection he inspired in the Florentines that, even when he was dead and of no further use to these economical businessmen, they were quite ungrudging in what they spent to honour his memory. Ordinarily, funerals were in theory controlled by the same kind of strict regulations imposed on wedding expenditure: there was a limit on torches and candles, no jewellery or armour or other trappings of much value might be buried with the corpse, and there was even a thoughtful provision that the mourning garments, the 'great cloaks' worn over the head and hanging down to the ground, should be only tacked together 'so as not to spoil the material, which would later serve to make clothes'. If any of these niggling economies were practised in Hawkwood's case they were not obvious. Even Donnina must have admitted that Florence put on a worthy show.

She herself, with her daughters, little John, and all the household at San Donato, were provided with handsome black outfits by the municipality. Hawkwood's body was first taken from his country home and laid in one of the city's churches. The empty bier, draped with crimson velvet and gold, was placed in the Piazza della Signoria and the procession formed round it. All the shops were closed by government edict. The foremost cavaliers of Florence carried the bier to fetch the corpse, which was then borne in full view, uncoffined as the custom was, regally swathed in cloth of gold, a drawn sword laid upon it and the commander's baton thrust between the stiffened fingers. The accent was appropriately military. Fourteen caparisoned chargers, led by soldiers who had served under him, paraded his crested helmet, his sword and shield, pennons, flags and all the panoply of chivalry. But the whole city turned out, including even the Signoria in person, ignoring protocol which normally discouraged their attendance on such occasions. There were scores of emblazoned banners, a forest of great wax torches. All the bells in Florence were tolling. Priests, monks, friars, and choristers swelled the procession, intoning their mournful psalms.

For a while, now, the body lay in state beside the font in the Baptistery of San Giovanni, the women lamenting over it in the Italian fashion that can still be witnessed today, especially in the south. Then the cavaliers took up the bier again and carried it across the street into the Duomo and set it down under the ornate catafalque prepared for it. The cathedral clergy conducted the funeral service and a eulogy was delivered, after which the dead general was lowered into a temporary grave in the choir, until the permanent tomb should be ready which the Signoria had already, even in his lifetime, resolved to provide.

115 When Hawkwood died, in March 1394, his body lay in state in the Baptistery of Florence, the octagonal building in the view below.

116 At the personal request of Richard II of England (right), Hawkwood's body was brought back to England and buried in the parish church of Sible Hedingham, Essex, where he was born.

So Hawkwood died – or 'entered the great sea', to use the noble euphemism that the Florentines favoured. But he was not destined to sleep in the tomb they had designed for him. The yearning of his latter days, to lay his bones in England, was unexpectedly gratified.

From England, from King Richard II, no less, came a request which the Signoria could scarcely refuse. Their reply is on record:

> Most serene and invincible Prince, most reverend Lord and our special benefactor: Our devotion can deny nothing to the eminence of Your Highness. We will leave nothing undone that it is possible to do, that we may fulfil your good pleasure. And therefore, although we hold that it reflected glory upon us and our people, to keep the ashes and bones of the late brave soldier Sir John Haukkodue, who, as commander of our army, fought most gloriously for us . . . nevertheless, in accordance with your request, we freely grant permission that his remains shall return to his native land, so that it shall not be said that Your Sublimity has uselessly and in vain demanded anything from the reverence of our humility.

153

Hawkwood's remains found their last resting-place in the parish church of Sible Hedingham where he was born. The tomb itself has vanished. The recess that once contained it can still be seen in the south wall of the church. It has a crocketed stone canopy and the punning emblem of the hawk is traceable in the decoration.

Did Donnina go there and supervise the monument – even to the inclusion of a figure representing Hawkwood's first wife? That is unknown. She certainly planned to go to England, taking with her the unmarried daughter, Anna, and her son. The Signoria sent King Richard another letter, full of respect and rhetoric, commending Hawkwood's widow to his royal protection. There is no evidence that she actually went. Anna married a well-connected gentleman of Milan, which should have pleased her mother. Young John is said to have settled in Sible Hedingham, but the subsequent history of the family is obscure.

It is in the Duomo, on the north wall, that Hawkwood's memory is most conspicuously preserved in Uccello's equestrian portrait. This curious monochrome painting calls for a word of explanation. Uccello, of course, never saw Hawkwood. He was not born until several years after the condottiere's death. The portrait began as a design for the marble tomb that was to have been erected in the newly completed nave of the church. When the tomb was not needed, the Florentine authorities decided to commission a fresco as a memorial: hence the sculptural quality of the portrait. The original fresco was poorly done. Uccello was employed to do it again, another impressive indication that Hawkwood's claim on the city's gratitude was not forgotten even forty years after 'the late brave soldier' had passed from the scene. Finally the fresco was transferred to canvas and hung in its present position.

With Hawkwood's death the domination by foreign condottieri ended, and the Italian-born captains took over, following the lead first given by Alberico da Barbiano. Soldiers of many nations continued in the various companies, but they soon ceased to hold high commands. Among the last to do so were Count Conrad of Eichelberg, whom the Italians called the 'Conte Corrado di Achilberg', and Bernardone da Serres, a Gascon of whom Hawkwood had thought well.

Conrad signed a contract with Florence in 1391 for an annual salary of 1200 florins so long as he stayed in Italy. The next year, this was changed to a life-long agreement, under which he guaranteed never to fight against the Florentine republic and to come to her aid whenever required. This does not seem to have prevented his developing close relations with her arch-enemy, Gian Galeazzo. When the latter was promoting, in the spring of 1396, one of his favourite disarmament schemes to eliminate the superfluous free companies, it was as his accredited representative that Conrad appeared in Florence to discuss the treaty.

Later that year it was Bernardone da Serres whom the Florentines appointed to Hawkwood's old post of Captain-General, and who, so far as any man could, replaced the Englishman. He had come to Italy many years before, usually serving the cause of the Avignon Popes, and acquiring several strongholds as a reward. These, and his past record, caused a little diplomatic awkwardness, since Florence acknowledged the Pope in Rome. When Bernardone's original six-month *condotta* came up for renewal, Rome's approval had to be obtained, and the republic arranged for the Pope to buy the lands granted to the general by Avignon.

When war broke out again between Milan and Florence soon afterwards, the Gascon proved a thoroughly satisfactory commander, and it was agreed, when his further employment was discussed, that 'no better or more trustworthy could be had'. He was Captain-General again in 1400 and held the position for another two years. Then, on 26 May 1402,

117 Alberico da Barbiano, Hawkwood's sometime comrade-in-arms, ravages the lands of Florence.

he was compelled against his better judgment to fight a battle against the Milanese army under Jacopo dal Verme.

The scene was familiar – especially to dal Verme. It was Casalecchio, on the banks of the pebbly River Reno, at the western outskirts of Bologna, where Hawkwood had faced him, turned him back, then pursued and defeated him, twelve years before. Bernardone was less fortunate. He had to defer to the wishes of Giovanni Bentivoglio, who had only recently made himself lord of Bologna and, acutely aware of his unpopularity with the citizens, was anxious not to be shut up with them for a siege. He therefore insisted that the condottiere should give battle outside, and, though the conditions were unfavourable, Bernardone had to agree. He lost and was taken prisoner. Bentivoglio's political assessment had been accurate. That night the Bolognese revolted, flung open the gates to the Milanese army (which, in accordance with Italian political tradition, contained many of their own exiled party leaders), proclaimed a free commune and invited Gian Galeazzo to be their overlord. Bentivoglio was killed in the rising. Bernardone gained his freedom by the simple expedient of signing a new contract with Milan. As matters turned out, however, his association with Gian Galeazzo, that avid collector of condottieri, was destined to last only for a month or two. Bernardone decided to quit Italy altogether and retired to his native Gascony.

118 Biordo Michelotti of Perugia is appointed Captain-General of the Florentines after the death of Hawkwood.

Simultaneously with the employment of these two old-style foreign commanders, the Signoria of Florence had been using Italians far more typical of the new epoch that was opening.

While Hawkwood was still alive, but clearly ageing, they had retained the services, by a *condotta in aspetto* dated 1 May 1393, of a well-known Perugian adventurer, Biordo Michelotti, but when Hawkwood died in the following spring, and they named Michelotti Captain-General in his stead, they found that the offer had been left rather too late.

Michelotti's sights had always been fixed upon his native city. In youth he had suffered the common fate of exile. The class war was particularly virulent and chronic in that nowadays delightful Umbrian town. Michelotti was born into the prosperous bourgeoisie, the *popolo grasso*, or 'the plump people', who in Perugia bore the party name of *Raspanti*, 'those who claw', with the appropriate emblem of a cat. Against them were arrayed the old nobility and the *popolo minuto*, or 'little men', whom the nobles claimed to champion. This party took a falcon as symbol and the name of *Beccherini*, thought to signify 'the butchers'. Both parties lived up to their names and the political life of Perugia was more vigorous than healthy.

A condottiere's life was the frequent choice of any spirited young fellow excluded from a settled career inside his own community. Michelotti took

157

to it and enjoyed success for a number of years, serving various masters and even, according to one tradition, fighting for the King of France against England. During these years, whatever the ups and downs of the parties in Perugia, he does not seem to have sought a chance to re-establish himself in the city. He was doing very well as a soldier of fortune and had little incentive to go home and become a nobody. He was biding his time. He would go back to Perugia as ruler of the city, if at all. He was the first of the new-style condottieri who used their military power to make themselves dictators.

In 1391 he was with dal Verme in the victory over d'Armagnac at Alessandria. When peace came next year, he transferred to Florence and looked like being the republic's first choice as successor to Hawkwood. But at this juncture came the long-awaited opportunity to return to Perugia.

That city had, for the moment, exhausted its capacity for internal strife. The pendulum had swung back to where it had been at the start of Michelotti's career. The nobles and their plebeian partisans were in, the Raspanti were out. But every one was heartily sick of the struggle and Pope Boniface IX was begged to arbitrate. Each party was doubtless confident that God was on its side and that His Vicar could not fail to see a fact so obvious. Hence the delighted welcome accorded to the pontiff when, in 1392, he arrived in Perugia in person. The city councillors donned fine new scarlet robes in honour of the occasion and the people danced through the streets.

This euphoria did not last long. Soon Boniface found himself in the common dilemma of the peace-maker when neither disputant will give an inch of ground. The monastery in which he was lodged became his refuge. He scarcely ventured to meet his excitable hosts in the narrow streets outside. His bodyguard stood ready to repel attack at any time.

Michelotti was watching the situation with the keenest interest from his fortress at Deruta, a day or two's ride to the south on the opposite side of the Tiber valley. He was a popular figure. His courage and charm had won him many friends in Umbria and the exiled Raspanti turned to him as their natural leader. The aristocrats, on the other hand, clinging to their precarious supremacy in the city, saw that he was potentially their most dangerous enemy. They sent messages offering him substantial inducements to keep out of the quarrel, an approach which would have succeeded with many condottieri.

At last the brawling factions in Perugia decided to give the Pope power to settle the dispute. Boniface thereupon promulgated his considered verdict: there must be reconciliation, and to achieve it the exiles must be

119, 120 Pope Boniface IX (right) played a major, though not finally a very effective, part in the return of Michelotti to his native city of Perugia. In 1392 he was invited to arbitrate between the warring classes. The miniature below shows the setting for such a scene, with a pope settling an ecclesiastical dispute.

122 The Porta Marzia of Perugia. Note the family towers in the background, built for defence in times of public disorder.

recalled and a balanced constitutional government set up. A month later, on 17 October 1393, Michelotti rode into Perugia with two thousand amnestied exiles exulting at his heels. Their first act was to wait upon the Pope, who was still lodged in the monastery of San Pietro, and pay their respects to him. Free elections then took place and a new Council was chosen, consisting half of the nobility and half of the merchants. The workers, needless to say, neither expected nor were offered any direct representation.

Michelotti knew his fellow townsmen too well to suppose that this happy compromise would endure. It lasted just a month. The Pope, indeed, was still there in San Pietro. It was Michelotti whose affairs had briefly called him away from the city again.

161

121 The city of Perugia, in the foreground the monastery of S. Pietro, where Pope Boniface lodged.

Trouble flared up. A nobleman killed one of the Raspanti. He was hauled before the *podestà* for trial. As that official was about to pass sentence, the verdict was challenged by Pandolfo dei Baglioni, a member of the leading aristocratic family. Convinced that the bad old days were come again, and that there was going to be no justice for the late exiles, the Raspanti took the law into their own hands. There was a massacre. Not only was Baglioni murdered in his own doorway but sixty of his relatives were hunted down and butchered. Another of the noble families withstood a three-day siege in one of those massive towers that still, especially in San Gimignano, remind us of the days when the Italian's home, even more than the Englishman's, had to be his castle. This other family, the Ranieri, were finally starved out. They were taken to court, where the *podestà* to his credit refused to give any judgment against them. Better for them if he had thrown them, for the moment at least, into the worst dungeon. Instead they were hustled back to the Ranieri tower, murdered and hurled from its windows.

This was the state of affairs when Michelotti came hurrying back. The Pope had thrown up his hands in despair and withdrawn across the valley to Assisi. When the condottiere took control into his own hands, imposing the order that no one else could, Boniface approved the arrangement. Only later, when he heard of Michelotti's growing popularity and prospects of permanence, did the unsuccessful arbitrator experience some pangs of understandable pique. He engaged a condottiere himself for a single month (and a singularly ineffective gesture that was, against a rival of Michelotti's ability and reputation) and strove to upset the new arrangement. But Michelotti was now firmly in the saddle, and it would have taken more than that to unseat him.

For several years he remained undisputed lord of the beautiful Umbrian city which sprawls, as someone has said, like 'a giant gnarled hand, laid on five hills', high above the valley of the Tiber and those soft landscapes made familiar by so many paintings. He did not renew his *condotta* with Florence, though he continued the association. He considered himself a sovereign now, an ally to be courted, not a general to be employed.

This was made clear by the style in which he celebrated his wedding. His chosen bride was Bertolda Orsini, of the ancient house of Roman aristocrats. She entered the city with a splendid entourage. They came riding up the steep road to the gates of the acropolis-like town, the ambassadors of Florence and Venice and many other notables swelling the numbers of her own kinsfolk and attendants. The women of Perugia came running out to strew flowers in their path, and to exclaim at the girl's beauty. She was a glittering figure, robed in cloth of gold, her hair starry with jewels and garlanded. It was a genuinely happy public occasion, for Michelotti had won the affection of many, and had brought peace to a community too long racked by uncertainty and violence. The city streamed with banners; balconies and archways were festooned and peasants lined up to add farm-produce to the more ostentatious wedding-presents.

Potentially, Michelotti was a unifying figure. His party support came from the merchant class. But his birth and military record made him a man the nobility had to respect, and his personal qualities endeared him to the *popolo minuto*.

123 Painted wooden chest used for the election of civic officials in Perugia, bearing the emblems of the Mercanzia and Cambio.

Even he, however, could not please everybody. His successful pacification of the city and his taking over of its government had left him with the Pope as a resentful, and for the moment powerless, enemy. Boniface was kept informed of all these doings by his late host, the Abbot of San Pietro. The abbot had his eye on a cardinal's hat. He soon realized that the surest way to win it was by the elimination of Michelotti, by any method, and the restoration of papal influence in Perugia. He was himself a member of one of the old patrician families, a Guidalotti, and therefore well placed to test the continuing strength of the underground opposition among members of that class.

Discussions of any political problem were apt to end in a conspiracy to assassinate the individual blamed for the trouble, and so it was in this case. Abbot Guidalotti soon found himself prime mover in a plan involving twenty or more determined enemies of the régime. Whether or not the Pope was an accessory before the fact, the abbot was able to assure his colleagues that the news would not be received with disfavour in Rome. As for the reactions of their fellow citizens, they optimistically assumed that a few shouts of 'The tyrant is dead!' would persuade every one to accept the changed situation without demur.

A Sunday in March, in 1398, was chosen. A time was appointed when most of the leading citizens would be hearing Mass in San Lorenzo's cathedral. With due regard for scriptural example, the abbot said that the signal to strike home with the poisoned daggers would be when he had saluted Michelotti with a fraternal kiss.

Sunday morning came. The abbot mounted his horse – for his monastery lay on an outflung spur at the extreme limit of the city – and rode to his family home, the Palazzo Guidalotti, where his aged father still lived. Here he was joined by the conspirators. The party then moved off to Michelotti's house, having made sure that they would find him there. The abbot announced that he had important news to deliver in person to his lordship. Knowing Guidalotti's status as a mouthpiece of the Pope, the condottiere suspected nothing and quickly came down to greet his visitor. Guidalotti grasped his hand and bestowed the Judas kiss, and his followers instantly surrounded Michelotti, hacking and stabbing with such desperate ferocity (despite the poison they had used as an extra guarantee of success) that the floor ran with blood.

Their mission accomplished, the gang suffered a fatal failure of nerve. Only two of the most resolute kept to the original programme, made for the principal piazza, and proclaimed what they had done. The abbot, whose status and calling might have made him the most acceptable spokesman, hurried back to his monastery with most of the others, if not

164

appalled by his own action at least alarmed by a new realization that it might have unforeseen consequences.

In that he was right. Michelotti's popularity had been underestimated. The proclamation was duly made outside the cathedral and the news instantly carried inside to the congregation. There was an angry rush for the doors. The preacher was abandoned in his pulpit. His listeners ran home to arm themselves. In no time the whole of Perugia was in tumult. Some of Michelotti's followers paraded a silver bowl with the blood which, they alleged, they had caught as it oozed from their dying leader's wounds. It was put on display like some relic of an accredited saint, and the banner of the city set up over it, a rampant silver griffin on a crimson field. This symbol still further inflamed the public fury. The old class hatreds were unleashed again. The Guidalotti palace was stormed and set on fire, the abbot's hapless old father perishing with numerous others in the course of the reprisals. The abbot escaped, for by this time he had decided not to trust even the massive walls of San Pietro, and had already set out on the road to Casalina.

In its hopelessly divided state the city was then just ripe to be taken over by Gian Galeazzo, and so, by one of his characteristic procedures, it very soon was.

For one reason or another, the Signoria of Florence were consistently unlucky in their attempts to find and retain a satisfactory replacement for

124 The banner of Perugia – a silver griffin holding a sword on a crimson field. Such a banner was set up over the blood of the murdered Michelotti.

Hawkwood. It is not surprising that for years afterwards they looked back wistfully to the time of that efficient and dependable Englishman.

In 1396, even while they were negotiating a contract with Bernardone da Serres, they were trying to secure an Italian commander on a permanent basis. They approached Cecchino Broglia, a Piedmontese who had fought under Hawkwood at Castagnaro. Although, since then, he had turned down their offer to employ him with a hundred lances, Gian Galeazzo having outbid them with a *condotta* for two hundred, and had fought for the Milanese at Alessandria, this did not count against him. The Florentine agent was instructed to assure him in confidence 'that they loved him much, and would welcome a decision on his part to live and die in Florence. They would do everything for his dignity and meet his requirements in the matter of recruiting troops.' Later these assurances boiled down to a firm offer of a one-year contract and a life-pension of 1200 florins. Broglia refused the terms as inadequate.

If Biordo Michelotti exemplifies the condottiere with political aspirations, Broglia will stand well enough for the brigand element so common in the profession.

After Alessandria and the 1392 peace, Gian Galeazzo had rewarded him with several fiefs, but Broglia was not content to stay quiet as a petty lord until his services were called upon. He preferred to move southwards into the Marches with his marauding band, sometimes making tiresome incursions into Florentine territory. His position was ambiguous. He held a *condotta in aspetto* from Gian Galeazzo, but when both Florence and Perugia protested to Milan about his activities the astute Visconti replied that he was not responsible for Broglia's doings. Gian Galeazzo often found himself embarrassed in this way by the uncontrollable behaviour of captains in his pay – Facino Cane was another offender – but he was adept at the deflection of diplomatic protests. Late in 1394 Broglia rode into Tuscany from the south and early in the following year he seized possession of the Aretine stronghold of Gargonza. On this occasion the Florentines prepared to throw him out, but first they sent a remonstrance to Gian Galeazzo, reminding him that he had guaranteed their dominions safety from Broglia's raids. This time Gian Galeazzo felt bound to do something. He called Broglia to heel, and the condottiere withdrew from the Arezzo region – only to move on, that summer, into the territory of Lucca. By June of the next year, 1396, Florence was again dispatching protests to the court at Pavia. It was in this period that the Signoria sensibly decided they might achieve more by getting Broglia on to their payroll, but, as already mentioned, their secret proposals to him met with no success.

He returned to his bandit-like existence in the Marches. Florence continued to feel she would prefer to have this rugged character fighting for, rather than against, her. In September 1398, she increased the offer. The life-pension would be 2000 florins, with a house provided in the city for his family. Broglia kept the talks going without committing himself. It was only six months since the assassination of his one-time comrade, Michelotti, and the political situation in Umbria was fluid. Broglia's understanding of such matters was probably slight. He became attracted by the notion that, as Michelotti had seized the *signoria* of Perugia, he himself might do something similar in the neighbouring city of Assisi. That he was not a native of the place, as Michelotti had been in Perugia, and not backed by one of its major parties, suggested no great difficulty. If he recognized a difference between the two cases it was probably rather that he flattered himself as too clever to be taken in by his enemies and murdered.

Broglia accordingly established himself in Assisi, where Cardinal Albornoz had built a massive papal fortress only thirty years before,

125 The fortress of Assisi, where the condottiere Cecchino Broglia established his brigand-like rule in 1398.

providing an ideal mountain-top headquarters for a brigand chief. He continued his haggling with the Florentines and meanwhile extracted protection-money from every state he was in a position to threaten with his mercenary bands.

'You know how eminent a man he is,' the Florentines wrote to their Venetian allies on 22 March 1399, 'and how important it is that we should have him on our side.' In July they wrote: 'We have reckoned up that over two months Messer Brolia and Messer Conte have received from the Pope, on promise of not injuring the Church territories for six months . . .' And the letter went on to list amounts totalling 32,300 florins.

The end of the affair is ironic. Broglia at last condescended to accept, for three years only, the proffered appointment of Captain-General of Florence. Within a few months of its being gazetted, he died of plague. Florence had to foot the bill for a magnificent funeral consonant with the dignity of his rank.

One cannot but sympathize with these councillors, for ever striving to protect their republic without wasting a florin of the taxpayers' money. Though far from being a democracy in the modern sense, Florence suffered, in her conflicts with Milan, the same crippling handicaps that inhibit a democracy confronted today with a dictatorship. Her government – the Signoria, selected from the city's four quarters and sixteen wards or gonfalons – could look forward to no permanent control of policy, and, though membership was restricted by conditions of age and parentage, making an oligarchy like that of Venice, it was extensive enough to produce clashes of opinion and interest, and to hinder the formulation of consistent long-term plans. The serving councillors looked splendid and lived impressively. During their term of office they lorded it in the Palazzo della Signoria, wore the *lucco* or gown of pink, violet, or crimson, were waited on by green-liveried servitors, enjoyed banquets, debated, and filed across the piazza in those ceremonial processions beloved by the painters. There were times when, hearing ambassadors, appointing condottieri, and approving treaties, the wealthy banker or wool-merchant could feel himself the equal of a Visconti or a Pope. But unless he was a fool, and Florentine businessmen seldom were, he knew that the moment would pass, and that in any case his power was shared. Gian Galeazzo was sole master of Milan, and would be so until his dying breath.

Thus, in the matter of condottieri, the Florentines could decide nothing without lengthy discussions, resolutions, and votes, a black bean for 'yes', a white bean for 'no'. If Gian Galeazzo needed another general for the secret plan maturing in his mind, he had only to crook a finger and beckon.

It is time to speak fully of Alberico da Barbiano, who in status was far more truly Hawkwood's successor than any of the captains whom Florence tried to enlist in her service.

As already mentioned, he had been the Englishman's neighbour for a few years in Romagna, his colleague in the horrible affair at Cesena and in other more honourable actions, his opponent on campaigns elsewhere. His strong and understandable resentment against the foreign companies ravaging his country had led him to form the all-Italian Compagnia di San Giorgio.

After his famous triumph over the Bretons in 1379 he had placed his forces under the banner of Charles of Durazzo, who came from Hungary to fight for the crown of Naples. In gratitude for Pope Urban VI's support, Charles sent Alberico and his company to threaten the Tuscan towns hostile to the pontiff. It was on this occasion, in March 1380, that the Romagnol knight found himself confronting the Englishman. Having taken Arezzo, Alberico menaced Florence, at that time defended by Hawkwood's brother-in-law, Lucius Landau, and the latter's brother Eberhard. There was a fight on 1 April. Eberhard captured Giovanni da Barbiano and others, along with seventy horses. Hawkwood then arrived to take over the supreme command from the German brothers and prepared to attack the Compagnia di San Giorgio, whose ranks contained a number of Florentine exiles. Alberico had a healthy respect for this particular foreigner. He declined battle and drew away. He had just demanded 20,000 florins from Lucca. He was glad to settle for half that amount and to retire into the solitary marshlands of the Maremma. Nine years later, he and Hawkwood were colleagues again in some rather abortive operations round Naples, from which Hawkwood was hastily recalled by the outbreak of war between Florence and Milan. Throughout this period Alberico was consistently occupied in the service of Charles and then, after his murder, of his little son Ladislaus, being rewarded for his loyalty with the title of Grand Constable of the Kingdom of Sicily.

In 1392, however, the fluctuations of the struggle for the Neapolitan throne dashed the immediate hopes of the sixteen-year-old Ladislaus, and Alberico himself was taken prisoner. This captivity lasted until late in the following year and seems to have been ended by the good offices of Gian Galeazzo, whom Alberico served for the next nine years. The circumstances of Alberico's entering the Milanese service are recorded in a reproachful letter written after he quitted it, following Gian Galeazzo's death, and still preserved in the archives of the Ambrosian Library. The writer, Uberto Decembrio, the duke's secretary, reminds Alberico how he had been languishing in miserable captivity, unable to pay the immense ransom demanded by the Duke of Venosa, whereupon Gian Galeazzo had

obtained his release, expending the sum of 27,000 florins for his ransom and other obligations. And when, his release effected, the count presented himself before this most gentle prince, first, the prince freely cancelled the debt for his ransom, and the price of a horse and other gifts; and then appointed him Captain-General of his armies, with a regular allowance of 500 ducats a month, and pay for 300 lances and 50 foot-soldiers. Further, he enfeoffed to him and his heirs two very fine and strong castles in the territories of Verona and Parma, with their revenues and jurisdictions.

One of these was Montecchio Emilia, where some of the ramparts are still preserved.

126 Montecchio Emilia, one of the castles given by Gian Galeazzo Visconti to Alberico da Barbiano. It later formed part of the estate of another famous condottiere, Muzio Attendolo Sforza.

The duke's secretary goes on,

On account of all this Count Alberico took solemn and binding oaths of fealty and homage for himself and his heirs to the said lord duke and his sons, and promised to the prince that he would serve him at all times loyally and faithfully, and that he would not depart from the service of the aforesaid lord or of his sons on any occasion, except with the consent and special leave of the aforesaid lord; but that he should be bound always and constantly to remain loyally in the service of the aforesaid lord and his children; even as it appears, on all these matters, in public documents, solemnly confirmed with the seal of the said Count Alberico in witness of the truth.

Before judging the condottiere too harshly, it would be well to study his defection in its historical context.

Meanwhile, all that lay in the future. It was towards the end of 1393 that the ransomed prisoner arrived to render thanks to his new patron in the bright audience-chamber at Pavia, and to join Jacopo dal Verme and the other condottieri who executed the military part of the Visconti design.

That Alberico was appointed 'Captain-General of his armies' does not imply that Gian Galeazzo had withdrawn any of his confidence in dal Verme, and there is no evidence that he ever did. As previously noted, the post of Captain-General did not necessarily imply supreme and unshared command. Gian Galeazzo – it was not until 1395 that he became 'Duke of Milan', buying the title from Wenceslas, King of the Romans, for 100,000 florins – maintained a sort of inner cabinet of men he fully trusted, and Jacopo dal Verme deservedly retained a position equivalent to that of a war minister. The rest of this inner circle comprised similar specialists in their respective fields, Pietro da Candia, the Bishop of Novara, Niccolò Diversi, a banker from Lucca, and Niccolò Spinelli, from the Regno, a man well versed in statecraft. The circle pivoted on the confidential secretary, Pasquino Capelli of Cremona, whose quiet and discreet demeanour masked, in that epoch of flamboyance, the vast influence he wielded. Gian Galeazzo knew how to delegate. 'Speak to Pasquino about that,' was his favourite answer to questions of detail.

In the military sphere it often suited him not to know too precisely what his hired generals were doing, so that if necessary he could disown them. With dal Verme, his trusted and permanent commander, who had been as it were his sword-arm since the day of his coup against Bernabò, his relationship was much closer. Dal Verme was sometimes sent on diplomatic missions, as well as maintaining an over-all supervision of the Milanese forces.

Alberico, for all his reputation, was just one of the group of condottieri that Gian Galeazzo liked to collect, whether he needed them or merely wished to render them unavailable to his enemies.

Another such was the famous Piedmontese Facino Cane, who owed his *nom de guerre*, 'the Dog', rather to his aggressive qualities than to his outstanding fidelity. In 1387 he had fought for Verona and been one of Hawkwood's numerous haul of prisoners at Castagnaro. He must have been ransomed promptly, for later that year he entered the service of Gian Galeazzo's friend, Teodoro of Montferrat, who encouraged him in raids on the territory of Savoy. In 1390 he was one of Carlo Malatesta's subordinate condottieri fighting for Gian Galeazzo. He was again captured by Hawkwood, and yet again, this time being severely wounded while harrying Hawkwood's retreat a year later. On 20 November 1393, about the date of Alberico's liberation, Gian Galeazzo lent Cane 4000 florins, free of interest but repayable on demand. In return the Piedmontese promised, as Alberico did a few weeks later, always to be available for the Milanese service if required. This loan immediately led to embarrassments with Savoy, since Cane used the money to start carving himself an unauthorized little dominion in those western mountains. Gian Galeazzo had to disclaim responsibility for his behaviour, and offered 'to place lands, goods, and persons under ban for the satisfaction of Savoy'. In 1395 and 1396 Cane served Orleans against Genoa and then Genoa against Orleans. In 1397 he was back under the Visconti banner again, but he must always have been a troublesome servant, obsessed with his own ambition to set up as a lord in his native region, at no matter what disturbance to neighbouring states. Towards the end of 1400 Gian Galeazzo had to exert pressure on his friend Teodoro and secure Cane's dismissal from the service of Montferrat.

Facino Cane has his distinctive niche in the gallery of famous condottieri, not so much for his prowess in the field as for his success in cultivating his own interests and building up his power until (as will be seen) that power had a decisive influence upon political events. Alberico da Barbiano is remembered for quite different reasons.

Subsequent historians, such as Machiavelli, regarded him as the father of the condottiere system. National pride, in part, made them play down the contribution of the foreign forerunners. In any case, Alberico was a more typical figure. Hawkwood, making his men-at-arms get off their proud chargers and employing those English archers with their devilish longbows, was an exception and had no imitators. His innovations left no mark on the tactics of the Italian wars. When he was gone, the Italian knights climbed thankfully into the saddle again and stayed there. That

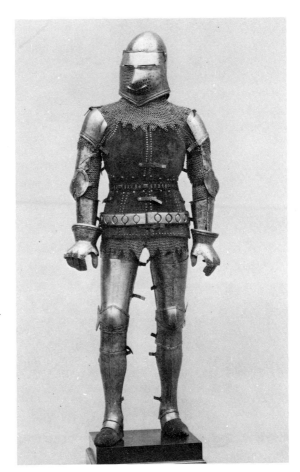

127 A suit of Italian armour, *c.* 1400. Machiavelli complained that condottiere battles were mere jousts in which no one was killed. It was true that in normal circumstances armour such as this gave almost total protection.

was Alberico's way. And to serve with him was the accepted form of apprenticeship for an adventurous young man.

Machiavelli wrote more than a century later, when the condottiere system was coming to an end:

All those who have been the arbiters of Italy's destiny, since Alberico of Romagna and his disciples, Braccio and Sforza, have adopted one method. Their aim has been to enhance their personal reputation by undermining the respect for infantry. They do this because, being landless men living on their acquisitions, they have found that to be followed by a few foot-soldiers won them no esteem, while they could not afford to keep up a big force of such troops. They accordingly confine themselves to cavalry, finding that with a modest company of horsemen they can command pay and respect.

Machiavelli's own prejudice must be allowed for, his contempt for mercenaries, his exaggerated descriptions of their lackadaisical fighting methods, and his ill-founded faith in the superiority of a patriotic citizen army, fighting on foot. But, discounting all these, one recognizes the truth of his broad picture. Alberico *did* make the mounted knight once more the most important factor in Italian tactics, and his pupils, however they differed in their modifications of his teaching, did not depart from the main principle he had reasserted.

In *The Archaeology of Weapons* R. Ewart Oakeshott gives a good idea of what it must have felt like to ride and fight under the conditions of that period: 'The principal – indeed the only – function of the great war-horse was to provide a platform, mobile, highly trained and supremely sensitive to the slightest movement of its rider, from which to fight.' Having discussed 'the prime importance of stirrups' Mr Oakeshott goes on: 'As armour became heavier, the saddle tended to be made with a higher ridge above the horse's withers, so that the rider's legs would not need to be spread at so wide an angle – in short, his "seat" upon his saddle would be more like the sort of stance he would take if he were fighting on his feet.' As Lady Apsley pointed out in *Bridleways Through History*, although the Crusaders had long ago observed the Saracens riding with short stirrups in the modern style, 'for centuries men-at-arms of Northern blood continued riding long with legs thrust out straight as stilts in the now characteristic high-peaked saddles.'

In *The Story of the Sforzas* L. M. Collison-Morley says it was Alberico 'who invented the visor to the helmet and the neck piece behind' and 'also had the horses protected by elaborate leather caparisons'. The first of these claims is misleading. Visors were known earlier, and the best type was in fact evolved in Germany, but Alberico may well have thought of some modification, or introduced visors where troops had not previously been equipped with them. He would certainly have paid more attention to defensive covering for the horses than Hawkwood ever did. The Englishman was all for mobility, and did not intend to expose his horses to the weapons of the enemy. Alberico meant them to share the full shock of battle.

So long as Gian Galeazzo lived, Alberico kept his promise of loyal service.

Genoa had passed into French hands in the autumn of 1396, a development unwelcome to Milan but one which, for the time being, the duke had to stomach. He therefore turned his attention east and south, resuming his expansionist schemes and exploiting the internecine feuds of the various cities, especially in so far as they weakened the position of his one truly

128 An Italian knight of about 1400, showing the long stirrup, the helmet with visor, and the elaborate horse armour.

obdurate enemy, Florence. In his more imaginative reveries he pondered the possibility that, with the great Tuscan republic neutralized, there would be nothing to bar his further advance. The papal lands were in their usual condition of weakness and chaos, and the Regno continued to be racked by dynastic competition. Given time, might he not fairly dream of dominating all Italy?

His immediate plans, for 1397, were to strike without previous declaration of war at his main surviving adversary in the north, Francesco Gonzaga of Mantua, simultaneously distracting Florence with raids upon her territory. Dal Verme was entrusted with the attack on the Mantuans, Alberico da Barbiano with the campaign in Tuscany. In this latter campaign the chosen tool was Pisa, Florence's traditional foe, a city which the duke had made his willing satellite by liquidating the previous doge and establishing one more susceptible to his direction.

That winter the preparations mounted. As a contemporary chronicler, Ser Naddo da Montecatini, wrote:

> The cursed Duke of Milan, to avenge the Pisans, sent over six thousand horses to Pisa in December and January, and again in March, with fine troops and good captains, chief among them Count Alberico da Barbiano. . . . After remaining there for two months, they added to their numbers and moved in the direction of Siena. . . . By 23 March they were at Mercatale di Greve, stealing horses and a large amount of corn and cattle, and taking numerous prisoners, both men and women.

Though Alberico had come to the fore as Italy's deliverer 'from the barbarians', it made little noticeable difference to the countryside whether it was ravaged by one of the foreign bands or by the Compagnia di San Giorgio.

This spring offensive filled the Florentines with gloom. To meet the danger fresh financial impositions were necessary. Even the priests were expected, for once, to dip into their purses. As for the poor businessmen, their reaction was typified by Datini's lament to his wife: 'War has broken out with the Pisans. The other merchants and I are all ruined. God provide what is needed!' He had just contributed 250 florins to a compulsory defence loan.

That was on 19 March. Tied by his business in Florence, he sent his wife, twelve miles away in Prato, detailed instructions that all the movable property on their farm should be brought within the town walls. Not even pieces of iron were to be left. If she and the servants had time to shift the straw, that too should be salvaged. 'Put it wherever you think best,' he added with a husband's cheerful disregard for such storage problems, 'for if the beasts cannot have oats, they must manage with straw.' The

176

previous night, he warned her, the raiders had been within twelve miles of Florence in the other direction.

While Alberico thus spread alarm through Tuscany, dal Verme was concentrating his army at Cremona. At the end of March he launched his surprise attack on the Mantuan stronghold of Borgoforte, where Hawkwood had once stopped the advance of the Emperor. It was well defended and the assault failed. Dal Verme had to bring up a siege-train and settle down to the lengthy formalities of investment and bombardment. It was not until the middle of July that he was able to send Gian Galeazzo the welcome news that the fortress had fallen. Dal Verme then went off to help Ugolotto Biancardo who was besieging Governolo, a smaller place some miles further to the east, situated on the Mincio just before it joins the Po after coming down through the city of Mantua. Here the Mantuans and their allies made a determined counter-attack. Carlo Malatesta arrived with a column of reinforcements and, making a sally from the defences, threw back the Milanese. Exploiting this initial advantage, Malatesta drove dal Verme back to Borgoforte and then across the Po again. Dal Verme lost not only all the ground he had gained but his siege-train, rivercraft, and food-supplies. But he had known such reverses before and triumphed over them. Helped by the lack of real unity in the alliance arrayed against him, he returned to the attack, and by the end of the summer Borgoforte was in Milanese hands once more.

Gian Galeazzo's programme went forward in the next year or two, step by step, in accord with his ever-flexible plans. In Pisa his satellite Doge Jacopo d'Appiano died in 1398: he was replaced by his son, Gherardo, who sold the city to Gian Galeazzo for 200,000 florins, despite the offer of the citizens to pay him the same sum and retain their liberty. Milanese troops occupied the city, the banners of Pisa were taken away, and on 31 March 1399 they were dipped in solemn salute before the duke in his palace at Pavia. In November the republic of Siena also yielded to him. Perugia followed suit on 21 January 1400. That city had been ruled briefly by Ceccolino Michelotti, brother of the murdered Biordo, but the arrival in Umbria of one of the duke's condottieri, Ottobuono Terzo, at the head of two thousand lances, persuaded him that it would be prudent to let Milan take over.

During this period Alberico da Barbiano had been busy in the north. Late in September 1399, his brother Giovanni had been captured, laden with plunder, while raiding the territory of Bologna. Instead of being put up for ransom in the usual gentlemanly fashion, he was executed by the Bolognese, at the insistence (it was said) of his old enemy, Astorre Manfredi of Faenza. When the condottiere conventions were at variance with the demands of the family vendetta, there was always the risk that the tougher line would be taken. Alberico certainly blamed Manfredi for his brother's death. He obtained the duke's permission to march against Bologna, but for the time being did not push matters to a military decision. Instead, he took a leaf out of his master's book, involved himself in political intrigues inside the city, and helped to engineer the downfall of its government, making a bargain with its new rulers for a combined attack on Manfredi's city of Faenza, thirty miles to the south-east along the Via Emilia. But greater matters were afoot, and soon the duke had need of him elsewhere, so this personal quarrel could not for the moment be pursued.

The greater matter was a threat to Gian Galeazzo from beyond the Alps. In despair the Florentines had seen one Italian city after another absorbed into the Milanese dominion. A strong ally they must have. But Venice was preoccupied overseas and there seemed no other adequate help forthcoming from within the peninsula. Their best hope lay in Rupert of Bavaria, the Elector Palatine who had just been chosen 'King of the Romans' after the deposition of Wenceslas. Wenceslas had played the Visconti game, selling Gian Galeazzo the ducal title he had craved. Rupert – for a consideration – would help Florence instead. That consideration was 200,000 florins down, and another 200,000 when he had completed four months' campaigning on the territory of Milan.

In the summer of 1401 Rupert and his German knights rode down through the mountains into Lombardy. The duke fielded a full team of his regular condottieri against them – Alberico, Facino Cane, Ottobuono Terzo, and others, even the veteran Jacopo dal Verme in person. What followed was an anti-climax, expensive to both sides. There was no major clash between the two glittering hosts, only a glorified cavalry skirmish before the walls of Brescia, garrisoned by Facino Cane and Ottobuono Terzo, whose men chased away a German foraging party. Rupert had arrived with weaker forces than expected and had not found the anti-Visconti Italians rallying to his banner as he had hoped. To make matters worse, plague was raging in Lombardy at the time. After his setback at Brescia in mid October, he withdrew slowly towards Germany by way of Padua and Venetia, less in conflict with the Milanese armies than with the Florentine Signoria over the second instalment of florins. It was indeed an unlucky period for the Florentines, who, it may be remembered, had only recently paid for the state funeral of a Captain-General who had never drawn sword in their defence.

Gian Galeazzo himself was not without his financial troubles. Even the vast revenues of Milan were not enough for all his requirements – not only (it is fair to recall) the hiring of condottieri and the subversion of governments but the building of Milan cathedral, the establishment of the Certosa, the great Carthusian monastery at Pavia, and the patronage of art and learning. Indeed, by 1402, some of his generals were beginning to knit their brows over the arrears of their pay. Alberico's gratitude was wearing thin after eight years and he was speculating about the prospects of alternative employment. Pope Boniface was at that time trying to detach some of the Roman condottieri in the duke's service, men like Bertoldo Orsini, Paolo Savelli, and Giovanni Colonna, and he made approaches also to Alberico.

But – and this fact posed all the adventurers with an agonizing dilemma – Gian Galeazzo's star was still very much in the ascendant. He had

129 The Certosa, the great Carthusian monastery just outside Pavia, is perhaps the Visconti's most lasting monument. Here Gian Galeazzo presents a model of the church to the Virgin.

130, 131 The Certosa under construction (above) appears – perched on a fantastic cliff – in the background of a painting by Bergognone depicting Christ carrying the Cross. The last part to be completed was the façade (below), built not by the Visconti but by their successors, the Sforzas.

survived the abortive invasion from Germany. He intended next to deal with Florence's traditional ally north of the Apennines, Bologna, now under the unpopular dictatorship of Giovanni Bentivoglio. That city disposed of, he would proceed at last to the attack on Florence. And when Florence yielded to him he would have himself crowned there as King of Italy.

The first stage of this programme went as planned. Late in May, as described in the preceding chapter, dal Verme defeated the Florentine and Bolognese forces. Following the overnight revolution inside Bologna, Alberico was one of the victorious army that rode in. Only the previous year Bentivoglio had described him venomously, in an appeal for help from the Venetians, as 'the creature of Milan'. Now Bentivoglio was dead, and one score settled, but Alberico still had another on his mind.

Gian Galeazzo's orders were to march on Florence. Alberico declined to start, pleading lack of provisions for so big an expedition across the mountains. 'I have a mote in my eye,' he is said to have murmured, 'Faenza!' Earlier he had entertained hopes of becoming lord of Bologna. Now he knew that the duke had other ideas for the city. Alberico was prepared to content himself with the lordship of Faenza. It would make a neat ending for the feud with Astorre Manfredi.

That summer he was not the only condottiere in a disgruntled mood. Facino Cane, supposed to assist dal Verme against Padua, betook himself instead to Milan, perhaps to suggest that the duke might give a little more thought to his victorious generals and a little less to the regalia he had ordered for his projected coronation in Florence. That city, after all, had still to be taken. Cane was ready enough to help, if adequately rewarded. In August, indeed, he was raiding the Florentines, but not faring very well.

It was one thing to beat off Cane in a skirmish. It was quite another to evade the strangling coils of 'the Great Serpent' as the duke was now called, not so much because of his family emblem as because of his tortuous aggressions. There was dismay in Florence, but not complete despair. Political divisions fractured the unity of her resistance, and some citizens, knowing the duke's flair for exploiting the internal disagreements of his enemies, felt that his victory was inevitable. But, as Hans Baron has shown in *The Crisis of the Early Italian Renaissance*, 'the experienced merchant-statesmen on the Arno must have discerned certain elements of hope beyond the seeming certainty of doom apparent to the average observer'. They guessed what the Milanese archives have revealed to modern historians, that the duke's endless aggressions had strained his economic resources to the limit. If only Florence could delay defeat, Milan would crack. But Florence herself was in grave difficulties, and her continued resistance, says Baron, 'required a measure of calm self-confidence and faith in native liberty and independence found nowhere else on the peninsula in the summer of 1402'.

Less well-informed Florentine citizens could only hope for a miracle – and that hope was realized.

The plague grew worse in Milan. The duke had seen other statesmen carried off by it elsewhere, often to the advantage of his schemes. But he was well aware that he himself was not immortal. To avoid the infection he moved out to his castle at Melegnano, then known as Marignano, eleven miles from the city. There, as one of his last ceremonial acts, he received the suppliant ambassadors of Bologna. On 13 August he was stricken with a fever. For the next three weeks doctors and astrologers muttered round his bed and in the ante-rooms, bandying rival remedies and prognostications. It made no difference. On 3 September Gian Galeazzo died. He was still just short of his fiftieth birthday.

There was no one ready to take his place. The three sons of his first marriage had died in infancy. His second wife, and first cousin, Caterina Visconti, had borne him two more. In his devotion to the cult of the Virgin he had named them Giovanni Maria and Filippo Maria. They were at this date only fourteen and ten respectively. They grew up into extremely odd characters, as befitted their peculiar and inbred heredity, but for the immediate future their joint inheritance had to be managed by a Council of Regency.

132, 133 Gian Galeazzo, Duke of Milan and greatest of the Visconti, died on 3 September 1402. He was buried in the monastery he had founded. Left: the effigy on his tomb. Right: his funeral procession, with the coffin (near the top) being carried to the Certosa.

Caterina presided over it. Jacopo dal Verme and Alberico da Barbiano were among its members. The others were Francesco Gonzaga of Mantua, the Count of Urbino, Pandolfo Malatesta, father of the subsequently notorious condottiere, Sigismondo, and Francesco Barbavara of Novara, whom Caterina (with something of her own father's exuberance) seems to have taken as her lover.

In the first critical days these regents, or whatever quorum was on hand to make the immediate decisions, acted with admirable prudence. The duke's illness and death were kept secret until the vital dispositions had been made to safeguard the position of the boys. The army was recalled to the capital. Dal Verme, as loyal to his late master as he had been throughout his life, saw that his wishes were respected. Of all the condottieri who had taken Gian Galeazzo's pay he was the only one who showed real loyalty to his memory.

The original harmony of the regents soon disintegrated. The special favour Caterina showed to Barbavara was more than the others could tolerate. Gian Galeazzo's unconsolidated conquests began to fragment. The generals, finding themselves free from any strong central control, began to grab territory in lieu of pay. Facino Cane rode off to Piedmont to carve himself a petty domain, Ugo Cavalcabò seized Crema and Cremona, Franchino Rusca installed himself in Como, Ottobuono Terzo, having failed to hold the Visconti conquests in Umbria, hastened home to Parma and set up as despot of his native region. There was anarchy everywhere. Bergamo was torn apart by political factions, Brescia was taken over by the Guelf party.

One by one the other condottieri, seeing no future for themselves under such conditions, threw off the Visconti allegiance and went to seek their fortune elsewhere. Carlo Malatesta and Alberico da Barbiano closed with offers already made to them by the Pope. Dal Verme alone tried to serve the monstrous adolescent, Giovanni Maria, whom he must now call Duke. Only when his position became completely untenable did he leave Milan and take service with the Venetians, for whom it is believed he died fighting against the Turks.

Alberico ended his career in the Regno. After his time with the Pope he went south again to Naples, and resumed his old appointment of Grand Constable to King Ladislaus. He held that post until his death in 1409.

By then a new generation of condottieri was coming to the fore, pre-eminent among them two of the many he had himself trained in the art of war. They were Muzio Attendolo Sforza and Braccio da Montone. Their friendship and rivalry provide a connecting theme for the complicated events of the period.

Pupils of Alberico

It may be remembered that, when Hawkwood was refortifying and extending Cotignola, he had found a co-operative neighbour in Giovanni Attendolo.

Giovanni must have had a proper respect for the famous English soldier. He himself was a rough diamond, with a brood of combative sons and a wife as bellicose as any of them. She was Elisa dei Petrascini and came from one of the most turbulent families in that martial region. Quick of tongue and temper, she was typical of those Italian women who have given the word 'virago' an international currency. She bore twenty-one children, mostly boys, who grew up to become professional soldiers – there was not much else for them to do in Romagna. Her daughters could, on occasion, match their brothers in ferocity. Muzio, born in the summer of 1369, was to become the most eminent warrior among those sons.

When not fighting, the Attendoli occupied themselves with farming their land. Their home was a bare stone house, their existence Spartan. Elisa was no housewife, or had simply given up the hopeless struggle. There were no regular meals. The family came in and ate when they were hungry, and when they were tired or drunk they sprawled on the mattresses strewn about the floor. They were brought up to despise comfort, let alone elegance. No hangings softened the gaunt walls. Only shields and cuirasses hung there, and they were not primarily for decoration.

This was the environment that formed Muzio. He grew up strong, truculent, a bare-hand-bender of horseshoes, a legendary leaper into saddles with all his armour on. The incident that started him on his career as a condottiere may sound very much like a legend but could well be fact. His great-grandson, Francesco Sforza II, Duke of Milan, used to tell the story as he conducted admiring guests round his castle, saying that the family owed everything to the axe that had stuck in the tree. The boy Muzio had been using this axe round the farm when some soldiers arrived, recruiting for the condottiere Boldrino da Panicale. Whether he was fifteen – the tale is usually dated 1384 – or only twelve, as another version has it, he must have looked promising material. The strangers tried to enlist him, chaffing him when he hesitated. At last he swung up the axe good-humouredly and prepared to throw it at a tree. If it stuck in the trunk, he promised, he would join their band. If it fell to the ground, he would bide at home. It stuck. That same night, without troubling to say good-bye or ask for parental permission, Muzio helped himself to one of his father's horses and rode after the soldiers. After a year or two he returned on a visit and was welcomed, having proved himself in the meantime. It is said that the proud father not only forgave him for taking the original horse but gave him four more, with which military capital he was able to win admission to the Compagnia di San Giorgio and serve under the great hero to young men of his generation, Alberico da Barbiano.

It is certainly as Alberico's pupil that he is known. His original commander, Boldrino, was a respected and popular leader, but he was murdered at Macerata, his angry soldiers forcing that town to do humble penance for his death. Indeed, for some time afterwards they carried his body with them in a handsome coffin, as holier men might have carried a saint, and continued to regard him as their captain. This gesture may have had a practical advantage behind the symbolism – perhaps it postponed a succession crisis that would have split the company – but these mercenaries were not without their sentimental loyalties and it was not unusual for a dead condottiere to be deeply mourned and resolutely avenged, long after he had held his last pay-parade.

Muzio never lost touch with home and family. The Attendoli were a united clan and Cotignola kept its place in the wanderer's heart. On one visit, when he was nineteen, he stepped into the midst of a typical local feud.

His brother Bartolo was betrothed to a girl who was abducted by Martino Pasolini, member of a neighbouring family with whom the Attendoli were regularly at odds. This time, for some reason, the Attendoli did not react. They shrugged their shoulders and let the girl go – it is over-late in the day now to speculate about the cause of their uncharacteristic complaisance. It was the Pasolini, oddly enough, who were deeply affronted. It was, they felt, an insult to the girl they had taken into their family, tantamount to a reflection on her virtue. Honour demanded that, as the Attendoli had not attacked them, they should attack the Attendoli. They did so without warning, killing two and wounding Muzio. This incident effectively cured the Attendoli of their apathy. They retaliated, and there were several homicidal affrays that must have considerably

186

134, 135 Grape harvesting and abduction: an unlikely combination, but typical enough of the home life of the Attendoli. This rough farming family conducted an endless feud with its neighbours the Pasolini over the abduction of a girl.

complicated the normal routine of the local farms. Giovanni and his sons were apt to launch surprise attacks upon the Pasolini when they were harvesting. They would 'spring out upon them from the corn like snakes'. The Pasolini had to toil sweating in their armour, their weapons laid ready amid the stubble. The vendetta was pursued so remorselessly that in the end Martino Pasolini and some of his closest relatives left the Cotignola district, and those who stayed on found it expedient to change their surname. There was a pleasing sequel long afterwards in 1405, by which time Muzio Attendolo had achieved fame. Martino came unannounced to his camp, disclosed his identity, and begged on his knees that the old quarrel might be made up. Muzio was in a good mood. A rough swashbuckling kindliness was the tradition of his clan, rather than coldly calculated revenge. He raised Martino to his feet, rebuked him for taking the risk without previously asking for a safe-conduct, and entertained him to a meal in his tent before sending him on his way completely forgiven.

Muzio served with Alberico for twelve or fifteen years. The physical promise of his boyhood was fulfilled. He was above average height, powerful and large of limb, small-waisted but with the massive hairy hands of his working farmer stock. He had a severe, on occasions alarming,

187

aspect. A hooked nose stood out from a weather-beaten face. His eyes were small and sharp, blue and deep-set under shaggy brows.

He was a man of few words, but those pithy and not without wit. 'If you have three enemies,' he used to say, 'make peace with the first, arrange a truce with the second – and turn on the third with all the strength you have.' He advised his son, Francesco: 'Never touch another man's wife. Never strike one of your servants or your comrades-in-arms – but, if you forget yourself and do so, get rid of him. And never ride a hard-mouthed horse.'

He remained quite illiterate. It was not until late in life that he learned to initial the letters he was by then dictating to his secretaries. For this clerical help he preferred to use monks, for, he said, the same hand could not hold the sword as well as the pen. Monks could be relied upon to remember all the tiresome details that were necessary to the businesslike running of a mercenary army. 'They are meant', he once remarked, 'to poke their noses into everything – there is nothing they do not meddle in, under the pretext of their religion.'

He loved to be read to. Of the ancient Roman writers he particularly enjoyed Caesar and Sallust, whose predominantly military flavour appealed to him. The scholar who translated these authors for him was rewarded with the gift of a house and garden. But, along with their terse and chiselled prose, Muzio could also appreciate the haunting cadences of the old romances that told of Charlemagne, Orlando and the Paladins, riding through landscapes not unlike the ones he knew:

> *High are the hills and huge and dim with cloud,*
> *Down in the deeps the living streams are loud . . .*

Nor was he untouched by romance in other guises. His weakness for women is said to have shocked even his own troops, who were not themselves of an ascetic habit. No doubt his advice about not essaying married women was born of experiences regretted.

He was in all senses a man of passions, but of passions he made some attempt to control. Once, when he was in Alberico's company, that famous commander found him hotly disputing the division of some plunder with two brothers who bore the picturesque nicknames of 'the Scorpion' and 'the Tarantula'. Alberico tried to arbitrate between them, but Muzio did not moderate his vehemence even when answering him. 'So,' said Alberico good-humouredly, 'you try to browbeat your general too?' The verb he used, *sforzare*, 'to force', started the nickname which Muzio and his descendants were to make famous in history. From this point it becomes convenient to refer to him as Sforza.

136 Braccio da Montone, one of a noble Perugian family, began his career, like Sforza, by serving in the company of Alberico da Barbiano. 'He combined', said a contemporary writer, 'military severity with a kind of civil modesty and courtly manner.'

It was while serving in the Compagnia di San Giorgio that Sforza formed his great friendship with Braccio da Montone, a friendship which in its early days bade fair to match any in the chivalric romances. Even if allowance is made for the over-neat antitheses shaped by the chroniclers, the two young men did present an effective contrast. Braccio had the impetuous courage of a Roland. Sforza, despite a rough temper, was more of an Oliver, cautious and self-controlled. Just as their dispositions differed, so did their social origins, and so too, eventually, the theories of warfare that became identified with their names.

Braccio was the elder by a year, born in 1368 at Perugia or at Montone, a remote mountain village north of the city, overlooking the valley of the upper Tiber. His father, Oddo Fortebraccio, was lord of Montone. 'Braccio', or 'the Arm', was thus an obvious nickname for the son (baptized Andrea) when he became a soldier of fortune. The mother, Jacoma Montemelini, came from the Perugian aristocracy, and the family sympathies were naturally opposed to the Raspanti party, the bourgeoisie, returned to power under Michelotti during this period. At an early age the future 'Braccio' was involved in the local political conflict. As a mere youth he was wounded, orphaned, and driven into exile, experiences that coloured the whole course of his life. For whereas Sforza, though thrustful enough, remembered his small beginnings and could only feel that he had risen, Braccio was nagged by overweening expectations of what was due to one of his blood. The lordship of Perugia beckoned him, just as it had tempted Michelotti to his doom.

Even in looks and manner the two young soldiers were strikingly different. Braccio, says Gianantonio Campano,

> was of medium height, with a long face and highly coloured, which imparted great majesty to his appearance. His eyes were not black, but very brilliant, sparkling with fun, yet with a certain gravity. Whether grave or gay, he was always well bred, so that even his enemies admitted that in any group of persons he stood out as a leader. . . . He combined military severity with a kind of civil modesty and a courtly manner.

Sforza was happy to soldier on under Alberico. Braccio's temperament made him hanker after his own command. His first attempt to leave the company and set up independently was not a success, and he returned richer only in experience. Doggedly he set to work again. He never had any difficulty in recruiting followers, for, as Campano testifies, 'he was beloved by his soldiers' and no one had a greater gift for rousing men to fight. His second venture was luckier. He made money and invested it in property at Foligno, twenty miles from Perugia, but disaster struck in the shape of a great fire in the town which destroyed all his possessions. The citizens expressed sympathy and, it is said, contributed to make good some of his losses. Knowing Braccio's reputation for savagery (despite all Campano's eulogies) one wonders how spontaneous these offers were. In any case they were not enough to restore Braccio's position, and he returned to Alberico's company once more.

His undoubted ability as a soldier provoked the jealousy of some of the other captains. They complained to Alberico that he was high-handed and insubordinate. They were probably right up to a point, though hardly to the extent of justifying their proposal that Braccio should be murdered. Alberico's wife was sufficiently in the general's counsels to know what was being discussed. She put in a word for the dashing young aristocrat, but Alberico preferred the advice of his officers. The lady then dropped a hint to Braccio. He departed hurriedly and went into the papal service, a purely professional relationship, needless to say, that in no sense reflected his views or sympathies. Braccio had no use for religion. He was, says a chronicler, 'impious and heretical in his private life. He believed neither in God nor in the Saints, he despised the offices and services of the Church, never heard Mass and was most cruel.' Though all such contemporary judgments must be read sceptically, most writers being keenly partisan on one side or another, this assessment is probably fair. Braccio believed mainly in Braccio.

The same chronicler concedes that he was brave and loyal at least to his comrades in war. Alberico saw this and admitted, too late, that his distrust had been unfounded. He tried to smooth things over and pressed Braccio to rejoin the Company. Braccio replied, with understandable hauteur, that he could not trust a commander who had behaved in such a way to a loyal lieutenant.

Sforza seems to have been left out of these intrigues. Possibly he was occupied elsewhere. Almost certainly his colleagues would have excluded him from their whisperings, knowing how close he was to Braccio, and, had Sforza known of the plot, he would have warned his friend without waiting for the intervention of Alberico's wife. The rivalry of the two young men was an honourable one, and even towards the end of their lives, when they had fought many hard campaigns against each other, they found it possible to meet and exchange good-humoured reminiscences about the skulduggery of their subordinates. Murder and treachery of that sort were not in Sforza's character. He liked to excel his comrades, not to remove them.

His own service with Alberico ended when he was about twenty-seven. During that time he had been fighting mainly in the armies of Gian Galeazzo. When he set up on his own account he accepted a two-year *condotta* from Perugia, but Gian Galeazzo did not care to see this promising young soldier in the service of a city he planned to annex, and he removed the potential difficulty by offering Sforza a *condotta* at double the pay. This Milanese engagement did not last long, however. Sforza, like Braccio, became the target of jealous slanders. The duke dismissed him. He left hastily and found fresh employment in the obvious place: Florence. This was in 1397 or 1398 when the republic was at war with Pisa, and Pisa, backed by Milan, had been lent the services of Alberico da Barbiano. Master and pupil thus found themselves on opposite sides. Nothing could more clearly have underlined the fact that, professionally, Sforza had come of age. He was, in his own right, an established condottiere.

It is a good moment to take stock of him, a burly, keen-eyed, rough-tongued adventurer, stalking through his camp in undress, a purple cap on his close-cropped head, his chin and cheeks similarly close-shaven so that helmet and visor would slip on without obstruction. He was a stickler for smartness but contemptuous of ostentation. Once, when his troops had just come out of winter quarters, he noticed a man with rusty armour. There was no time for him to clean it. The troops were going straight into action. Sforza ordered him to fight with his visor up as a punishment. On the other hand, when another soldier paraded through the camp with a helmet too pretentiously plumed, the men took their cue from Sforza and greeted him with a chorus of hisses. It was part of the *condotta* system that troops should be reviewed at regular intervals by the employing government, and checked for numbers, fitness, arms, horses, and everything specified in the agreement. Sforza never feared such inspections. His men had no rivals. In their discipline and turn-out they seem to have enjoyed the sort of reputation that Hawkwood's company had won in its palmiest days.

Hawkwood and Sforza had, indeed, several characteristics in common. Sforza too was never a cruel man. He took care of his own troops first. After that, he was not fond of wanton butchery, and he checked his soldiers – if he could, which was not always – when they turned to plundering and rape. He was scrupulous in money matters and always paid his debts, so that his credit was excellent if he ever needed a loan. He abhorred dishonesty and disloyalty, and showed no mercy to those guilty : a man who stole forage was tied to a horse's tail. Ridicule, which he could not bear himself, was his favourite instrument of punishment. When one of his high-born young officers disobeyed orders and kept a mistress in camp, disguised as a page, it amused Sforza to dress the knight in women's clothes and expose him to the raucous comments of the whole company. He could have been more sympathetic, for his own love-life was notorious. In this he did not resemble Hawkwood. Nor did he in religious observance. Hawkwood had never been conspicuous in that field – he had been quiet, correct, and English. Sforza, on the other hand, was as pious as Braccio da Montone was impious. He heard Mass daily, and if ever, owing to some critical military situation, he was forced to miss the ceremony, he made up for the omission by hearing two Masses on the following day. He confessed regularly and took the sacraments in the most devout manner.

None of this, as already implied, inhibited his sexual activities. It was during this Florentine period that he began his association with Lucia Tregani. Lucia was well born and not without moral scruples. She was unmarried, and yielded to Sforza on the understanding that marriage would follow. This was one of the debts he did not pay. In that age the position of Christian marriage was even more equivocal than it is now. In theory the Church's authority was unchallenged, but in practice the Church found it expedient not to lay too much emphasis on this aspect of

137 Muzio Attendolo Sforza, the illiterate son of a poor farmer
who became one of the most powerful condottieri in Italy.

its moral teaching. There were too many bastards in the most elevated
circles of society, bastards cheerfully acknowledged by their progenitors
and readily admitted to great inheritances when legitimate heirs were not
forthcoming. Legal marriage was not so much a moral essential as a useful
device for cementing an alliance, and, as the same person could scarcely
expect the chance to exploit it more than once or twice, it was something
to be used sparingly. If Sforza did not marry the girl he had seduced (though
they had a long and happy relationship) it was probably because his
cautious instinct warned him to preserve his liberty. Many a condottiere
had advanced his career by marrying the daughter – albeit only the
illegitimate daughter – of an important client. Hawkwood and the other
captains had wedded Visconti girls. Such an opportunity might well come
Sforza's way in the future.

Whatever calculations went through his head, he did not marry Lucia
Tregani, though their relationship seems to have been more stable and
affectionate than many a more sanctified union. Their first child, a son,
was born at San Miniato on 23 July 1401, and in the course of the next
eight years Lucia gave birth to half a dozen others. That first boy was

193

named Francesco. He was to become the great Francesco Sforza, whose eventual marriage to his master's daughter, and the great inheritance that went with her, were to demonstrate in the next generation the importance of a condottiere's preserving his freedom of marital manœuvre.

Sforza's reputation was steadily growing as the fifteenth century opened. Inevitably he acquired both friends and enemies.

His services to Florence made a favourable impression on one of the republic's allies, that Rupert, King of the Romans, whose abortive incursion into Italy against Gian Galeazzo has already been described. It was the habit of princes (it will be seen again in the case of Bartolomeo Colleoni) to honour a condottiere by giving him permission to bear their arms. Rupert granted Sforza the right to use his own lion rampant. Sforza had been using the emblem of a quince, a *cotigna*, a typical heraldic pun on the name of the little town to which he always looked back with affection. The German suggested a combination of the two devices, the quince being held in the lion's paw, and Sforza gratefully adopted the idea. Later, the Sforza coat of arms was completed with a helmet bearing a winged dragon and a human head.

The gesture of regal friendship was welcome, but Rupert was in no position to further Sforza's career. He soon withdrew to his own side of the Alps, to cope with the manifold difficulties of his Teutonic world, and a few years later he was dead, without again attempting to influence the affairs of Italy. Of more consequence to Sforza in the long run was the hostility he aroused about this same time in an obscure colleague named Tartaglia. This developed into a permanent feud. The two condottieri, both employed by Florence, had to be kept apart, and so did their followers,

138 Left: a damaged terracotta of the Sforza coat of arms from the family house at Cotignola. At the top was the helmet with the Visconti dragon swallowing a man (see *ill. 64*), beneath it the lion granted to Sforza by Rupert, King of the Romans, with a quince (*cotigna*) in its paws.

139, 140, 141 Right: Muzio Sforza's patron, Niccolò d'Este (far right) and two of the famous men he attracted to his court at Ferrara, the artist Pisanello (top) and the scholar Guarino da Verona.

whose instinctive loyalty made them quick to take up the quarrels of their commanders. Many years later it was the vindictiveness of Tartaglia that was to produce the worst rift between Sforza and his one-time brother-in-arms, Braccio da Montone.

That first decade of the fifteenth century is more than usually confused, even by the high standards of confusion consistently maintained in the military and political history of Renaissance Italy. It was the decade of Milanese chaos after Gian Galeazzo's death, when his patiently constructed dominion flew apart and everyone, including many of his late condottieri, scrambled and fought for the pieces. In Milan itself Gian Galeazzo's elder son, the unbalanced Giovanni Maria, held the dukedom, bolstered and managed (so far as he was manageable) by one army commander after another – the brutish Ottobuono Terzo or the cultured Carlo Malatesta of Rimini or Facino Cane. The younger brother, Filippo Maria Visconti, was relegated to Pavia, that traditional repository for junior partners, and as the years passed he became little more than Facino Cane's hostage.

In this tangle of events, now not worth the full unravelling, Sforza found fresh employment with the Marquis of Ferrara, Niccolò d'Este, who had inherited his state and a whole crop of troubles at the tender age of ten, though the troubles had been considerably lessened by the death of his most dangerous enemy, Gian Galeazzo. Niccolò d'Este is chiefly remembered as one of those princes who built round themselves a brilliant Renaissance court. His boyhood taste was moulded by a tutor, Donato da Casentino, who had been the friend of Petrarch and Boccaccio. It was developed in manhood by the society of the artists and scholars he befriended, men such as Pisanello and Guarino da Verona. First, though, Niccolò had to fight for his inheritance, and it was lucky for him that,

like so many of his contemporaries, he found the combination of soldiering and scholarship agreeable. His immediate task was to discipline his unruly vassals and to deal with Ottobuono Terzo when that ambitious adventurer made himself despot of Parma and Reggio, uncomfortably near the borders of Ferrara. In this task the book-loving marquis found a congenial colleague in the illiterate Sforza. Who knows how much their association contributed to Sforza's respect for the Classics?

Whatever improving conversations they may have shared by the camp-fire, or as they rode across the interminable levels of Lombardy, their main business was sterner. Fighting Ottobuono was no kid-glove affair. The issues were too grave, the passions too deeply roused.

The struggle reached its climax in 1408. Sforza encountered Ottobuono in a cavalry skirmish, knocked him out of the saddle, and was about to finish him off. There seems, on this occasion, to have been no question of ransom. It is hard to think of any one who would have wished to ransom Ottobuono. At that moment, however, the enemy counter-attacked. Ottobuono struggled to his feet and escaped. It was Sforza's brother, Michele Attendolo, who was taken prisoner, the best soldier in the family after himself. Again there appears to have been no idea of ransom, following a brief period of honourable captivity. Instead, defying all precedents and professional etiquette, Ottobuono half-starved Attendolo and the other prisoners, and even subjected them to torture, until after four months of misery they managed to escape. Outraged by such behaviour, Sforza vowed revenge. It would be easy to comment that, under stress, the rough peasant from Romagna was quickly revealed beneath the thin veneer of chivalry, but the sad truth is that Niccolò d'Este, that blue-blooded humanist, was his willing confederate in the treachery whereby that revenge was achieved.

The marquis invited Ottobuono to a peaceful discussion under flag of truce. The venue was a clearing in woodlands outside the town of Rubiera, a few miles down the Via Emilia from Ottobuono's stronghold of Reggio. Ottobuono, with one of those lapses from normal scepticism that so often terminated promising careers in this period, took the invitation at its face value and arrived unarmed, riding a small Spanish jennet instead of his usual charger, and with the minimum escort consistent with the new dignity to which he aspired. He then saw, with what dismay can only now be guessed, the marquis riding to meet him with a fully armed party, including his recent captive, Michele Attendolo, and the formidable Sforza, the latter mounted on one of the mettlesome horses he always preferred, but which, on this particular occasion, even he seemed to be having some difficulty in controlling. As Ottobuono did not immediately call off the conference it may be assumed that there was something else he did not notice at all – the additional figures lurking in the trees that fringed the meeting-place.

Ottobuono did voice a protest that the rules had been broken. Sforza, striving ineffectually to quieten his unruly mount, shouted that personally he made it a rule *never* to go anywhere unarmed. Further argument on this point was difficult. His horse seemed to have taken the bit between its teeth and was careering round the field. Ottobuono's suspicions may have been lulled by malicious amusement at seeing his rival condottiere's vain struggles to master it. Suddenly its unpredictable wheelings brought Sforza to Ottobuono's side. Before the other man could back away from this undesirable proximity, Sforza achieved a remarkable and almost instantaneous control over the cavorting charger. Ottobuono found his own right hand gripped, then felt – perhaps his last sensation – Sforza's dagger driven home with such tremendous violence that the point emerged and pierced the jennet. If he did feel anything more, it was not for long. He tumbled from the saddle. Michele Attendolo slipped from his own horse and completed the murderous work. Before Ottobuono's helpless escort could escape, they were overwhelmed by more of the marquis's men rushing out from their ambush in the trees. It is not a pretty story, nor is its epilogue: Ottobuono's body was carried to Modena and there barbarously mutilated by some of the people he had driven into exile when he established his petty despotism.

Sforza continued a little longer in the service of Ferrara, until Reggio and the easterly half of Ottobuono's territory had been brought safely under the rule of the marquis. There being no further active employment for him in that region, he next accepted a contract from Baldassare Cossa, who, born into a noble Neapolitan family, had begun his variegated career as a kind of pirate and was ending it as a Pope, or Anti-Pope as the Avignon faction insisted, under the style of John XXIII. It is his tomb, by Donatello and Michelozzo, that one comes upon with mild surprise in the Baptistery at Florence: it is there because, after his deposition and imprisonment for a whole catalogue of scandalous doings, he humbled himself and was allowed to end his days as the mere Bishop of Tusculum.

142 Tomb of the Anti-Pope John XXIII in the Baptistery at Florence.

He was in the first flush of his glory, however, when Sforza went to him. He was determined to recover Rome for the Papacy. The city had been lost to King Ladislaus of Naples a year or two before, and since then the papal elections and other business had been carried on perforce in Tuscany. John 'had the soul of a condottiere', wrote Janet Penrose Trevelyan in her *Short History of the Italian People,* and he naturally turned to men of that profession to secure his objectives. Sforza found himself enrolled once again under the same banner as Braccio. The Pope also stirred up the Angevin party to renew their claim to the Neapolitan crown, and the tide of war began to flow for a time against Ladislaus.

About the same date as he changed masters, Sforza changed mistresses, or, to be more exact, gave up Lucia Tregani for a legal wife, Antonia, the widowed sister of a Sienese nobleman, Count Salimbeni. It was the kind of social advancement for which he had so far-sightedly preserved his bachelor condition. Antonia brought him background and status. She also brought him a dowry including four castles. In due course she bore Sforza a son, Bosio, who was developing into a good cavalry officer when he met an early death in action.

What, though, of the affectionate and faithful Lucia, who had provided Sforza with companionship and seven children during the preceding ten years? Lucia, having no choice, accepted the situation, accepted even, indeed, the husband thoughtfully provided for her. He was Marco Fogliano of Ferrara, one of Sforza's own captains. No doubt they were both used to obeying orders. She settled in Ferrara, taking Sforza's children with her. Francesco was allowed to share the stimulating and humane education of the marquis's children, though it is interesting to note that the marquis did not return the compliment when, a few years later, he wanted military training for his own son: it was to Braccio, not to Sforza, that the boy Leonello d'Este was sent at fifteen for his apprenticeship as a soldier. There may be no significance in the fact. The two great rival condottieri had their continual ups and downs, and Niccolò's choice at a particular moment may have been dictated by a sense of parental responsibility rather than his own preference.

Leonello, incidentally, was no more legitimate than Francesco. The Marchioness Gigliola was childless, a misfortune which her husband offset by fathering a plentiful progeny elsewhere. '*Di qua e di là del Po,*' sang his irreverent and envious subjects, '*tutti figli di Niccolò!*' ('On this side and that of the Po, all are the children of Niccolò.') As Ella Noyes wrote in *The Story of Ferrara,* 'The most careful historians have found it impossible to number his children.' The palace rang with the pattering footsteps of the numerous offspring, Leonello and others, born to him by his beautiful

Vgo Aldrouaodino fu fiolo n̄ale de' quefto Nicolo e mori del 1425.

leonello fu & fiolo n̄e d'quefto

143 Leonello d'Este, Niccolò's son, later ruler of Ferrara and patron of one of the most cultivated Renaissance courts.

mistress, Stella dall' Assassino, and accepted of necessity by his wife. No one in the schoolroom could point the finger of scorn at the condottiere's bastard.

Sforza meanwhile continued his social progress. The Pope owed him 4000 ducats and could not pay. He did what an earlier pontiff had done in Hawkwood's case. In lieu of the money he offered the lordship of Cotignola. A settlement which the Englishman had accepted without undue enthusiasm filled Sforza with extravagant delight. Cotignola might be an obscure little place, but was it not his native town, the ancestral home of the Attendoli? He declared it to be the proudest moment of his life. Not long afterwards the new lord of Cotignola was appalled to receive news that almost the whole place had been gutted by fire, though fortunately his own home, where his redoubtable old mother still lived, had escaped destruction because it was built of stone. He promptly sent a generous contribution so that the other people could rebuild their houses and improve them.

He was fortunate to have the money available. Pope John was proving an unreliable paymaster. Sforza began to grow tired of so unsatisfactory a position, and he disliked serving with another commander, Paolo Orsini, who was his inveterate enemy. From Naples King Ladislaus sent counter-offers, tempting him to change sides. Sforza accepted. The Pope was furious. He commissioned a caricature of Sforza, dangling by one leg like a hanged traitor, over a scurrilous inscription sneering at his rustic origins: '*Io sono Sforza, villano di Cotignola . . .*' ('I am Sforza, a peasant from Cotignola').

Sforza did not care. A bright new chapter of his career was opening, the Naples chapter, in which his fate would once more be interwoven with that of Braccio da Montone. Ladislaus made one condition. Sforza's son, Francesco, must be brought down from Ferrara as a pledge of his father's loyalty. The boy came, now eleven years old, full of the graces inculcated by the Este household. The king was charmed, insisted that he was 'a divine thing' (*una cosa divina*), and made him Count of Tricarico, with the lordship of several towns. The omens looked good for the Sforza family.

144 Naples in the fifteenth century, scene of the final phase of Muzio Sforza's career.

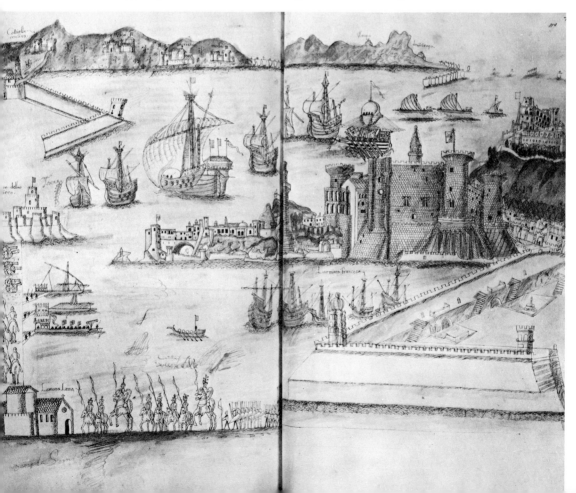

The rivals   14

When he rode south to Naples Sforza was, in a sense, riding out of the Renaissance and back into the Middle Ages.

Then, as ever since, the southern half of Italy was far behind the north in its development. Here were neither free republics nor dynamic dictators. This was the Regno, 'the Kingdom', with a court and a creaking feudal apparatus to which there was no obvious alternative.

Naples itself was a blend of breathtaking beauty and unspeakable corruption. Long galleys lay at anchor in the incomparable bay, shadowed by the cliff-like walls of the Castel Nuovo. Cogs, round of rump and square of sail, brought in the merchandise of the Mediterranean. Green hills, not yet built over, hung their tapestry behind the houses that crowded to the waterfront. Further away, Vesuvius sprawled deceptively comatose, its ancient scars veiled with foliage. Behind and beyond this skyline lay a world of backward baronies, with none of those oases of enlightenment provided by the little principalities of the north.

Ladislaus, who had inherited the disputed crown as a child and fought for it as a youth, had now worn it without serious challenge for over ten years. He was still in his early thirties, aggressive and ambitious, his taste for war matched only by his pleasure in political intrigue. He liked tournaments and women. The other fortress on the harbourside, the old Castel dell' Ovo, he used to accommodate his harem. His elder sister, Joanna, shared this intense sexuality and her lack of morals was notorious. She was his heiress-presumptive, for he had no child of his own. Her marriage, too, had been barren. The dynastic conflicts of Naples promised to continue indefinitely.

For the present, however, Ladislaus held his throne by an effective combination of military strength and astute diplomacy. The Great Schism was a help, and he worked to prolong it: with two Popes in opposition he could be sure that Anjou's claims to Naples would never win the backing

145 Ladislaus, the last Angevin king of Naples, a state which remained basically feudal in structure long after the rest of Italy was divided between dictators and republics.

of a united Church. When it came to a fight, he was quite ready to campaign himself, but he also believed in enlisting the best condottieri available.

Alberico had been retained as Grand Constable of Naples until his death in 1409. There were then, by common consent, two outstanding mercenary captains in Italy, his two most brilliant pupils, Braccio and Sforza. Which was the better was a topic for endless argument, and soldiers divided on the question. Leaving aside the characters and temperaments of the two commanders, the disputants concentrated on their respective theories of warfare, claiming to discover a fundamental difference therein which the records do not make quite so striking to the modern reader. Braccio, it was emphasized, believed in using soldiers in small detachments, giving more scope for initiative to his junior officers. This, says L. M. Collison-Morley, was 'his contribution to the military science of his day'. Sforza, on the other hand, clung to the old tradition favoured by Alberico, the use of massive forces, flung in at the right place and time. If it ever occurred to any contemporary soldier that there might be something to be said for either method, and that every tactical situation should be judged on its merits, he was wise enough to hold his tongue. There were the two schools of thought, as irreconcilable as the two papal courts then or as the supporters of rival football clubs today. They were actually known as the Sforzeschi and the Bracceschi, and the labels lasted after the deaths of the competing generals. Like 'Oxford' and 'Cambridge', 'Freudian' and 'Adlerian', they served to indicate the prejudices of the man whose engagement was being considered.

Ladislaus had already had dealings with Braccio. In the year of Alberico's death, looking no doubt for the best replacement, the young king had been attracted to him. Braccio, he found, had a consuming ambition to become lord of his native Perugia. Ladislaus promised to help him to this objective, which fitted in well with his own grandiose schemes to extend his power northwards – he dreamed of a kind of Gian Galeazzo operation in the reverse direction. The Perugians, however, got wind of Braccio's design. They had not long escaped from the Visconti domination and had no wish to lose their liberty again, but if a new master was inevitable they preferred to be subjects of a distant ruler in Naples rather than submit to an exiled countryman who would stir up the bitterest animosities inside their small community. They accordingly approached Ladislaus and made an alternative proposal: they would accept his overlordship if he would disown the Perugian exiles he was then supporting and if he would prove his good faith by executing Braccio. This seemed to Ladislaus a most reasonable suggestion, with many advantages over his original plan. He agreed, and went to work at once, summoning Braccio to visit him. The condottiere prudently excused himself on the grounds of indisposition. He knew enough about Ladislaus to guess that his health would not benefit from the journey. The king was furious, threw off all pretence, and sent troops against him. The Perugians, though disappointed in their hope that Braccio would be liquidated, had little choice but to keep faith with Ladislaus as the lesser evil. For the remainder of his reign they were his loyal dependants.

After this affair Ladislaus knew that Braccio's sword would never be at his disposal. Braccio, as he had demonstrated once before during his early days with Alberico, had a prejudice against serving under men who had considered murdering him. He had gone over to the Florentines, the consistent enemies of Naples, and accepted a long-term contract to command their forces. On 2 January 1410, he had driven the Neapolitans out of Rome. On this occasion he amply justified his reputation for cruelty, for – if the records are to be believed – he amused himself by dropping certain prisoners from the highest towers of that unhappy city. Unhappy indeed Rome was at this date, ruinous and derelict, moribund compared with the great mercantile centres like Florence and Milan. One almost wonders why its depleted population clung to the site, but where else, in that era of jealously guarded local rights, could the citizens possibly have removed themselves? They had no choice but to haunt their ghost-town, cowering in its shadows as kings and condottieri and cardinals raged in and out with their savage soldiery. Other occupying powers were no better than Braccio. It is said that Ladislaus, when he held Rome, stalked the city himself as a plunderer in the grand manner, demanding loot and beheading those who could not satisfy his greed.

Since Braccio was now in the service of his enemies, the king had taken the obvious course in engaging Sforza. It proved a good investment. Although Ladislaus campaigned in person, his improved results during the next season or two owed much to the experience and flair of his general, and to the disciplined troops that Sforza brought with him. Rome was recovered, the Papal States largely overrun, and by the summer of 1414 Tuscany invaded and Florence threatened. It looked as if Ladislaus was about to accomplish his most ambitious schemes of conquest. It was then, in the middle of the campaign, that sickness struck him down. In pain he was carried in a litter from his Tuscan camp to his castle in Naples, but scarcely had he arrived there than he died, on 6 August.

Sforza found himself with a new employer, who was at once proclaimed Queen Joanna II. The altered situation was full of opportunity and danger.

146 Queen Joanna II, who at the age of forty-five, on the death of her brother Ladislaus, became ruler of Naples, is one of the most colourful characters of fifteenth-century Italy. After one year she was confined by her barons and those of her party, including Sforza, were thrown into prison.

The opportunity lay in Joanna's sex and character. Any woman would necessarily be more dependent upon her general than would a man, especially a youngish man like her brother, capable of taking the field himself. As to her character, the queen had only the most limited interest in politics and administration. She would lean readily on the advice of the man who gained her confidence.

The danger lay in these same facts. That confidence would be given not on merit but for quite irrelevant reasons. Like the first Queen Joanna a generation earlier, who had scandalized even Naples with her four marriages and the rumoured murder of one of her husbands, the new monarch had a nymphomaniac bent, which determined her choice of advisers. She was at the dangerous age of forty-five, dangerous less to herself and her throne than to the men, like Sforza, whose careers were bound up with her capricious favour.

She celebrated her accession by taking a lover of twenty-six, Pandulfo Alopo, and appointing him Grand Chamberlain with complete control of finance and patronage. Alopo is described as ill-bred, shifty, and effeminate – the almost inevitable description to be expected from such a man's unsuccessful competitors, and perhaps a fair one, though his capacity to please his mistress casts some doubt upon the effeminacy. It is possibly significant, however, that the queen was immediately struck by the appearance of Sforza when he attended her Council and that she developed a new and uncharacteristic interest in military matters, detaining him for *tête-à-tête* discussions after the formal meeting had broken up.

This was a juxtaposition that Alopo viewed with understandable alarm. The condottiere, the very antithesis of himself, could well stimulate Joanna's thirst for change. Sforza was a man of her own age, one in whom the undeniable charms of maturity were combined with a virility that had not yet begun to diminish. He was famous alike as a soldier and as a lover. In sheer physique he dominated the council-chamber. Clearly, he was a rival to reckon with.

Worst of all, he appears to have been by now a widower. It was his sister, Margherita, who in his absence governed the castle of Tricarico in the remote hills of the Basilicata, the fortress with which the late king had endowed the boy Francesco. She was not the only member of the Attendolo family to follow their most successful representative in search of fortune in the Regno. But Antonia Sforza must have been dead by now, or Alopo could not have spread the rumour that this northern upstart was daring to think of sharing not only a bed but a throne.

Was there anything in the whisper? Did Sforza ever dream, in fact, of becoming King of Naples? It seems unlikely. His native caution would have been against such a gamble, doubly hazardous in the feudal south, where the mystique of hereditary royalty was still potent and the unruly barons, disunited in all else, would have closed ranks to oppose a self-made intruder. If there had been anything very solid in Alopo's allegations the rest of the councillors would not have acted as they subsequently did.

To begin with, Alopo's influence was strong enough to put Sforza behind bars in the Castel Nuovo. He spent four months in one of its dungeons. It was then that he learned to form the initials of his name, which he afterwards used to write on documents. It was a modest educational achievement for four months of enforced leisure, but the Castel Nuovo was not designed to promote the intellectual improvement of its captives.

That Sforza ever saw the full light of day again was due to the insistence of his former colleagues on the Council. Joanna's misgovernment was shaking the realm to its foundations. Rebellious barons were in arms. They held towns like Capua and Aquila which it was essential to recapture. Who could accomplish that mission but the great condottiere? Alopo saw that his own supremacy was doomed unless he solved the problem. He bowed to the demands of his colleagues, and Sforza was set free. But, making a virtue of necessity, he made a compact with his potential rival which effectively removed the danger he had feared. Sforza married the Grand Chamberlain's sister, Catella. This had the effect of taking him out of the marriage market, and, from Sforza's own point of view, assuming that he had never fancied his chances as a royal consort, it was as advantageous a match as he could have expected, and a guarantee of Alopo's future goodwill. To bind their interests even more closely together, Alopo saw that he was given the appointment of Grand Constable of the Kingdom, the proud office once held by his old captain, Alberico. It carried a salary of 8000 ducats. Sforza was also given the lordship of several castles, including Benevento and Manfredonia. His late captor had behaved most handsomely. So long as Alopo kept it up, Sforza was quite happy to work hand in glove with him. There seemed no reason why they should not, between them, run the country.

In the campaigning that followed his release, Sforza found himself in congenial opposition to Tartaglia, whose comradeship he had found so insufferable in the days when they had both served Florence. He laid an ambush for him, but Tartaglia managed to cut his way out. The incident was not in itself important, but it helped to rejuvenate their old antipathy, and it had more serious consequences a little later.

It was about this time, too, that Francesco's marriage was arranged. The promising boy was now fifteen, a usual age for bridegrooms. The girl chosen was Polissena Ruffo, a young noblewoman of Montalto in Calabria. She was a good match, bringing with her a dowry of 20,000 ducats and the lordship of several towns. Francesco rode down into the foot of Italy to wed her, with a smart escort of his father's veterans to impress her family. But the marriage ended tragically. Poor Polissena was destroyed by the very richness of her endowment. She lived just long enough to bear Francesco a daughter. Then both mother and baby were poisoned by an aunt in order to get hold of the property. When one starts exploring the by-ways of the Quattrocento one wonders if the most diabolical of the condottieri matched some of their civilian contemporaries.

Sforza, meanwhile, had troubles of his own. The various incidents in his life at this period are not all easy to date, and it is impossible to shuffle them into precise chronological sequence – to say, for example, exactly how his affairs stood on the day of Francesco's wedding. But the first two and a half years of Joanna's reign, mid 1414 to the end of 1416, were full of vicissitudes, of which Sforza suffered his share.

The queen's scandalous way of life soon convinced the barons of the Regno that she had better marry again, taking an acceptable husband who would be equal to the dignity and responsibility of his position. She agreed to wed a Bourbon of French royal blood, James, Count of La Marche, but she would not make him King of Naples, merely 'Vicar-General, Duke of Calabria and Prince of Taranto'. So Alopo advised her, reckoning that, so long as she did not fully share her throne, he would still retain his controlling influence. The same thought occurred to the faction opposing him.

James reached Manfredonia on the Adriatic coast in the middle of the summer of 1415. He was given a warm welcome by the nobility, who set forth with him as escort across the peninsula to his waiting bride in Naples. Sforza seems to have been in the company, which was to be expected, in view of his office as Grand Constable and the fact that Manfredonia was one of the castles awarded to him.

The barons' first-hand acquaintance with James quickly satisfied them that he was the man for their purpose. What had been only a provisional scheme was confirmed and put into action before the cavalcade reached its destination. Sforza was known to be Alopo's man, and clearly he was the most dangerous adversary. He was arrested. James was proclaimed King of Naples. As soon as the party arrived in Naples Alopo was seized and put to death, while Joanna was placed in confinement, powerless to take any political measures of her own.

For the second time in two years Sforza found himself a prisoner in Naples. He was lucky to have escaped with his life. But he had done nothing to excite the same virulent resentment as the young Grand Chamberlain – he was an outsider drawn into the affair by his profession, he was a great soldier whom even the most hostile baron could respect, and he had never been Joanna's lover. He might live, but for the time being he could not be allowed to go free.

This time he was kept captive in the Castel dell' Ovo, the grim fortress rising from a rocky islet within bowshot of the shore. It had housed famous and tragic prisoners before, such as the sixteen-year-old Conradin, last of the Hohenstaufen, prior to his public beheading in the city square in 1268. More recently, Ladislaus had found its isolated position convenient for lodging his women.

That autumn was unpleasant for Sforza, and so was the year that followed. He was put to torture because his various castles would not surrender to the new government and their possession was judged vital to the control of the country. Sforza refused to divulge the passwords so that they could be taken over. His tough physique and unconquerable will defied the pressures put upon him.

His sister, defending Tricarico, showed herself a worthy upholder of the family name. Messengers arrived to demand the surrender of the fortress. Margherita Attendolo confronted them sword in hand and clad in armour. They stated their business. She had them arrested. They protested that they had come with a safe-conduct. She retorted that she herself had given no such assurance and recognized no promises but her own. She offered her grim guarantee that, if any further hurt was done to her brother, the envoys would die a horrible death. It is said that Sforza's subsequent liberation was accelerated by the relatives of these hostages she retained at Tricarico.

Simultaneously Sforza's castles outside the Regno, his older possessions in Romagna, came under threat from another quarter. To see why, it is necessary to turn back to Braccio, and find out how he was faring while his rival languished in the Castel dell' Ovo.

The death of Ladislaus and the consequent slackening of Neapolitan efforts in central Italy had revived Braccio's old dream of making himself lord of Perugia. He had latterly been serving Pope John as governor of Bologna, building up his personal strength as chance offered, with the seizure of a castle here and a castle there. Michele Attendolo and his company had enrolled under his command, for his strictly professional contests against Sforza were no reason why Sforza's relatives should decline commissions from him. It was in fact owing to this amicable relationship with Michele that Braccio at first promised not to lay a finger upon his old friend's possessions in Romagna. At this point, however, Tartaglia makes another of his brief but sinister appearances in the story. Fresh from Sforza's attempt to ambush him, from which he had escaped by the skin of his teeth, Tartaglia indicated strongly that there was no place for sentiment. *He* was Braccio's friend and colleague, Sforza was and had been for years his opponent. Tartaglia demanded the castles for himself. Braccio hesitated for some time, embarrassed by the dilemma. Finally, since Sforza was a captive in the Castel dell' Ovo and might never emerge alive, Braccio preferred to keep Tartaglia's goodwill. It was an understandable decision but, as it proved, not a happy one. Sforza was enraged by what he felt to be a mean betrayal of their youthful comradeship. Braccio had kicked him when he was down. Their relations were never the same again. Though they were able, years later, to meet and shake hands and laugh together, there was henceforth an underlying bitterness between them.

A more immediate consequence was the anger of Michele Attendolo, who was placed in an impossible position by Braccio's changed attitude. He could no longer serve such a commander. The atmosphere was electric. If Tartaglia had had his way Michele would probably have been murdered. As it was, Michele was befriended and helped to escape by one of Braccio's junior officers, a man so remarkable that he deserves notice from the moment of his first entrance.

147 The Castel dell'Ovo, Naples, where Sforza was imprisoned from 1415 to 1416.

Niccolò Piccinino was, as his nickname suggests, a very small man, but sheer personality enabled him to triumph over this handicap, just as his iron will counterbalanced his poor health. Born in 1386, he was a Perugian like Braccio, but whereas his leader was of noble family Piccinino was a butcher's son and started his working life as a weaver. The two men, in fact, personified the traditional class alignment of nobility and *popolo minuto* against the prosperous bourgeoisie.

Piccinino had a lively intelligence. He acquired a smattering of education, the three Rs at least, which was more than most of his fellows. Weaving bored him. He was drawn to an adventurous career, from which at first sight his diminutive stature seemed to disqualify him. Fortunately, he had an uncle serving with Bartolomeo da Sesta in Romagna, and this personal introduction procured him a trial as a page. He soon demonstrated that brute strength was not everything. A little man – this little man, at all events – could ride and fight and kill with the best. He won his right to be numbered among the men-at-arms. He also won the hand of his commander's daughter, and she brought him the appropriate dowry for a would-be condottiere, three horses. Soon he came to suspect her, rightly or wrongly, of infidelity. It was perhaps inevitable that in this department of life he could not conquer a nagging sense of inferiority. It was said that he allowed the woman to bear her child, then murdered her. Perhaps that was just a camp-fire story. It was not entirely consistent with his acknowledgment of the child as his own son, though that could have been dictated by a wish to put the best face on the matter and to pretend he had not been cuckolded. But whether the savage story was true or not, Piccinino left his father-in-law's service and enlisted under Braccio, a move that requires no particular explanation in view of Braccio's renown and the fact that they were both Perugians. He soon attracted Braccio's notice. He could hardly fail to, especially when he defeated two opponents in a tournament. On that occasion Braccio placed the victor's crown upon his head. Later, as a more lasting mark of his approval, he gave Piccinino his daughter in marriage, which would have been odd if he had thought him the murderer of his first wife. Piccinino was unswerving in his loyalty to Braccio and became, after his death, the principal exponent of his military methods, the acknowledged leader of the Bracceschi, just as Francesco Sforza carried on his father's tradition and headed the school of the Sforzeschi. In the next generation those two were to be paired in perpetual rivalry like Braccio and Muzio Sforza before them.

Meanwhile, in the period following Joanna's accession to the throne of Naples, Braccio was extremely well placed to further his ambitions in Umbria. Not only had Perugia lost her strong protector but Braccio was

148 Niccolò Piccinino, the little butcher's son from Perugia, who became Braccio da Montone's companion-in-arms and, after his death, one of the leading condottieri in Italy.

almost simultaneously freed from his obligations to his latest employer, Pope John XXIII. That pontiff had been sufficiently ill-advised to submit himself to a great assembly of the Church, the Council of Constance, where he was deposed for 'causing scandal to the Church of God and Christian people by his detestable and unseemly life and manners'. There were, at that moment, two more rival Popes instead of the usual one. The Council of Constance made a clean sweep of the whole trio and after a lengthy interval for the necessary formalities and negotiations elected a new one, Oddo Colonna, in 1417. He took the name of Martin V. He was generally acceptable and his election ended at last the Great Schism which it had suited Ladislaus to prolong. But during the two-year interregnum, when there was effectively no Pope at all, Braccio was a completely free agent, and was able to raise funds for his own Perugian adventure by selling to the citizens of Bologna the freedom of their own city, which he had been governing in the name of the now deposed and captive Pope. The ultimate constitutional value of the transaction was dubious, as the Bolognese were fully aware, but at least they were relieved of Braccio's presence and were masters of their own affairs until such time as a stronger authority overcame them. They paid him 82,000 florins, which enabled him to enlist a good many additional lances. With these, and a number of Perugian exiles belonging like himself to the noble families, he set off to conquer his native city.

Perugia was always a tough nut to crack. A typical hill-top city, sixteen hundred feet above sea-level and nearly a thousand above the Tiber flowing at its feet, the place had immense natural advantages. These were enhanced by the robust tradition of the inhabitants, who prided themselves on being the most warlike people in Italy. They had long been alive to Braccio's ambitions and determined that he should not get a foothold in the place, knowing well that it would touch off an explosion of class war with the usual reprisals. The news that Braccio was at last marching against them, and in such force, caused deep dismay but did not produce any talk of surrender. The gateways were barricaded, a proclamation was issued that no one should leave the city, and the population made ready for a desperate defence.

They had, in point of fact, a good chance of repelling him. Though citizen soldiers were no match for mounted men-at-arms in the open field, they could give a good account of themselves when they fought from behind battlements. To storm Perugia would be a formidable task, even with the most elaborate siege artillery. To starve it would take time, and would inevitably result in the ruination of the surrounding countryside, which was all very well for a foreign invader but would be short-sighted policy for a general hoping to be accepted as the future lord of the city.

Braccio duly arrived with his host, toiled up the steep mountain road, and encamped beneath those massive walls, parts of which dated from Etruscan times. Perugia must have presented a discouraging appearance to any besieger. Within the walls almost every house was itself a miniature fortress. Medieval chroniclers claim that seven hundred towers soared above the rooftops, like the dozen or so still to be seen at San Gimignano.

Braccio made his military demonstration. The Perugians were not overawed. Indeed we are told that some, spoiling for a fight, made a sortie and surprised the unwary besiegers. Later, Braccio attempted to storm the defences. His men penetrated a little way into the town but were thrown out again, even the Perugian women hurling down stones and scalding water. Braccio withdrew for the moment. But, if he could not gain possession of the city neither could the citizens enjoy possession of the *contado* round it, so long as the condottiere prowled like a wolf outside. Such a situation could not continue indefinitely. If he would not leave their territory, he must be fought in the open. To help them in this risky enterprise the Perugians engaged another eminent condottiere, Carlo Malatesta.

The battle was fought on 15 July 1416. The place was close to the Tiber, where the road to Assisi crossed the river on a thirteenth-century bridge that continued to span it until blown up during the German retreat of 1944. It was a countryside always much fought over, this dipping valley between the jealous neighbour towns of Assisi and Perugia. Even the future St Francis had once soldiered and been taken prisoner there. The actual spot on which Braccio clashed with Malatesta was between Sant' Egideo and the river, which was about a quarter of a mile away. It has been said that this was the occasion depicted by Uccello in the picture more usually described as *The Battle of San Romano*, and that the bare-headed fair youth is Galeazzo Malatesta, but there is no proof of this, and the picture more probably represents a Florentine victory over the Sienese, the central figure on the white horse being that same condottiere, Niccolò da Tolentino, whose splendid portrait by Andrea del Castagno hangs beside Hawkwood's in the Duomo at Florence. The period is much the same. Tolentino died in 1434.

If that spirited picture does not portray the Braccio battle, it might well have done, for the struggle on that torrid July day was no less heroic. It went on for seven hours. The heat, for a man in heavy armour and the padded clothing he needed under it, must have been almost intolerable. The dust was choking. 'Most dolorous', wrote the chronicler Fabretti, 'were the sighs that were heard to issue from the helmets.' One can believe it.

Braccio had foreseen that it was going to be thirsty work. He had gone to the unusual length of accumulating countless jars of water behind the lines, so that when one of his detachments retired to re-form after a charge there was an ample supply even for the horses as well as the men. It may be that this provision was inspired by some recollection of Sforza, who, though he could endure cold and most other hardships, was well known for his susceptibility to heat and thirst. When Sforza fought in such weather, he always insisted that a pack-horse should be kept handy for him with wine and water. By extending the idea, and arranging for the comfort of his men, Braccio made a decisive contribution to the result of the battle. For, in the end, Malatesta's men – tortured with thirst and lacking any such organized relief – began to break away and straggle down to the river-bank. The sight of the first such stragglers presented their parched comrades with an irresistible suggestion. As soon as Braccio observed a serious degree of disarray in the ranks facing him, he ordered a general charge. It ended the business. Carlo Malatesta and his nephew, Galeazzo, were both captured along with hundreds of their exhausted followers. 'It was strange to note,' wrote the chronicler, 'that the humblest of Braccio's soldiers were driving prisoners before them like a herd of cattle.'

This battle, the dust-pall at least of which must have been visible to agonized watchers on the battlements of Perugia, convinced the citizens that it was useless to resist Braccio any longer. His most obdurate opponents were outvoted by those who urged that a prompt and graceful bowing to the inevitable would be best in the long run for all concerned. Messengers were quickly sent to Braccio's camp, offering him the lordship. Those who had lately busied themselves with piling up missiles and preparing douches of boiling water were now equally active in hanging rich cloths from their balconies and gathering flowers to strew before his feet. When Braccio rode into the city, the voices that a few months earlier had deafened his soldiers with threats and execrations now chanted with quickly generated enthusiasm: '*Evviva Braccio, Signore di Perugia!*'

In the event, things did not turn out too badly. The worst fears were not realized. Braccio's reputation for cruelty was not maintained so far as his native city was concerned, and he made a statesmanlike effort to conciliate all parties in that faction-riven community. He diverted them from these squabbles by constructive schemes at home – still further strengthening the walls that had so lately defied his siege, and adding a pleasant loggia of four arches in front of the cathedral – and by attractive prospects of increased influence for Perugia in the world outside. How far these could have been fulfilled, it is hard to say, but the establishment of Braccio's despotism was certainly followed by eager demonstrations of support from the smaller towns of the neighbourhood, symbolized in the sending of their banners to Perugia on the feast-day of St Ercolano, the local patron. And, no less certainly, Braccio did manage to imbue his countrymen with a new and dynamic spirit. He had a great contempt for idlers, *i consumatori della piazza*, as he termed them, 'those who wear out the public square'. Once master of Perugia, he ruled unchallenged for the remainder of his life, and seems to have been justified by his general popularity.

As Braccio's fortunes soared to their zenith, Sforza's were at their nadir. Very soon, however, things took a more favourable turn. There was a natural reaction in Naples against the French husband who had virtually usurped Joanna's throne and used his position to distribute honours and key posts to his fellow countrymen. In November 1416, there was a coup headed by Ottino Caracciolo. Joanna was set at liberty, her husband's domination ended, and he and his various protégés ejected from the realm. Less than six months after Braccio's triumphal entry into Perugia, a no less happy Sforza emerged from the gloom of the Castel dell' Ovo and was restored to his office of Grand Constable. He never, however, re-

149 Rome in the early fifteenth century (right) was a half-empty city living on its past, but still important as the seat and symbol of the Papacy.

covered his old standing with the queen. The dead Alopo had been replaced with a new favourite, Giovanni Caracciolo, a cousin (but no friend) of the other Caracciolo who had led the coup against the French. Giovanni had all the charm that Joanna looked for in her ministers. He had also genuine ability. But Sforza could not get on with him, and their antipathy blocked the condottiere's road to further advancement.

Sforza was not long kept hanging about the court. Soon he had more congenial duties in the field. There was still in effect no Pope. The cardinals were still enmeshed in a tangle of procedures, far away in Constance, while Rome was occupied by the new lord of Perugia, who had arrogated to himself the title of *Almae Urbis Defensor* ('Protector of the Bountiful City'). Sforza was given the task of expelling him and regaining possession for Naples. In the summer and autumn of 1417 his horsemen tightened their grip on Rome, advancing from Ostia and the coast. Braccio's troops withdrew before them. Sforza's rode in through streets half-blocked with rubble and the silt of old floods. Nothing flourished but the weeds between the flagstones. An English chronicler about this time mentions the wolves that he had seen with his own eyes, hunting stray dogs in front of St Peter's.

Yet if Rome had become little more than a name, it was still a potently evocative name, and competing princes would do much to claim control

215

of it. It was obviously of particular importance to any Pope, and any occupying power had a valuable bargaining counter. It happened that, almost as soon as Sforza had taken the city, the cardinals elected Martin V, a native of Rome and all the more eager to restore it as the papal capital. A bargain was therefore struck. Sforza, as the general appointed by Naples, should be guardian of Rome until such time as it was fit and ready for His Holiness to return. Martin, for his part, would confirm Joanna in her own disputed title to the throne of Naples. That dispute had raged, off and on, ever since any one could remember, the rival dynasties being Angevin (as was Joanna herself) and the House of Aragon, that had long ruled Sicily and wanted the southern mainland too. As Joanna was approaching fifty, and childless, and proposed to nominate an heir of her own choice, it was desirable for her to obtain papal recognition.

Hostilities between Sforza and Braccio continued in a desultory way over the next year or two, as hostilities were apt to do in the conditions of that place and period, when it was easier to let a state of war drag on, without much positive action, than to achieve a settlement round a conference table. Italy, though a populous and well-developed country by the standards of Europe at the time, was empty by comparison with the crowded peninsula of today. Armies were for the most part cavalry columns of modest size, traversing certain well-trodden roads between cities unfortunate enough to attract their attention, but leaving whole tracts of territory in grateful ignorance of what was going on. Now and then a set battle or a siege gave the chronicler a definite event to record for that particular summer season, but neither side had the resources to maintain continuous fighting.

The campaign of 1419 was more energetically carried on than most. There was a hard-fought engagement in June on the Via Cassia between Viterbo and Montefiascone, just south of the Lake of Bolsena. Braccio won handsomely. Sforza was wounded. The fighting continued sporadically through the summer, extending across Umbria into Romagna. In his anxiety to restore the situation Sforza went so far as to patch up his ancient feud with Tartaglia, and induced him to change sides. This insincere reconciliation was sealed with a marriage that must truly have been one of convenience: Tartaglia's son was given one of Sforza's daughters, presumably one of his children by Lucia Tregani.

The personal lives of Sforza himself and of Braccio at this time are, as nearly always with the condottieri, most sparsely documented and tantalizing in their silences. It is known, however, that Sforza contracted a third marriage at about this date, so Catella Alopo must have died. Now, at about fifty, he married the widowed young Countess of Celano, who brought him her previous husband's castles and bore him a son, Gabriele, who did not inherit the Sforza taste for soldiering and eventually became Archbishop of Milan. Of Braccio's private affairs even less is known. He had a wife, Nicolina da Varano, and a small son, Carlo, who is heard of many years later as a condottiere.

As the military results of the 1419 season had been disappointing, Pope Martin's mind turned to the possibility of achieving his aims by diplomacy. Two years after his election he was still in Florence, lodged in the splendid Dominican monastery of Santa Maria Novella, but ever hankering, as he paced its green-frescoed cloisters, for the triumphal entry into his native Rome which seemed inadvisable until his power was more secure. In January 1420, he sent for Sforza as the man who was supposed to be facilitating his return. Sforza, though the servant not of the Pope but of the queen, had no choice but to obey the summons.

Long ago, in the then revered columns of the *Encyclopaedia Britannica*, Noel Valois described Martin as 'a good and gentle man, leading a simple life, free from intrigue', but this last phrase accords oddly with his policies, which closely affected Sforza, in the matter of the Neapolitan succession. Over the next year or two Martin was to align himself in turn with Joanna against Louis III of Anjou, with Louis against Joanna and Alfonso of Aragon, and finally with Joanna and Louis against Alfonso. Such papal permutations made the most cynical condottiere look like a faithful hound. Or, to change the comparison, as Peter Partner comments in *The Papal State under Martin V*: 'The understanding of Martin V with Filippo Maria Visconti was a singular instance of two formidable foxes running together.' True, as Partner says, 'at the time of his election the tenacity and firmness of purpose, the ruthless will to dominate, which were at the basis of Oddo Colonna's nature, were hidden beneath an exterior of shifty affability'. Even so, there were those at the time who had had a taste of his true character even before he had started his journey to Italy. 'I had a very fine white horse here, bigger than any in the entire court,' lamented a member of the Teutonic Order, 'but one day the Holy Father sent word to ask me to lend him the animal for his journey, as he was short of white horses. . . . If the Pope lays hands on him, I am sure I shall never get him back, so I might as well make it a present. Please send me another horse – only make it a black or a brown one.'

Martin, like Sforza himself, was essentially a man of the world. Both preferred to work for an ultimate objective that they could sincerely believe was good rather than bad. But neither, having lived for some fifty years in an imperfect human society, was too squeamish about some of the intermediate stages. Martin had been elected to end the Great Schism, to

217

restore the Church's authority in Italy, and to make Rome great again. To achieve this objective he would exploit rival condottieri and Neapolitan claimants, and mobilize every kind of support, from his grasping Colonna kinsmen to his Florentine financial backers. He was a client of the Medici, whose power was now in the ascendant though as yet not supreme.

The Florentines were pressing Martin to make his peace with Braccio and recognize as a *fait accompli* the latter's dominion over the various towns and castles he had seized in papal territory. Martin intimated to Sforza that, in view of his failure to beat Braccio, they had better work for a *rapprochement* of this kind, unpalatable though it might be. So the olive branch was duly extended, and in February 1420 Braccio made his impressive entry into Florence.

As befitted the lord of Perugia, he had arrayed himself gorgeously in purple, with gold and silver embroidery, and mounted his four hundred followers on the biggest chargers he could find. The procession was reinforced with a welcoming party of civic dignitaries and foreign ambassadors. Together they all made their way through the cheering crowds to where the Pope awaited them with as benign a smile as he could muster. He greeted Braccio publicly as Papal Vicar of Perugia, Assisi, Orvieto, and all the other places whose lordship he had forcibly seized during the past few years.

Sforza also had to mask his chagrin and welcome his old comrade with diplomatic compliments. It cannot have been the happiest of days either for the Pope or for his military champion. That night the Florentine urchins chanted ceaselessly under their windows:

> *Papa Martino –*
> *Non vale un quattrino!*
> *E Braccio valente*
> *Che vince ogni gente!*

Such was the popular estimate. Pope Martin was not worth a farthing. Brave Braccio was the one to conquer all comers.

150 Pope Martin V.

218

Changing partners 15

The last years of Sforza and Braccio may be likened to a set dance in which the participants advance, retire, turn about, clasp hands, separate again, and pause facing each other from the sides opposite to those they originally occupied. In the struggle for the Neapolitan succession no two people shared identical interests, and there was thus a continual change of partners, in which the two condottieri were always in demand.

The superficial harmony exhibited at Florence did not last. Sforza was not happy in Joanna's service. Her favourite, Giovanni Caracciolo, had altogether too much power. The Pope shared his disapproval of Caracciolo, and, as the queen was clearly devoted to him, Martin decided to withdraw his support from her and recognize her rival, Louis of Anjou, as King of Naples. This was a cool breach of faith. Rome, which the Pope triumphantly entered at last on 30 September 1420, had been given to him in return for his recognition of Joanna's title. Now the 'good and gentle man . . . free from intrigue' not only reneged on that understanding but seduced her general as well. Sforza was commissioned to fight for the Pope's new nominee, Louis, and in due course marched against Naples, assailing that city at the Capuan Gate.

Joanna meantime, under Caracciolo's able advice, made counter-dispositions. She turned for help to Louis's cousin and rival, Alfonso of Aragon, who already held the twin kingdom of Sicily and maintained an historic claim to Naples as well. If he would aid her now, he should be recognized as her heir. It was a fair offer from a childless and ageing queen. Alfonso, however, though he later became famous under the tag of 'the Magnanimous', was realistic enough to ask for guarantees. An agreement was drawn up, in which Joanna promised that he should 'receive the Castel Nuovo and Castel dell' Ovo on the first sighting of the Aragonese sails'.

Simultaneously, both to strengthen her military position in general and to ensure that she did not depend excessively on Alfonso, Joanna engaged the services of Braccio, so that the rivals, so lately reconciled, were once more arrayed against each other. They had merely moved to opposite sides. Braccio and his troops arrived in Naples in early June 1421. She not only gave him Sforza's old post as Grand Constable but created him Prince of Capua. Braccio, now indulging higher and higher ambitions of extending his own power through Italy, was delighted with this addition to his dignities. He opened vigorous hostilities against Sforza who was investing the city from the north.

Alfonso sailed in from Sicily, with an army largely composed of Catalans, about the end of June. Whatever he thought of Braccio (and there could well have been jealousy between them) he formed a warm estimate of the condottiere they were both fighting. Observing Sforza's behaviour from a distance during one of the battles in the bay, he called to a captured officer and told him: 'Your commander is the bravest captain of our time. Go and tell him so from me.' The prisoner was released to do so, and to add the royal promise that in future Alfonso's archers would not deliberately aim at Sforza. Not to be outdone, Sforza sent back word that his own men would be instructed not to molest the Aragonese flagship.

Courtly exchanges of this kind were not thought incompatible with acts of treachery and revenge. Tartaglia was still fighting under Sforza's banner, but he had never been a satisfactory subordinate, and he now fell increasingly under the suspicion that he was contemplating a change. He did not always carry out orders and it was noticed that, if any of his men fell into Braccio's hands, they were treated with conspicuous leniency. Compromising letters from Alfonso were intercepted. Tartaglia appeared to be receiving gifts of horses from the same source. Sforza was not left with the sole and embarrassing responsibility of dealing with this fellow soldier whose son had married his daughter. It was the Pope and Louis of Anjou who satisfied themselves of Tartaglia's guilt and ordered his punishment. The suspect was occupying a house at Aversa, outside Naples on the Capuan road. It was surrounded during the night and Tartaglia was dragged naked from his bed. A confession, true or false, but probably true, was extracted by the ruthless methods of the time. Then, without further ado, he was hustled into the piazza and put to death. Loyalty still existed at humbler levels: Tartaglia's men were enraged at this treatment of their captain, and, though the Pope made them attractive offers to remain in his pay under a new leader, they preferred to disband. Before long, the majority were to be found fighting on Braccio's side.

Exchanges of this sort were the easier because the two armies were so close. Naples was divided between them. On the one hand stood the queen

151 Alfonso of Aragon, the successor of Joanna, reunited Sicily and Naples in one kingdom.

with Alfonso and Braccio, on the other hand Louis of Anjou and Sforza, backed by the Pope in Rome and the Medici bankers of Florence. There was practically a stalemate, a confrontation that was tedious to condottieri accustomed to a war of movement and expensive for their employers.

This state of affairs was brought to an end by general agreement. Martin was adept at negotiating such compromises. His thirteen-year pontificate was milestoned with concordats and deals of one sort or another. This time he was aided by the willingness of the professional soldiers to wind up the affair. Braccio and Sforza were largely the arbiters of the situation, Braccio in particular. He was anxious to get away and look after his other interests. He had received tempting offers to intervene in the struggle then proceeding between Venice and Milan. He was already Prince of Capua, and Joanna was now prepared to reward his services with the governorship of the Abruzzi, the rugged territory that extended eastwards behind the Papal States and linked up conveniently with his possessions there and in Romagna. So Braccio, arguing from a position of strength, induced Sforza to make his peace with the queen. Once the two condottieri had sorted things out between them, the other parties fell into line. Caracciolo retained his place at court. The two royal claimants promised to withdraw from the kingdom, though Louis of Anjou went no further away than Rome.

Thus, to continue the simile of the formal dance, ended the first figure.

Fresh figures, and complicated ones, were evolved in the months that followed.

Caracciolo felt that Alfonso, as heir-presumptive, threatened his own domination of the queen. Much as he disliked Sforza, he regarded him as an insignificant menace in the political field, and wondered if he could not safely play him off against the Spaniard. Sforza looked ready for a change. Neither the Pope nor Louis seemed anxious to employ him and he had no funds with which to pay his men. That was the recurrent problem of a condottiere, how, having collected a good team, to maintain it in being when there was a shortage of contracts.

It would have been unwise to go behind Braccio's back, for he was still Grand Constable of the Kingdom, apart from holding the other high honours granted by the queen. Caracciolo sensibly used Braccio as his go-between in approaching Sforza. The two soldiers met by appointment in Braccio's tent, pitched in a meadow beside the road by which he was travelling to Umbria. It was a most amicable reunion. They talked frankly and at length, reviving memories of their early adventures together in Alberico da Barbiano's company and good-humouredly exchanging revelations of the treacheries attempted against each other by their respective subordinates. Sforza, for instance, Braccio assured him, had been perfectly right to execute Tartaglia. Tartaglia had been guilty. He deserved his fate for being found out.

It was a typically professional gossip the two men enjoyed in that roadside encampment, very much like the unbuttoned talk of opposing lawyers about hard-fought cases on which the files are closed. They understood each other. They knew how far to trust each other, and where to draw the line. They could never recover the whole-hearted comradeship of the good old days, but they would always have more in common than with the Popes and princes they served.

Braccio could afford to be magnanimous. On the face of it he had been the more successful. He had achieved his original ambition to become lord of Perugia, and in a few years since then he had reached out in many directions until by this date, there is no doubt, he was entertaining dreams of power on a much vaster scale. If Sforza had dreams, it is harder to guess their nature. Of humbler social origin and no education, he was perhaps agreeably surprised to find that he had come as far as he had and was acceptable in the royal council-chamber of Naples. But were his sights really set no higher? Certainly in 1422 his first concern must have been to maintain his position. Braccio's assurances that he would now be *persona grata* with Queen Joanna again, and that Caracciolo was positively anxious to secure his support, offered a welcome prospect for the immediate future.

He spent that night in Braccio's headquarters, and the next morning rode several miles with him along the northward road. They parted with the utmost cordiality. They were never to meet again. Sforza turned back. When in due course he presented himself in Naples, the queen received him with all her one-time warmth.

Partners changed again when the dancers grouped themselves for the figure of 1423.

Alfonso had not observed the agreement that he and Louis should both stay away from Naples and the Regno. He and his Catalan followers were much in evidence, causing friction with the Neapolitans. Joanna herself was irritated and began to regret that she had promised Alfonso the succession. He was presuming altogether too much. She was not dead yet – and she could change her mind. Relations became strained. Alfonso decided to act first.

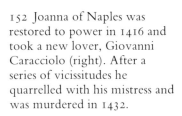

152 Joanna of Naples was restored to power in 1416 and took a new lover, Giovanni Caracciolo (right). After a series of vicissitudes he quarrelled with his mistress and was murdered in 1432.

In May he arrested Caracciolo, rightly judging him to be the prime mover of the opposition against him. Joanna quickly took refuge in the Castel Capuano, a favourite royal residence just inside the Capuan Gate. It was a place of some strength, first built by the Norman King William the Bad and subsequently improved by that tireless castle-builder, the Emperor Frederick II. Besieged there by Alfonso's troops, the queen dispatched an urgent appeal to Sforza. He had only limited numbers at his disposal, but he responded with all his old energy. He attacked the Catalans from behind and routed them, taking a host of prisoners and a great deal of booty. Then, judging his own force insufficient to hold the position, he persuaded Joanna to leave the Castel Capuano and withdraw to Aversa. He found her amenable enough, but adamant on one point: at all costs her beloved Caracciolo must be freed from Alfonso's clutches, and to achieve this Sforza had to exchange (with what private regrets may be imagined) the Catalan prisoners who had just fallen into his hands.

At Aversa, when the fugitive queen had recovered her breath, she denounced Alfonso and revoked his nomination as her heir-presumptive. Louis of Anjou, who had so long contested the throne, was now taken into her favour and promised it on her death. He was at once created Duke of Calabria. To complete the reshuffle, Alfonso called in Braccio, so that once again the two condottieri found themselves on opposite sides.

153 The arms and portrait of Louis III of Anjou, who for long disputed the succession of Naples with Alfonso of Aragon.

154 The castle of Aquila, in the Abruzzi, besieged by Braccio da Montone during the winter of 1423–24.

Braccio was still in the north and did not answer the Aragonese summons with much promptitude. He wished first to settle accounts with the city of Aquila, which was stoutly Angevin in its sympathies and had closed its gates against him. Set high in the rugged mountains of the Abruzzi, Aquila had been founded by Frederick II for strategic reasons, and for similar reasons Braccio could not tolerate its being in hostile hands. Was he not Governor of the Abruzzi? But who, the Aquilans doubtless retorted, had given him that authority over them? Queen Joanna – and was not he now leagued treacherously with that lady's enemies? They defied him. Braccio sat down before the city with his army and began a siege that lasted all through the second half of 1423 and into the next year.

Alfonso had at first taken refuge in the Castel Nuovo at Naples, from which he had been delivered by the arrival of his fleet from Sicily. Sforza seems not to have been unduly troubled by the threat of anything Alfonso could do. Braccio was the serious opponent. Why wait for Braccio to tire of besieging Aquila – or even to capture that loyal city – and to ride triumphantly south when it suited him? Far better to give Braccio a surprise, to march north in the depth of winter and catch him at a disadvantage with one of those attacks from the rear Sforza had just so successfully brought off outside the Castel Capuano.

With this object, and also no doubt because the season made the upland routes difficult or impassable, the approach was made from the Adriatic side. Aquila stands on a hill rising from the broad valley of the Aterno, which joins the Pescara and enters the sea near the town of that name. Aquila itself is 2360 feet above the sea, but it is surrounded by much higher peaks, the most notable being those of the Gran Sasso, whose limestone summits soar to eight and nine thousand feet. Braccio had a bleak setting for a midwinter siege.

The new year, 1424, had just begun when Sforza, accompanied by his son, now an experienced young campaigner of twenty-two, and by Michele Attendolo, approached the River Pescara along the flat coast, proposing to cross near its mouth and then turn inland up its valley towards Aquila, some sixty miles away. Braccio heard news of his move and sent down a contingent to defend the usual ford. Sforza decided to go a little further downstream and make a crossing, which he was confident was practicable, almost at the river's debouchment into the sea.

It was Monday 3 January, a date declared inauspicious by the astrologers, but Sforza would not wait until the morrow. An east wind blew shrewdly off the sea, driving the salt water into the river-mouth and churning it into alarming waves where it clashed with the current swirling down from the hills.

Sforza himself, mounted on his charger, Scalzanacha, was with the vanguard when they reached the bank. Five men rode into the water and passed across safely. Young Francesco went after them, with Michele Attendolo close behind. Sforza followed with a small troop of men-at-arms. It was rough going but not unduly dangerous. Though now in his mid fifties, the veteran cared little for a January soaking.

Braccio's men were waiting for them and advanced to the attack. Sforza turned in his saddle and signalled to the rest of his party to come over. But they hesitated for a fatal minute, unnerved by the tawny maelstrom of seething water and sand. Sforza bellowed against the wind that there was no danger. Then, impatient and furious, he turned back into the river to demonstrate the fact and shame them into obedience. His example had the effect he wanted. The troop plunged into the waves. But one of the pages got into difficulties, panicked perhaps, and Sforza leaned over to give him a supporting hand. Scalzanacha stumbled and rolled over, throwing him from his seat. The horse was up again in a moment, but the condottiere, weighed down by his armour, had no chance.

226

155 The young Francesco Sforza inherited his father's position as a condottiere
    leader after Muzio was drowned on his way to attack Braccio before Aquila.

DIVVS FRAN SPHOR HVIVS IMPERII
PATER ET ASSERTOR BELLI PACISVE ARBITER
AC SEMPER VICTOR VIXIT VIVIT VIVET

Now for the first time the spotlight picks up Francesco Sforza, who, on the score of wider historical significance, must be reckoned the most eminent of all the mercenary captains.

Rallying the men he had, he attacked the enemy with such *élan* that they soon abandoned all attempt to contest the crossing. Only then, in all probability, did the young man learn for certain that his father was dead, and how it had happened. Sensibly making use of a boat that was found on the northern bank, he hurried back to find the main body of the army, which had just been cast into the deepest gloom by the news of their leader's drowning. Francesco was his father's son and they recognized it. The promptitude with which he assumed command, mastering his own grief and heartening the men, won their devotion from that moment.

Perhaps the unfortunate circumstances of Muzio's death, leaving an element of guilt and shame in the minds of his followers, made them especially determined to avenge him. There was nothing unusual in their ostentatious marks of mourning, in the darkening of their helmets and the decking of their horses, as well as themselves, with black. Such observances recur frequently in the records, whenever a company is bereaved of a popular commander. Sforza's soldiers were more remarkable in that they did not merely swear vengeance, they very soon exacted it.

In giving Francesco, without question, the place left vacant by his father, the men's sound judgment was quickly endorsed by Joanna. The queen was distressed by the loss of the general she had liked as a man, and who had at least, in all their vicissitudes, been more often on her side than not. With her well-known propensities she could not fail to be attracted by his son. Francesco had all Muzio's virility and physical advantages, coupled with the more polished manners inculcated in his genteeler childhood. Pope Pius II relates that, when nearing sixty, he looked like a young man, so tall was he and upright in carriage. It may be imagined how favourably he impressed Joanna when he was twenty-two. She confirmed him in possession of his father's lands and castles, and treated him as the chief commander of her forces.

In the early summer he moved against Braccio, who was still besieging Aquila. The capture of that defiant city was a challenge he could not ignore. His prestige was now deeply involved.

Francesco had the support of Michele Attendolo. There were strong papal forces as well, commanded by Jacopo Caldora, a Neapolitan condottiere engaged by Martin V. For all his diplomatic gestures at Florence three years before, the Pope had never been reconciled to Braccio's conquest of central Italy and his thinly veiled aspirations for the future, so incompatible with Martin's own determination to maintain

228

the temporal power of the Church. Any effort to overthrow the lord of Perugia could count on the Holy Father's prayers and material support. Finally, as was to be expected in any Italian campaign of this nature, the army was leavened with Braccio's fellow townsmen and political opponents, those Raspanti whom he had failed to win over and had been compelled to drive into exile.

Braccio received estimates of the combined forces advancing against him and knew that he was outnumbered but was not unduly alarmed. He had respected his dead rival, but he had never feared him, and he certainly did not fear his son, a young man trained (he believed) in the fundamentally inferior methods adhered to by his father. He had given old Muzio a thrashing before now. Francesco should present no problems.

In this confident mood Braccio observed, from his camp on the level ground below Aquila, the approach of his enemies down the opposite mountainside, which was so steep that they had to lead their horses. He disdained to attack them at a disadvantage. Let them come down and settle the matter in fair fight: the Aquilans, watching from their battlements, might then be at last persuaded to abandon their hopeless resistance. He contented himself with dispatching a force to cut off the escape-route of the relieving army when in due course they turned to flight. Then he called his pages to arm him, and finally, donning his helmet, a particularly splendid affair adorned with a silver garland and balls, he rode forward to do battle.

It was no courtly contest that followed. Braccio had possibly underestimated the bitterness and determination of his adversaries. Michele Attendolo ordered his men to go for their opponents' horses, a tactic common enough in some medieval battles but not favoured by condottieri, who considered it both unsporting and wasteful, captured horses forming a valuable part of the spoils of victory. The Attendoli, however, were concerned with revenge rather than loot. A thousand of Braccio's men-at-arms were unhorsed in this way, and many of them, once down, were given no chance to get up again. The attacking forces were not taking prisoners – the Perugian exiles were filled with the special blood-lust that is stirred by civil wars – and Braccio's men had to fight back with equal savagery. This battle raged for eight hours. The issue was decided by a sortie of Aquilan townsmen, fresh to the conflict and eager to seize this chance to end the siege.

Even Braccio saw that the day was lost, and after the slaughter he had witnessed he knew the mood of his enemies. His one chance of personal survival was to avoid recognition. It must have been a decision of exquisite bitterness when he took off that conspicuous helmet with its silver garland and threw it away. It was a useless act. There were plenty in that struggling mass who knew the face better than the helmet. It was a fellow Perugian who gave him the wound that eventually proved fatal.

Although no quarter was being given, the fallen Braccio was in fact picked up, carried to safety, and treated with the utmost compassion. Jacopo Caldora, the Pope's condottiere, surrounded him with the best doctors available, who made every effort to heal him of the wounds he had sustained in head and throat. They held out optimistic hopes of his recovery, but it seemed that Braccio had lost the will to live. He lingered for three days, refusing all nourishment and declining to utter a word. As the precise nature of his throat-wound is not recorded, the gruesome thought inevitably occurs that perhaps the poor man was physically incapable of doing either, but the tradition of the broken heart is most generally accepted. One story, however, suggests darkly that Francesco Sforza hastened his end by nudging the surgeon's arm when he was cleaning the wound. This rumour was spread by the Aquilan poet, Ciunillo, but is so contrary to Francesco's character that it has never been widely accepted. If any such dirty work was done it was far more likely the act of some embittered Perugian with personal motives for revenge.

Another picturesque legend supports the broken heart tradition and has been used to emphasize the scale of Braccio's pretensions. Before leaving for the siege of Aquila he handed a small coffer to his wife, telling her it was to remain locked until his return and she must open it only in the event of his death. When Nicolina did examine the contents she found two articles within – the sceptre he had meant her to hold as a queen, if his plans of conquest reached their logical conclusion, and the black veil she would need as his widow if they did not. Whether or not this is another romantic story to be dismissed, the death-or-glory symbolism fits Braccio's life and character.

So, within the space of a year, perished the two pre-eminent condottieri of their generation. Pope Martin's rancour pursued Braccio to the grave – which, the pontiff decreed, should be in unconsecrated ground outside Rome. Perugia quickly submitted to his authority. Within two or three months, on 29 July, Martin rode in triumph into the city and reclaimed it as his own. At a later date there was another solemn entry, quieter and sadder but in a way no less triumphal – when Braccio's bones, redeemed from their first dishonourable resting-place, were brought back to the city that remained obstinately proud of him. No bells rang. The streets were shuttered. In silence the unending procession of magistrates and citizens followed his remains to the church of San Francesco al Prato. When that church was threatened with subsidence in the nineteenth

156 A later artist's reconstruction of the battle outside Aquila at which Braccio da Montone was fatally wounded.

century they were removed once again, this time to be exhibited, rather unfeelingly, in the University Museum, where a flamboyant Latin inscription appealed:

> O you who pass by, pause and weep. I, born in Perugia, was received in Montone as an exile. Mars made me master of my native land of Umbria, and of Capua also. Rome obeyed me, the world was my audience, Italy my stage. But Aquila marked my downfall, wherefore my sorrowing country enshrined me in this little urn. Alas, Mars upraised me, *Mors* brought me low. So go your way.

It was not in churches or in museums that the memory of Braccio and Sforza was kept green, but rather at countless camp-fires and in soldiers' taverns, where for the next few generations their battles were refought, their tactics criticized, their legendary prowess inflated at each retelling. The survivors of Braccio's company rallied at first mainly to his diminutive but fearsome lieutenant, Niccolò Piccinino: he saw to it that his

231

157 Filippo Maria Visconti, the younger son of Gian Galeazzo, was able to seize supreme power in Milan after his elder brother, the vicious Giovanni Maria, was murdered in 1412.

master and fellow countryman was not forgotten. Francesco remained the natural as well as the hereditary leader for the Sforzeschi. Queen Joanna herself bade him and his younger brothers assume the Sforza nickname as a permanent tribute to their father.

Despite the favour showered upon him at Naples, the young man did not remain there long. He had attracted the attention of a Milanese admiral who was serving the queen. This man recommended him to Filippo Maria Visconti, the younger son of Gian Galeazzo and by this time Duke of Milan. Within a few months of his triumph over Braccio at Aquila, Francesco Sforza began his connection with the great northern duchy, a connection that opened with a modest command of fifteen hundred cavalry and three hundred foot-soldiers and ended only when he was master of the whole state.

Before that story can be told it is necessary to go back twenty years or more and see what had been happening in Milan.

The decade of Giovanni Maria Visconti's tyranny at Milan, 1402–12, offered many chances for unprincipled adventurers like Facino Cane but small appeal to commanders of Hawkwood's or dal Verme's stamp.

Giovanni Maria can scarcely be said to have governed. He had little opportunity and less inclination. So long as he could enjoy the show of power and the freedom to express his sadistic fantasies, he cared nothing that his father's great political design lay now in ruins.

Gian Galeazzo's will was quickly disregarded. Two of Bernabò's sons, Carlo and Ettore, emerged from long exile and made an aggressive bid to recover what their branch of the family had lost, seventeen years before. The late duke's widow, Caterina – their own sister and half-sister, respectively – was overthrown along with her lover, Barbavara. She died in 1404, 'poisoned by her son', said rumour, as rumour was apt to say. Giovanni was quite capable of the crime, but he did not commit every act of which he was capable. By that time, the already disunited Council of Regency had melted away. Carlo and Ettore, for all their boldness – and Ettore especially, one of Bernabò's bastards, was described as 'a man without fear' – proved unable to consolidate their victory and provide an effective government. They were ejected, but returned again. The duchy continued for some time as the arena for a sanguinary free-for-all struggle, in which the condottieri snatched what they could and acknowledged whichever authority suited them, or none at all.

In such a boiling cauldron scum naturally rose to the top. That is hardly an unfair description of Facino Cane, who of all these competing generals secured the most control over the new duke. Giovanni's caprices are legendary. He was reputed to amuse himself with man-hunts through the midnight streets of his capital, setting forth with his huntsman, Squarcia Giramo, and a pack of famished hounds to chase citizens imprudent enough to walk late. In 1409, when the crowds greeted him with plaintive

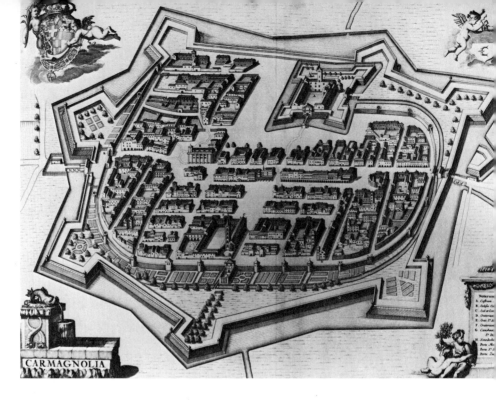

CARMAGNOLIA

cries of 'Peace! Peace!' he had the demonstration savagely broken up by his mercenaries, with two hundred fatal casualties. Thereafter he decreed it a hanging offence even to utter the words *pace* and *guerra*. The very priests had to chant *dona nobis tranquillitatem* instead of *pacem* as laid down in the missal. Even if the more lurid stories are discounted, it is impossible to doubt the duke's excessive and most unpleasant oddity. While he amused himself with this or that depravity, it was Facino Cane who protected him and quietly feathered his own nest.

A Piedmontese himself, Cane singled out a youth from the same region as promising material for the future. Francesco Bussone was of peasant stock, a shepherd's son, fresh-complexioned, chestnut-haired, and not unhandsome. He came from a village south of Turin, Carmagnola, later to give its name to the song and dance famous in the French Revolution. Long before that, however, the name was adopted by Bussone, and it is as 'Carmagnola' that history mentions him. He was brave, able, and ambitious. Cane summed him up. 'He's of the type that, once he's tasted a few honours, will never be satisfied. He has more ambition than any peasant who ever lived.' Cane held him back for the time being, not wishing to build up a dangerous rival. Carmagnola could afford to wait. He had been born in 1390. He was only twenty-two when his great chance came.

158, 159 The condottiere on whom Filippo Maria Visconti relied during the early years of his reign was Francesco Bussone (right), born at the small town of Carmagnola (left) and always known by that name.

In that year, 1412, Cane's position seemed secure. The duke was no problem. His younger brother, Filippo Maria, was for practical purposes a prisoner in Cane's hands. A nervous young man of twenty, superstitious, afraid of the dark, of thunder, and indeed of most things, he was confined to the Castello of Pavia, where his father and grandfather had known so much happiness. He might well remain there indefinitely, unless his perverted brother conceived a whim to murder him.

Suddenly the situation changed. Cane was taken ill while besieging Brescia and was carried to Pavia. Perhaps by coincidence, or perhaps encouraged by the knowledge that the commander-in-chief was temporarily out of action, a group of Milanese noblemen chose that moment to remove their odious duke. Giovanni was struck down with repeated dagger-blows in the church of San Gottardo. The body lay in its blood, neglected, until (according to a story which introduces that stock character of sentiment, the whore with a heart of gold) a prostitute crept near and strewed it with red roses. The news of the assassination was carried post-haste to Pavia, only an hour or two's ride away. Cane roused himself on his death-bed and bade his officers swear allegiance to Filippo Maria as the rightful heir. He must have known that his own hours were numbered, for he went on to advise his wife, Beatrice di Tenda, to marry again – and to secure the new duke as her husband.

235

At first sight this might have seemed an odd union, for she was twice Filippo's age, but on reflection it was seen by all to be a marriage of the greatest convenience. The Archbishop of Milan urged it upon the young Visconti: by it he would secure the loyalty of Facino Cane's troops, together with all the territory they occupied and the vast personal fortune their dead leader had collected, amounting to almost 500,000 florins. Beatrice for her part could never have hoped to retain this inheritance for herself, even the money, let alone the power, so that her best chance of enjoying it, and then indirectly, was to take it as a most welcome dowry to the new duke.

Filippo being anything but a warrior himself, the troops needed a new commander at once. Carmagnola had always earned Cane's approval and it is likely that his name had figured in the commander's dying recommendations. At all events Carmagnola became, from this time forward, increasingly prominent in the Milanese service. He and the duke were almost of an age, twenty-two and twenty respectively. Filippo was glad to escape from the tutelage of a veteran scoundrel like Cane and deal on more equal terms with a contemporary.

Filippo acted with impressive promptitude, almost suspicious promptitude, one might say, remembering the ruthless way the Visconti family habitually treated their near kin. Giovanni was murdered and Facino Cane died on the same day, 16 May, and without hesitation the timid, secretive Filippo leapt into action. No doubt, like his father who had similarly spent years of his youth as a nonentity at Pavia, Filippo had often let his imagination play with the notion of some great change in the balance; but whereas Gian Galeazzo had been forced to bide his time patiently, Filippo responded unhesitatingly to a situation that should have taken him by surprise. Did it? True, he rewarded the rose-strewing prostitute with extravagant liberality and punished the assassins with no less extravagant savagery, but these gestures were as conventional as mourning observances. They do not prove a complete lack of foreknowledge or a sincere regret that he was now duke and his own master.

Once assured that Carmagnola and the rest of Cane's mercenaries would back him, he marched upon Milan. Ettore Visconti tried to bar his entry. Filippo, however, had the support of Vincenzo Marliano, castellan of the Porta Giovia, that huge red-brick fortress which was to become Filippo's favourite home – his 'lair' would hardly, in this context, be too melodramatic a word. Marliano not only held this key-point on Filippo's behalf and refused admission to Ettore, but also used his authority to rally the citizens and occupy other parts of the city. There were a few days of confused fighting. Then Ettore and his partisans were driven out, and

Filippo made a triumphal entry, welcomed by a population hoping for better times and sure at least that he could not be as bad as his brother.

Ettore withdrew no further than the ancient city of Monza, barely ten miles to the north-east. Carmagnola was sent in pursuit. There was a brisk engagement, in which Ettore was worsted. For all his fearlessness, he turned in flight, but Carmagnola's men shot him down, and he bled to death. His sister Valentina still held out in Monza, but, spirited woman though she was, she knew that Ettore's death had robbed Bernabò's descendants of their most credible leader. She surrendered on terms that reasonably safeguarded herself and the other survivors of her branch of the family.

These opening events of his reign convinced Filippo that Carmagnola was the man for his business. The killing of his cousin, so much more final than his capture with all its subsequent embarrassments, was not the least gratifying of the successes reported to him. He gave Carmagnola a free hand, and the young condottiere quickly demonstrated his ability.

City by city, castle by castle, he re-established the ducal authority as it had existed in Gian Galeazzo's day. Where he met with resistance, he struck great hammer-blows and beat it down. Determined opponents, once defeated, met not with chivalry but with cruel punishment designed to deter others in the future. When he took Lodi after a surprise attack, he exposed the lord of that city in an iron cage, a torment from which the wretched captive was delivered only by the duke's formal death-sentence. On another occasion, Carmagnola crossed the Adda by pontoon-bridge in December. One of the enemy swam under water in an attempt to file through the chain linking the boats. Carmagnola's watchful sentries caught him in a net. Carmagnola rewarded his courage by marooning him, naked as he was, on the central fragment of the original bridge whose destruction had made the pontoons necessary. When Filippo degli Arcelli defied him from the walls of Piacenza, Carmagnola seized his adversary's son and brother and had them impaled before his eyes. Mercy was not the Milanese way. The duke and his general were well suited.

Filippo did not fail to show his appreciation. He created his young commander Count of Castelnuovo di Scrivia and had him invested with impressive ceremonies in Milan cathedral. He allowed him to bear the Visconti arms, that grisly but not inappropriate device of a serpent engulfing a man. He permitted him to marry the beautiful Antonia Visconti, who was probably his own half-sister by one of Gian Galeazzo's infrequent love-affairs. The new 'Count of Carmagnola', as he was usually called, set up house in a magnificent palace, the Broletto Nuovo, that was conspicuous even in opulent Milan. There, children came in as rapid and regular succession as the military victories of the previous years. But they were all daughters – Antonia, Margherita, Isabella, Luchina . . . The ennobled peasant lacked only a son to inherit his honours.

To be precise, he lacked one other thing, the duke's real trust. Between the two men there was nothing comparable with the lifelong relationship of Gian Galeazzo and Jacopo dal Verme. Filippo trusted nobody, least of all a condottiere. He had so far found Carmagnola indispensable, but that was no recommendation. He wanted no one else, ever, to attain the supremacy that Facino Cane had enjoyed.

Filippo had exchanged the virtual imprisonment of Pavia for the voluntary seclusion of the Porta Giovia at Milan. He seems to have been genuinely sensitive about his appearance, ugly from the start, and later corpulent, for he would never sit for his portrait, but his extreme reluctance to appear in public, his refusal on one occasion even to emerge and greet the Emperor Sigismund, was positively neurotic. James I of England was no less morbidly afraid of assassins, but James was never a recluse. Filippo's special and not unreasonable fears must have been intensified by a general agoraphobia. Even when he quitted the castle shadows for one of his country villas he would not travel by road, but crept through the green Lombard plain in a strongly defended state barge along canals specially dug for the purpose.

His visitors – even Carmagnola – had to be circumspect in word and behaviour. They must never, for example, glance out of a window, or the duke, in chronic fear of conspiracy, would assume that it was a prearranged signal to confederates outside. Filippo was quite capable of changing his room more than once in the course of a single night: he was a poor sleeper and the move disturbed him less than it did his guards. He maintained checks and double-checks on everybody. Carmagnola was not exempt. He knew how unsafe it was to conceal anything from his master. An efficient administrator, Filippo made his information service a priority. Though he seldom stirred outside the Porta Giovia, he had an uncomfortably exact knowledge of what was being done a hundred miles away.

Carmagnola had plenty of courage, and needed it to fish in such murky waters. He had also the toughness, the salty wit, and the avarice of the peasant, along with the poker-faced craftiness of the market-place. Without that last quality he could not have held his own with such a master.

He knew what to expect if he outlived his usefulness. What had happened to Beatrice di Tenda, once Filippo had secured her first husband's troops and treasure? Within a few years the redundant duchess had been accused of adultery with a good-looking page, Michele Orombello. The evidence

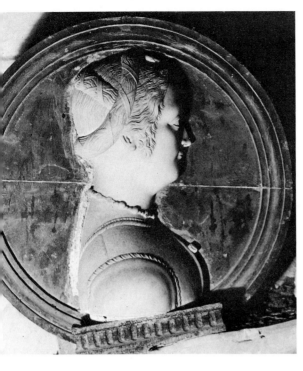

160 The unhappy Beatrice di Tenda, wife first of the condottiere Facino Cane and then of Filippo Maria Visconti. She was executed on a trumped-up charge of adultery when her second husband tired of her.

was dubious. She was known to love music. He had tried to enliven her dreary existence by playing to her on the lute, and he had been imprudent enough to sit on the edge of her bed during the recital. Though the duke's marriage seems to have been a purely nominal relationship, such familiarity was not to be tolerated. The unfortunate couple were put to torture. Beatrice maintained her innocence. The young man broke down and gasped out the required confession, which she still vehemently contradicted. She was beheaded. Orombello was also executed, and, for good measure, two of her waiting women who were assumed to have witnessed more than conduced to the duke's dignity. If a duchess could be treated so, Carmagnola could have no illusions about what might be done to an unwanted general. There is some irony in the manner of his own end and the direction from which it came, as we shall see.

Meanwhile, throughout that first decade of Filippo's long reign, the count advanced steadily in favour.

He dealt with rebellion wherever it raised its head. He restored unity and authority in the duchy and made safe its frontiers against outsiders who had exploited past Milanese weakness and had encroached upon Visconti territory.

Ever since the death of Gian Galeazzo the Swiss had been trying to improve their position in the Alpine valleys that stretched down towards the Lombard plain. There were not merely infringements of the border but friction over tolls and dues. The St Gotthard Pass was the life-line of Milanese trade with Europe north of the Alps. Any threat to cut that route had to be taken seriously. On several occasions Carmagnola marched, without any decisive results, against intruding forces from the neighbouring Swiss cantons, but it was not until 1422 that he met them in a pitched battle, the most interesting military operation of his career.

This engagement took place at Arbedo, near Bellinzona, on 30 June. Several thousand men were involved on each side. The Milanese had numerical superiority, though as usual the exact figures are not known. They consisted chiefly of mounted men-at-arms with supporting crossbowmen. Carmagnola shared the command with another of the duke's condottieri, Angelo della Pergola. The men of four Swiss cantons were marshalled on the opposing side. They were those typical sturdy infantrymen whose staunchness so often, in their heyday, shattered the columns of chivalry launched against them. At Arbedo only about a third of them carried the long pike. Twice as many wielded the halberd, barely six feet in length, and combining its ugly spear-point with a battle-axe.

Carmagnola had never met this kind of enemy before. As men, these independent mountaineers were very different from mercenaries. Their mode of warfare was equally unlike the cavalry charges that decided most issues in the plains of Lombardy.

He made an initial and costly mistake by ordering one of those charges. He lost four hundred horses in a few moments, impaled on the unwavering pike-points of the Swiss. He did not repeat the error. He made all his men-at-arms dismount and form tightly knit masses, their lances levelled in the best Hawkwood tradition. The crossbowmen were disposed on both flanks. Then he attacked again.

Now both sides were fighting in roughly the same way. It was lance and sword against pike and halberd, with the bolts from the crossbows taking some toll of the Swiss rear ranks. The Swiss, too, were outnumbered and the sheer weight of the Italian masses began to dent their line. One Swiss leader was sufficiently dismayed to plant his own halberd in the ground in token of surrender. Pergola saw the signal and wanted to accept, but Carmagnola's blood was up. He could not forget the sight of his horsemen breaking on the Swiss pikes. No, he shouted, men who did not give quarter did not deserve to receive it.

At that moment, however, he made his second mistake. Glancing round to the flank, he saw what he took to be the vanguard of another Swiss

240

161 At the hard-fought Battle of Arbedo, four Swiss cantons challenged the power of Milan. The Milanese remained in possession of the field.

army known to be in the neighbourhood. Fearing that in the moment of victory his men might be caught and rolled over by the wave of a massive counter-attack, he did the only sensible thing, and halted his advance so that ranks could be re-formed. Then, as he braced himself to withstand the onslaught of the fresh column, he saw his error. They were not a second fighting force, only a crowd of Swiss foragers, some hundreds in number, who were gaping at the scene of carnage without showing any eagerness to take part in it. Those few minutes of delay cost Carmagnola the superlative triumph he might have won. The Swiss army was given the chance to withdraw in good order. They had been badly mauled. They admitted to the loss of four hundred men and most likely lost more, though the Milanese casualties were higher, because of that wasteful cavalry charge. Both sides learned from the encounter. The Swiss saw that the pike was a better weapon than the halberd, and thereafter they adopted it more widely. Though Carmagnola had missed his chance to rout them, he could claim a decisive victory, one of the very few that were won over Swiss infantry in the Italian wars.

The victory at Arbedo was the high-water mark of his career in the service of Milan. His very success was ambivalent in its effect upon the duke. His popularity with the soldiers was alarming. Filippo's naturally apprehensive temper was played upon by jealous courtiers like Zanino Riccio and Oldrado da Lampugnano. They made clever use of the astrologers, to whose advice and equivocal suggestions the duke always paid anxious attention. Security officers reported upon Carmagnola's doings. Even had he been as single-minded and loyal as a dal Verme their investigations would doubtless have produced some apparent grounds for suspicion. As Carmagnola was Carmagnola, it is likely that he provided a certain amount of evidence to justify the duke's forebodings. He had been allowed, for instance, as a special favour requiring a decree of the Grand Council of Venice, to invest some of his recently gained wealth in Venetian bonds. It was a privilege seldom granted to foreigners, and it was a warning light to Filippo that his general was taking out an insurance policy against the turns of fortune.

Venice looked like being Milan's main adversary in the near future. The 'Most Serene Republic' had reached a turning-point in her policies. For centuries she had been eastward-looking, a great sea-power, drawing her wealth from the Levant and the vast Asian continent beyond. Secure and isolated amid the swamps and lagoons that were her original *raison d'être*, she had mostly kept aloof from the squabbles of the Italian peninsula. Only in the last generation had the Milanese expansion begun to cause her serious concern and involve her in the struggles to control some of the intervening states such as Verona. Now a powerful group was coming to the fore in Venice, the 'mainlanders', who argued that in future the republic must take a strong line in Italian affairs and block the spread of Milanese influence, reviving under Duke Filippo. It was all very well for the argosies to bring the wealth of the Orient up the Adriatic to the wharves of Venice, but how could those wares be re-exported overland to France and Germany if Milan could seal off all the Alpine passes between? When, in the same year as Carmagnola's victory over the Swiss, the Milanese recovered possession of Genoa, the one sea-port capable of serious rivalry with Venice, forebodings darkened along the Rialto. These developments coincided aptly with a change of doge. In the following year, 1423, Doge Tomaso Mocenigo died, upholding the traditional eastward-looking policy to the end, and striving with his last gasp to prevent the election of a 'mainlander' who would plunge the state into military adventures of which no man could foresee the end. Mocenigo's effort was vain. Francesco Foscari, the leading exponent of the new policy, was a convincing propagandist and an astute political operator. At the tenth ballot he won enough votes to make him doge. No one could have foreseen that this man, already in his fifties, would hold office for the next thirty-four years, a period of triumph followed by tragedy, in which there would be three costly wars with Milan and the Venetian treasury would have to call on two-thirds of its reserves.

This, then, was the change in Venetian policy that made her a major land-power in Italy and made her for the first time a prominent employer of condottieri. It was natural that Carmagnola should cast a pensive glance in her direction.

There were changes, too, at this time in his own situation. Filippo appointed him governor of the newly recovered port of Genoa. It was an honour but one that had to be eyed sceptically. It was an office of profit but not of military influence. Though Carmagnola remained nominally Captain-General of the Milanese forces, the number under his effective command was reduced to a mere token three hundred men-at-arms. Whatever uneasiness he may have felt, he had no choice for the time being. Leaving Antonia and their small daughters in the handsome palazzo in the capital, he obediently took up his duties in Genoa and set about the administration of that city with becoming zeal. One task entrusted to him was the equipment of a new fleet, in itself a significant indication that Filippo meant to compete with Venice at sea.

The duke evidently felt that he had now manœuvred Carmagnola into a position where he was relatively harmless. It was safe to make the next move. Without warning, he sent an order depriving him of his supreme

243

military command and specifically appointing another man to the newly commissioned fleet.

For all his craftiness, Carmagnola appears to have been taken by surprise. He wrote in protest. His letter was ignored. He wrote again. If the duke had no use for his services, could he at least have permission to offer his sword elsewhere? Still there was no reply.

It says much for Carmagnola's courage and self-confidence that he decided at this point to confront his master face to face, without formally applying for the audience which he felt certain would be refused. Fortunately, the duke had temporarily left his stronghold for one of his country castles at Abbiategrasso, some fifteen miles west of Milan, and this somewhat reduced the risks of the encounter. Taking a small troop of his most dependable men-at-arms, Carmagnola slipped secretly out of Genoa and rode north at top speed. He reached Abbiategrasso unheralded and demanded to see the duke. After a long delay the answer was brought to him that His Highness was indisposed. The count would perhaps discuss his business with Zanino Riccio? But the count would not, being too well aware of that courtier's role in the intrigues against him. He reiterated his demand for an audience. It was obdurately refused. The story goes that as Carmagnola turned away and crossed the courtyard, he happened to glance up and saw Filippo skulking behind the battlements above him; he shouted up to him angrily, warning him that he would rue this day.

The gloves were off. Filippo sent Oldrado da Lampugnano with a column of horsemen to overtake and arrest this insubordinate servant. Carmagnola evaded them. His family was still in Milan. He dared not show his face there. He sent secretly to Antonia, bidding her join him. He should have thought of that earlier. His palazzo was already cordoned off, his wife and children under house-arrest, his possessions confiscated.

These, and other circumstances, suggest that whatever prudent calculations had gone through Carmagnola's head, he had not been contemplating any immediate act of disloyalty to his master. Clearly he had no definite understanding with Venice, for he did not at once turn to the republic. He first went to Savoy and offered his services to the duke, Amadeus VIII, but that ruler was too cautious to offend his neighbour in Milan. Thereupon Carmagnola had to turn about, cross northern Italy incognito and make his way to Venice, where the new doge, Foscari, gave him a welcome that must have gone far to obliterate the humiliations of the preceding weeks.

It was about this time, most significantly, that Filippo Visconti, having dispensed with one condottiere, engaged another: the young Sforza, Francesco, came north from Naples to take service with Milan.

Carmagnola was taking service with the state which, if not the most formidable military power in Italy, was the wealthiest, the most highly organized economically, and in political terms quite the most stable.

These first years of Doge Foscari's régime were a period of unforgettable pageantry and splendour for the city. A population of nearly two hundred thousand people swarmed on its islets, and lived well on an export trade estimated to yield a profit of twenty per cent. Venetian prosperity was at its zenith. The Turkish capture of Constantinople lay nearly thirty years in the future, the voyages of Vasco da Gama and Columbus, with their fateful economic consequences, would not be made until the end of the century. In 1425 the Serenissima, the Most Serene Republic, had plenty of reasons for serenity. Three thousand merchant-ships were kept busy, some convoys sailing as far as England and the Low Countries. Three hundred galleys ruled the waves for Venice: new warships slid off the stocks at the Arsenal at the rate of almost one a week. Foscari sought to reproduce this naval security with some comparable strength on the *terraferma*, and the opportunity to engage the foremost Milanese condottiere was too good to be missed.

This thriving and dynamic commercial society was run, paradoxically enough, with a degree of state interference and control that a modern businessman often imagines to be the peculiar innovation of his own century. Even the merchant ships were built in the Arsenal and remained state property, being merely chartered to the private trader. They sailed in convoys, whose numbers, sailing-dates, ports of call, and freight-charges were rigidly fixed. In countless details there was an insistence upon standardization and inspection. Yet instead of the Venetian trader being strangled by bureaucracy he somehow flourished and combined rich returns with an international reputation for reliable value.

Venice had begun as a kind of democracy which had hardened into an oligarchy of a mere two hundred noble families. Their members – some

162 Under Doge Francesco Foscari (left, receiving the Statutes from the head of the Carpet-Makers' Guild), Venice began to concern herself actively in the politics of mainland Italy. One of his first acts was to engage Carmagnola, then on bad terms with Filippo Maria Visconti.

thirteen hundred individuals listed in the *Libro d'Oro*, at once an electoral roll and a social register – constituted the Grand Council which nominally controlled the government of the republic. Effective power lay with the doge and various small bodies, of which the famous Council of Ten gradually acquired predominance. Whatever the disagreements in these inner councils, and the animosities between certain families, there was such an over-all respect for the constitution that Venice was singularly free from palace coups and popular revolutions alike. Milan might be racked by the feuds of the Visconti cousins, Rome by the clash of Pope and Anti-Pope, Naples by the dynastic claims of Angevin and Aragonese, Florence by the rivalry of various families before the triumph of the Medici, and smaller cities like Perugia with perennial outbursts of violence between the classes, but Venice seemed to glide smoothly forward, year after year, like the doge's Bucentaur sailing across the lagoon. An extremely efficient secret police contributed much to this stability. Venetian justice, sinister though it might appear, was carefully and on the whole fairly administered. It was not invariably harsh, it could be relatively humane in cases that did not involve state security, and it was generally impersonal. Innocent men did not have to fear the caprice of a dictator as in so many cities at that time.

Businesslike in all things, the Venetians did not allow their warm welcome to encourage Carmagnola in any exorbitant demands. The

246

condotta they negotiated with him was the outcome of long discussions in which almost every point was contested. They knew his value. They knew also his difficult situation. For the moment there was no state of war, and they could afford to haggle. By the end of a month or so, during which both sides had made concessions and Carmagnola had been forced to make a personal appeal to the doge, the document was ready for signature. He had not secured nearly all he wanted, or what he was sure that he deserved, but as a fugitive, with a mere handful of followers, he must take the best terms he could get. When war came, he would be in a stronger bargaining position.

A short period of uneasy peace remained. Foscari was working for an alliance with the Florentines, who in the past had shown themselves the staunchest opponents of Milanese expansion. It would help too if Savoy could be brought in to threaten Milan from the rear. Duke Filippo, well aware of what was going on, made some counter-moves of his own. He decided to remove Carmagnola, either by poisoning or by abduction and execution. His information services told him that the condottiere was no longer in Venice itself but at the inland city of Treviso, some twenty miles distant, where he was mustering the men and horses stipulated in his contract, an operation virtually impossible to carry out on the over-crowded islands of the capital. The duke therefore sent his agents to Treviso, ostensibly to buy dogs. The Venetian counter-espionage being even more efficient, the Milanese party were neatly picked up, interro-gated under torture, and quietly disposed of. The Duke of Milan's implica-tion in the affair was not publicly mentioned. He was still in theory a friendly power, and the diplomatic courtesies had to be maintained.

This happened in the late summer of 1425. Within six months the doge had attained his objective of a league against Milan – and Carmagnola his aim to become commander-in-chief of the allied forces. The Florentines were content to accept the Venetian choice. The condottiere they had especially loved, Braccio da Montone, had been killed eighteen months earlier. Sforza the elder was dead, Sforza the younger had gone to Milan. Piccinino, who had taken over Braccio's company, had also accepted an offer from the duke. Carmagnola was not merely, as Machiavelli wrote later, 'one of the outstanding soldiers of that day'; he was almost the only one available to accept the baton.

The Venetian-Florentine alliance was ratified on 27 January 1426. Two or three weeks later, at a solemn ceremony in St Mark's, Carmagnola was proclaimed Captain-General of the combined forces, with 'all the pre-rogatives, facilities, and honours' exclusive to that position, not to mention a personal salary of 1000 gold ducats a month.

247

From this point Carmagnola's career is overshadowed by a great question-mark. Indeed, there are several question-marks.

Why did he, a commander previously renowned for initiative and energy, a man still only in his middle thirties, become suddenly a byword for inertia?

One suggested answer is that he always hoped for a *rapprochement* with Filippo and did not want to exacerbate their quarrel by inflicting too much damage on Milan. 'He played a double game from the first,' wrote F. Marion Crawford in his *Gleanings from Venetian History*, and his subsequent behaviour can be interpreted, though not conclusively, in support of this theory.

An alternative explanation of his inactivity in the field might be found in the fact that his wife and daughters were hostages of the duke. But, as Joseph Jay Deiss points out in *Captains of Fortune*, Antonia and the girls were of the duke's own Visconti blood, and so 'useless as hostages' – though in view of what the Visconti family could do to their nearest and dearest it would be a mistake perhaps to attach undue importance to this relationship. Deiss adds the ingenious suggestion that the duke, himself childless, was mainly concerned to keep Antonia and Carmagnola separated lest they produced a son with a plausible claim to be heir to the dukedom. Another uncertainty, in any case, discourages too much reliance on this 'hostage' explanation: historians differ on the length of time Antonia and her daughters were held in Milan. Deiss thinks that the duke did not release them until 1432. Marion Crawford, an earlier writer but one who drew upon a wealth of authorities, declared explicitly that 'on the twenty-fourth of March' – that is, in 1427, when a single year of hostilities ended in a treaty very unfavourable to the duke – 'Carmagnola and his wife made a sort of triumphal entry' into Venice. It seems on balance more likely that the condottiere was reunited with wife and family for most of the time that he served Venice. It is known that he was able to betroth his third daughter, Isabella, to young Sigismondo Malatesta of Rimini, and that the dowry was actually paid over, though the engagement was repudiated by Sigismondo after Carmagnola's death. There would not have been much time for this betrothal to have been arranged if the girl had remained a hostage in Milan until the final weeks of her father's life.

Too little attention has perhaps been given to a third possible reason for Carmagnola's puzzling lack of vigour in prosecuting the war against his late master: that he was, as he complained himself, a sick man. Soon after he had taken up his command in 1426, he suffered a fall from his horse while wearing full armour. No obvious injury was noted. He seemed merely to be badly shaken. But from that date he was continually subject to pains and fits of dizziness. His doctors advised him to try sea-bathing in the Adriatic or, better still, the warm springs at Abano Terme near Padua, whose therapeutic properties had been recognized in ancient times. Thereafter, whenever his military responsibilities permitted it – and occasionally when according to his critics they did not – Carmagnola was liable to leave his headquarters for a course of treatment. Were these journeys necessary? The Venetians had their doubts. Once, they sent their own doctors to the camp; these examined the patient, advised against the thermal baths so early in the year, and prescribed (in the best tradition of army medicine down the ages) a powerful purgative instead. Who was right? After all these centuries, lacking any accurate data, no one can say. At all events, it is quite conceivable that Carmagnola was not malingering but was genuinely suffering, throughout those years, from after-effects of his fall that no one could have detected or understood in the current state of medical knowledge. A temporary remission of these symptoms would explain an occasional flash of his old brilliance, such as he displayed in his victory at Maclodio.

Whatever the true reason for Carmagnola's torpor, he certainly behaved quite uncharacteristically in that first campaign. He laid siege to the Milanese fortresses at Brescia, but left the planning of the elaborate entrenchments to the Florentine general under him. He was then a passive witness of the first attacks, and shortly afterwards departed for treatment at Abano Terme. Whether by good luck or shrewd calculation, he returned to his headquarters a few days before the Milanese surrendered, just in time to claim the whole credit for a victory in which he had scarcely played any part.

Meanwhile, another of his subordinate commanders, Francesco Bembo, had sailed up the Po with a flotilla of small craft and then, turning up the tributary River Adda, had made a military demonstration unpleasantly close to Pavia itself. So, whatever the shortcomings of the Captain-General, the 1426 campaign ended very much to the advantage of the League. Pope Martin, who was on the whole indulgent to Filippo and had tried from the first to avert this alliance against him, now stepped in again and persuaded the parties to make peace. This was done on 30 December. The duke had to agree to the release of Carmagnola's family and to the surrender of various fortresses.

Even if he did keep the first of these promises, he most assuredly broke the second, for by the end of the winter the Venetians were instructing Carmagnola to renew hostilities. He was reluctant to do so. Was it his persistent malaise? Or disinclination to leave the family with which he

Da Lecho a Olgina fono miliari iiii. Da
Olgina a Briuio. iiii. Da Briuio al porto de
iberfago. iii. Dal porto pdicto. ale tre Corne
in Adda. iii. Da le tre Corne doue fe fara la
chiufa in Adda p far mōtare la qua ī lo cauo
qual fe fa de pfente per la uale de la rocheta
p nō poterfi acōciare de nauigare p adda fin
un pocho defopra dala torre de porto doue
p dicto cauo fe retorñara cū le naue in adda
qual fera miliari. ii. & dal dicto loco doue p
dicto cauo fe ritornara in adda fin a Trezo
fono miliari. v. doue e la bocha del Nauilio
de martexana per lo qual fe nauiga fin a Mi
lano, e da la dicta bocha del nauilio a Mila
no fono miliari. xx v. fono in fumma miliari
xlvi. da Lecho a Milano p aqua. Per q̃fto po
cho defigno fe puo inĩedere e conofcere che
fe nauigara dal laco de Como fin a Milano.

163 The upper course of the Adda, rising (top left) in Lake Como and flowing south to join the Po just above Cremona. It was along the Adda that the Venetian commander Francesco Bembo made an expedition in the direction of Pavia in 1426, and the river was of crucial importance in the later war between Venice, Sforza and the Ambrosian Republic.

had just been reunited – if indeed he had? Again, the tantalizing gaps in the evidence excite conjecture. For two or three months the Captain-General dallied and disputed with his impatient employers. There would be a shortage of grazing, he had not enough men or enough money, the men he had were inadequately trained . . . By June the excuses ran out, and the erstwhile fire-eating warrior rode forth with his army.

Nothing much happened. Although young Sforza and the bellicose little Piccinino were in the field against him, they did not bring him to battle. Possibly their zeal was restrained by their supreme commander, Carlo Malatesta, whose generalship is not rated highly by the historians: like most of that famous Rimini family, Carlo found it useful to supplement his modest revenues with mercenary soldiering. He was as cultured as his notorious nephew, Sigismondo, but a far pleasanter and less passionate character. At this date he was sixty-three. He must have found his

250

two dashing subordinates a considerable handful, representing as they did the two opposing schools of military thought, as well as being bitter personal rivals who could not forget the recent tragic deaths of their respective teachers. The son of Muzio Sforza and the faithful lieutenant of Braccio da Montone were a strange pair to run in double harness.

There was some marching and counter-marching during that summer, and much tedious digging of entrenchments, but only one brisk skirmish in which the main casualties were some of the Venetians' cavalry horses. In September Carmagnola informed his employers that he was retiring into winter quarters.

There was incredulous indignation in Venice. Though two commissioners – 'commissars', they might be termed today – were regularly attached to Carmagnola's headquarters to spy upon him and make independent confidential reports on all his doings, this premature termination of the campaign took every one by surprise. The commissioners recommended that the Captain-General should be publicly reprimanded, but caution prevailed in the inner councils of the republic and no open action was undertaken that might humiliate him. Carmagnola must be handled with care. He was, none the less, given blunt instructions to bring his troops out again.

He obeyed. The marching and counter-marching were solemnly resumed. It seemed to all that he did not mean business, he was simply going through the motions of warfare until the autumn indisputably set in, and he could retire once more without argument to the comfort of permanent billets. Sforza and Piccinino gave up hope of decisive action, even the elderly Malatesta grew slightly restive. They could not themselves force a decision unless Carmagnola gave them a chance. A commander of his experience and reputation, leading forces of such magnitude, could not simply be attacked, irrespective of circumstances.

Again looms the question-mark. Was he a sick man, playing for time, counting the days until he could decently declare the season closed? In which case he must suddenly have rallied some of his old dynamism, and made, as sick men can, a tremendous effort. Or were his manœuvres a sham from the first, designed to mesmerize his opponents and lull them into complacency?

At all events, Carmagnola went over to the offensive. One misty morning, on 11 October, he advanced against the Milanese camp at Maclodio, near the River Oglio, midway between Lodi and Brescia. He knew the ground, and it well suited the plan he had in mind, having swampy fields crossed by raised causeways that offered tempting passage for bodies of troops but also had the effect of channelling them along predictable lines exposed to missiles. Carmagnola had some particularly lethal new weapons to try, powerful crossbows mounted in threes on wheels, projecting long spears with a terrifying velocity. The autumn mist, wreathing the dank levels of the river-valley, combined with the occasional line of trees or thicket to provide the cover essential to his plan.

This was clearly a massive ambush, designed to swallow the whole army arrayed against him. From the start, his own troops were disposed with this end in view, large numbers being sent to concealed positions from which – if only Malatesta swallowed the bait – the enemy could be assailed from every direction. A force of two thousand men was reserved for the final stroke that would cut off the Milanese escape-route. Carmagnola gave the command of this division to the Florentine condottiere, Niccolò da Tolentino.

These far-sighted dispositions, together with the deliberate feebleness of Carmagnola's opening attack, followed by that difficult and always risky ploy, a feigned retreat that must not turn into a genuine rout, suggest that he fought the battle precisely as he intended to, and that on this one day at least in 1427 he displayed all the qualities that had once made him Filippo's outstanding soldier.

Carlo Malatesta fell into the trap. Elated by the ease with which the first assault was repelled, convinced that Carmagnola had shot his bolt and that resolute action could now inflict a decisive defeat upon him, he gave the order that unleashed the eager Sforza and Piccinino in pursuit. Nor was he backward himself, but went galloping into the haze with the rest of them.

The resulting débâcle equalled Carmagnola's rosiest expectations. At his signals, company after company emerged from their places of concealment. Strung along the embanked causeways, the Milanese horsemen bunched helplessly, finding themselves targets from every side. To turn and ride back was difficult. To escape completely was impossible, once Niccolò da Tolentino had cut the road behind. Malatesta, Sforza, and Piccinino surrendered their swords, and when those illustrious three had given in, who wanted to make a hero's last stand? Carmagnola took ten thousand prisoners at a trifling cost to his own army. The captured arms and banners were piled up in glistening heaps. The fruits of victory were almost an embarrassment in their profusion.

It is a pity that no painter of those days was on hand to make a conversation-piece out of Carmagnola's supper-party that night. It would have grouped most of the foremost living condottieri in one picture, captors and captives amiably exchanging reminiscences and professional gossip. That the atmosphere *was* cordial seems abundantly clear from the sequel:

252

Sforza and Piccinino were set free the next morning, Malatesta was handed over to one of Carmagnola's Venetian subordinates, who promptly gave him his freedom too, without ransom. Almost all the prisoners were released within a few days. To feed and guard them all would have been a task beyond Carmagnola's resources. But his liberation of the most distinguished individuals would have been remarkable indeed if his wife and family had still been hostages in Milan.

This generous treatment of the vanquished did not find favour either in Venice or Florence, though the victory itself was received with delight. It was not easy, in the circumstances, to criticize the Captain-General, but there was a good deal of murmuring. Why had he given back to the duke an army which, though admittedly disarmed, was otherwise as good as new? Why had he not pressed on to the gates of Milan?

Carmagnola had no wish to spend the winter besieging Milan, a city with a tradition of desperate resistance. What would the Venetians have wanted him to do with ten thousand prisoners? Short of turning them over as galley-slaves – an unthinkable solution to a condottiere – there was nothing that could be done with them, except perhaps to earn their goodwill for future seasons. When the Florentines suggested that he might at least have hanged one particular Milanese officer against whom they harboured resentment, Carmagnola answered with hauteur that a general did not kill prisoners. It was an admirable reply, but scarcely consistent with some of the blacker incidents in his own record.

164 Niccolò da Tolentino, one of the commanders of the Venetian republic under Carmagnola at the victory of Maclodio. He is seen here at another stage in his career, fighting for his native Florence at the Battle of San Romano.

253

If the victor excited criticism it was not surprising that Filippo should express less than satisfaction with the expensive team of generals that had led his army to disaster. Francesco Sforza was openly accused of treachery and consigned to the castle at Mortara.

Privately, however, the duke explained that there was no ill-feeling and that this was just one of his devious methods of tackling another problem. Sforza must for the moment submit to this slur upon his reputation. It would be more than made up to him in the future. In reality, the duke emphasized, Sforza had his complete confidence. So much so that he was now entrusting him with a task of importance and delicacy. Lucca was in danger from Florence and must be saved, but Lucca would not accept Sforza's services if he went as a highly suspect loan from Milan. Regretfully, therefore, the duke must go through the motions of disgracing and dismissing him, so that he could appear in the Tuscan city as a free agent. It was an old trick, especially favoured by the Milanese dukes, and once more it worked. Sforza was released and went to Lucca. He was such a success there that the people offered him the lordship of their city. Sforza declined the honour, possibly influenced by a generous bribe from Florence to withdraw from the scene. This was discreetly disguised as arrears of pay still owed to his late father. Sforza went off to the old family home at Cotignola – and with suspicious promptitude Piccinino found himself freed from his Milanese commitments to continue the protection of Lucca.

The direct hostilities between Milan and the Venetian-Florentine alliance had petered out and were not resumed after the winter. A second peace treaty was made in the spring. No one knew how long it would last, and the allies insisted on Carmagnola's signing a new two-year *condotta* with an option on his services for a further two-year period. The Florentines also continued their friendly cultivation of Sforza. They approached him at Cotignola with an offer for his services, but Filippo, knowing well that it was only a matter of time before the conflict was renewed, was determined to keep Sforza on the Milanese side. Once more the personal despot had a special advantage over a republican committee: the duke could tempt his condottiere not only with money but also with a bride.

Bianca Maria Visconti, Filippo's only daughter, was to be of considerable importance later. His first marriage, to Facino Cane's forty-year-old widow, was certainly childless and probably unconsummated. After putting her to death, he had remained unmarried for a long time, until for purely diplomatic reasons he had sought a union with Maria of Savoy. This too had remained unconsummated. A dog howled at their first encounter, and the superstitious duke had declared, whether sincerely or

254

165 Bianca Maria, only child of Filippo Maria Visconti, promised at an early age to the condottiere Francesco Sforza.

not, that this was an ill omen it would be fatal to ignore. The new duchess made no recorded complaint: when first told that she must marry this grotesque creature she had burst into hysterics, and his neglect suited her. Unfortunately, she was to find herself condemned to a secluded existence, spied on at every turn and restricted to the company of her own sex. Filippo was not going to be fobbed off with some putative heir whom he knew could not be of his own blood.

Despite his two unproductive marriages, he was not incapable. He had a mistress, Agnese del Maino. Bianca Maria was their only child, and as more years passed it looked increasingly probable that he would have no other heir, legitimate or otherwise. Bianca's eventual husband would therefore be well placed as successor to the Visconti dukedom. Sforza could not ignore the bait dangled before him. As the child was only seven or eight at this time, however, there was no immediate opportunity of testing the duke's sincerity. Sforza could do no more than hope for the best and avoid any commitments that would make such a match impossible. The war, when it was resumed, found him under the banner of Milan.

This was at the beginning of 1431. Carmagnola was the decidedly reluctant Captain-General of the Venetian forces. The Most Serene Republic had loaded him with honours, making him a viscount and hereditary lord of Chiari, with another estate in the region of Brescia. If he successfully invaded Lombardy he would of course regain the estates previously granted by the duke and later confiscated. Indeed, if he actually overthrew Filippo, he might himself become duke. The prospects were dazzling. Carmagnola nevertheless displayed no enthusiasm and even tried unavailingly to lay down his command. He must have known in his heart that he could not win another victory like Maclodio.

Peace would have suited him better, a peace that would have enabled him to patch up his quarrel with Filippo without having to forfeit the benefits he had received from Venice. The duke corresponded with him, ostensibly seeking his good offices to preserve the peace, but more probably hoping to seduce him from his present allegiance. Or so it struck the Venetians, to whom Carmagnola prudently showed the correspondence. They warned him not to be taken in by fair words from Milan. They became doubly suspicious themselves lest he should betray their interests.

Carmagnola's inept handling of that year's campaign encouraged those suspicions. His winter surprise-attack on Lodi was a fiasco. So was his attempt to seize the castle of Soncino, where he had relied on treachery but found himself repulsed with the utmost vigour. He went back there in May with strong reinforcements: Sforza gave him a thrashing. In June the Venetians tried to capture Cremona. If they could do so they would

255

hold the entire line of the River Adda down to its confluence with the Po. Carmagnola besieged the city by land, while a flotilla of Venetian galleys under Niccolò Trevisani blockaded it by water. Trevisani was utterly routed by a Milanese fleet commanded by Eustachio Pacino, and Carmagnola's failure to intervene made a bad impression in Venice. He blamed lack of information. The Venetians wondered. They wondered still more when in October, after what seemed like a summer frittered away in lethargy, he failed to support a Venetian commander who had secured a foothold on the city walls. The Cremonese themselves believed that only Carmagnola's slowness had saved their city from falling.

That winter the murmurs gathered strength in the council-chambers of Venice. Carmagnola was in the Brescia region. When it was learned that the Milanese had been prepared to evacuate Soncino, the very place he had tried twice to capture in the preceding spring, and that he had not seized even this opportunity, it was hard to resist the conclusion that he was playing a double game.

At a secret meeting on 29 March it was decided to take action.

A special envoy, Giovanni d'Imperio, was charged with the duty of bringing Carmagnola to Venice, without in any way arousing his suspicions. In the ordinary course of events the condottieri were not encouraged to visit the city. Even the Captain-General, though he had been welcomed there with every show of honour on more than one past occasion, had to apply for permission before entering the capital. Sometimes Carmagnola had been kept waiting for weeks.

He was now asked, in the politest possible manner, if he would 'give himself the trouble' of travelling to Venice to discuss a new plan of campaign for the year that was opening. Giovanni d'Imperio had clear instructions. The count was to be treated with the utmost deference, even flattery. On the other hand, if he started to excuse himself, inventing military necessities or pleading ill-health, he was to be put under arrest and held in the castle at Brescia. With so famous a general, in the midst of his own army, this might not have been the simplest of tasks. The Venetian envoy was no doubt exceedingly relieved when Carmagnola made no demur but set out with him on the several-day journey eastwards, past the shores of Lake Garda and Verona, and finally through Padua where (still further to lull any possible misgivings) he was saluted with every mark of honour. The party reached Venice on 7 April, when the city was preparing for the festivities of Easter, less than two weeks away.

Eight noblemen welcomed Carmagnola and escorted him to the Doge's Palace, where, he was told, Foscari expected him to dinner. What followed was pure Jacobean drama, lacking only the blank verse. Carmagnola dismissed his own attendants at the door. He was kept waiting a few moments in an ante-room. Then Leonardo Mocenigo appeared and expressed the doge's profound regrets: owing to sudden indisposition he was unable to receive the count, but looked forward to doing so tomorrow. Carmagnola murmured his sympathy and, still attended by the eight noble Venetians, started across the courtyard in the direction of the canal where his boat was waiting. His escort, however, pressed round him and indicated a small portico.

'This way, Sir Count,' they said, according to the oft-told story.

'But that is not *my* way,' he objected.

'You are mistaken. It is the best way.'

The door opened. Some jailers sprang out and hustled him through to one of the dungeons within.

'I am lost!' he is said to have shouted as he was dragged into the shadows. He had no illusions about his chances.

His trial began two days later. He was refusing food. Weak as he became, he held out against the first of the tortures that were applied on the third day of his interrogation. Eventually, after one arm had been broken and his feet had been painfully burned, he made the confession his examiners were determined to extract: he admitted treason to Venice in the past and the intention of committing more. It was not a satisfactory case, and it looks as though some, including the doge, had many reservations. The trial was interrupted by the Easter celebrations, which gave the judges longer to ponder and discuss the evidence, and the hapless prisoner more time to speculate about the result. Machiavelli, in *The Prince*, records how that result was determined by political necessity: 'Perceiving that Carmagnola had become cold in their service, they yet neither wished nor

166 'Between the lion and St Theodore' was the traditional Venetian place of execution. Here Carmagnola was beheaded on 5 May 1432.

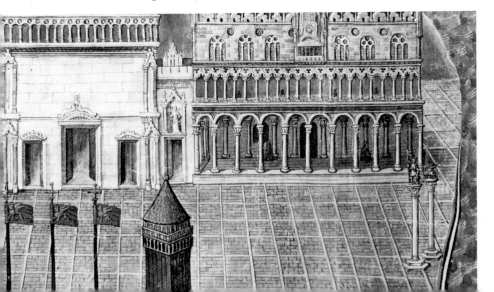

dared to dismiss him, from a fear of losing what he had won for them; and so, for their own security, they had no option but to put him to death.'

The court gave its verdict by secret ballot on 5 May. Despite that secrecy, it was credibly rumoured afterwards that Doge Foscari had voted for acquittal. If so, he was in a minority. The sentence, which *was* published, ran as follows:

> That the said Count Francesco Carmagnola, a public traitor to our dominion, be led today after nones, at the usual hour, with a gag in his mouth and with his hands tied behind his back, according to custom, between the two columns of the Piazza San Marco, to the usual place of execution, and that his head be there struck off his shoulders, so that he die.

That evening the sentence was duly carried out with the pageantry with which Venice marked all occasions, grave or gay. Carmagnola was arrayed in his best – a full-sleeved crimson tunic, scarlet cloak, and velvet cap tilted at his usual jaunty angle. But under the cloak his arms were pinioned and a wooden gag prevented any last cry of protest, and his legs in their tight scarlet hose had lost their soldierly stride because of the unhealed burns on his feet. His old hound was allowed to trot beside him as he limped towards the block in front of the cathedral.

The news that the sentence had been carried out was taken to his wife at the convent where she was lodged with her daughters. She was assured that the republic would deal fairly with her if she expressed regret for the part she had played in Carmagnola's intrigues with her Visconti kinsman. She was required to hand over a list of her jewels, but promised a pension on condition that she retired quietly to Treviso. There would be provision also for her daughters. Isabella's betrothal to Sigismondo Malatesta was now off. The young Rimini condottiere declined to marry the daughter of a convicted traitor.

Carmagnola's body was carried first to the church of San Francesco della Vigna, decently attended by two dozen torch-bearers, but before the interment could begin there was an interruption. Carmagnola had made his last confession to a Capuchin monk, who now appeared and announced the general's dying wish, which was to be buried in the cloisters of the Frari. This was observed, but Carmagnola was not allowed to lie there for ever. Eventually his body was removed to Milan and laid beside his wife's in the greater church of San Francesco. For Antonia had not been content to remain in Treviso as the pensioner of the government that had executed her husband, and she had taken an early opportunity of escaping to the city of her birth.

Sforza and Milan

With the tragic ending of Carmagnola's story attention can be turned again to the young Francesco Sforza, whose ambitions and eventual triumph provide the central dramatic thread through the complex events of the next decade or two.

Sforza was now thirty. Eight years had passed since he had inherited his father's company and come north to take service with Filippo Visconti. He had had his setbacks, sharing in the humiliations of the Maclodio disaster, but since then he had restored his prestige by defeating Carmagnola elsewhere. So far from wanting to dispense with him, the duke had tried to ensure his continued availability by a vague promise of marriage to his only child, and in the very year of Carmagnola's execution this promise was turned into a formal betrothal between the general and the little Bianca Visconti.

Sforza combined many of Muzio Attendolo's robust basic qualities with the polished manners and wider intellectual horizons provided by his upbringing. His father's boyhood had been spent on the farm at Cotignola, his own had included spells at the courts of Ferrara and Naples. The first Sforza had been illiterate, though with a touching respect for a world of scholarship and literature that he dimly apprehended beyond his reach. The second Sforza was an impressive orator and a graceful conversationalist, who in later days would hold his own with such sophisticated friends as Cosimo de' Medici, Pope Pius II, and Federigo of Urbino.

None of this had been allowed to soften him. Indeed, it would not have occurred to his contemporaries that there was any reason why it should. In Renaissance Italy there was no assumption that intellectual interests and artistic appreciation were incompatible with effective action in politics and war. Sforza learned the soldier's trade under his father's tutelage, just as his father had learned it under Alberico da Barbiano. Sforza was physically strong, tough and active. He slept well and enjoyed homely fare. He was accessible, open-handed, and sociable. Throughout his life he never forgot the rank-and-file soldiers who had served under him, but would hail them in the street and even remember names of horses they had ridden. Needless to say, such a man inspired loyalty. In his youth in the Regno he won the devotion of the Simonetta family in Calabria, and they followed him to the north, Cicco Simonetta becoming his confidential secretary and Giovanni eventually writing his biography. The continued employment of these southerners inevitably provoked the jealousy of the Milanese and Sforza was told that he would be more popular if he got rid of his secretary. He refused with a laugh, saying, 'If I did, I should only have to replace him with another Cicco, even if I had to make him myself out of wax.'

That was typical of the good-humoured, down-to-earth attitude he had inherited from his father. Though it must often have been pointed out to him that Muzio's drowning had occurred on a day when he had advanced in defiance of bad omens, Sforza cared nothing for the superstitions to which many of his contemporaries, even the most intelligent, gave credence. When an astrologer asked for the date and hour of his birth, he said he had no idea, but his secretary no doubt had it written down somewhere.

On a mission to Florence in 1435 he made the acquaintance of Cosimo de' Medici, who the previous year had returned in triumph from his brief and comfortable exile in Venice and had begun the long period of Medici domination. The two men became life-long friends. The astute banker gave good advice and encouraged Sforza in his policies. In the end, working closely together, they were among the handful of statesmen who gave Italy the spell of relative peace that opened with the treaty at Lodi in 1454. In personal matters, however, the soldier did not invariably follow the advice of the businessman. When Cosimo urged him to save money for his children (by that time, Sforza had several and was devoted to them) Sforza answered that he had never been a merchant and did not intend to become one now. 'If my children are good, there will be plenty for them. If they are not good, then nothing I can save for them will be enough.'

In appearance the young Sforza must have been striking. It was common to compare him, when older – and invincibly established – to the noblest of Rome's military emperors, Trajan or Hadrian. The similarity of type was perhaps deliberately emphasized in his portraits and medals.

On the whole he was one of the more likeable of all the condottieri, just as he was quite certainly one of the most historically important, but he was a man of the Quattrocento and he had the streaks of cruelty and

260

cunning so common in his time. He could torture and execute one of his officers, Sarpellione, for suspected treachery, an action condemned even by his friends. In the case of two other disloyal captains, Troilo Orsini and Pietro Brunoro, he persuaded his own brother Alessandro Sforza to forge letters framing them, so that his enemy, Alfonso of Aragon, believed them traitors to both sides, and consigned them to his dungeons in Spain.

There was a romantic sequel to this affair. One of the condottieri, Brunoro, had a mistress named Bona, a mountain-bred girl of stamina and spirit. She had campaigned at his side in male dress. Now she agitated for his liberation, approaching all kinds of influential personages, including (it is said) the gentle King Henry VI of England. Ten years of persistence won her lover's freedom. They were married and joined the Venetian service in the Greek islands. Brunoro fell in the defence of Negroponte against the Turks, and it is unlikely that Bona survived the appalling massacre when the city fell. Sforza, however, cannot be blamed for these subsequent vicissitudes. Originally, Brunoro and his fellow officer had been guilty of allowing two towns, Iesi and Fabriano, to fall into Alfonso's hands. In turning the tables upon them with forged letters, Sforza had done no more than Hamlet did to Rosencrantz and Guildenstern.

Filippo Visconti and his two chief generals formed a trio of effective contrasts – Sforza, the good-looking and strapping cavalier, Piccinino, compensating for his diminutive stature and poor health with an aggressive ambition and ferocity that kept him at the head of his competitive profession, and the duke himself, ugly, obese, neurotically timid, yet somehow, through sheer cunning, a match for them both.

He liked to keep them guessing. To Sforza he had promised his only child, but it was Piccinino to whom he entrusted the supreme command of his forces, and who, when the Emperor Sigismund came to Milan in 1431, was given the honour of handing him the golden orb, symbol of sovereignty.

Sforza and Piccinino had particular reasons for jealousy. It was expected of them: were they not carrying on the traditional rivalry of their teachers, Sforza senior and Braccio? At first they were both in the Milanese service, competing for Filippo's favour. Later, when Sforza switched to the Venetian side, they were opponents on the battlefield. It is hard to say which of the two relationships engendered the more animosity. In his life of Sforza, Giovanni Simonetta compares the two men with that love of neat antithesis with which Renaissance writers trimmed truth to a graceful literary shape. 'Niccolò', he generalizes, 'was more eager to fight and join battle at the first opportunity, to surprise his enemy by his speed, to wear

167 Francesco Sforza, the only condottiere to rise from humble origins to a dukedom.

him down by incessant attacks, preferring light cavalry to infantry. . . .
But Francesco had incomparable skill and knowledge, and tired out his
opponents with Fabian tactics and sieges, placing much importance upon
his infantry. . . . He did not underrate his adversary or attack him rashly.'
The reference to infantry is worth noting and there seems no cause to
doubt Simonetta's reliability on this point. Though in other ways
Francesco Sforza carried on a tradition inherited through his father from
Alberico da Barbiano, he obviously did not exalt the horseman and ignore
the value of the foot-soldier.

262

Sforza and Piccinino were but two outstanding condottieri in a rich period. They had some notable contemporaries. There was Erasmo da Narni – Gattamelata, 'the Honeyed Cat' – a veteran who had served many masters and had commanded Braccio's cavalry. Two years after Carmagnola's death, Venice was glad to engage him though by that time he was sixty. There was Bartolomeo Colleoni, a year older than Sforza, who had been prominent among Carmagnola's officers. Another of those officers was the gallant Florentine, Niccolò da Tolentino, who had helped Carmagnola so effectively at Maclodio – but he, within a year or two, was to be taken prisoner by the Milanese and to die in captivity, a fate unusual in his profession. The too-gentle Carlo Malatesta had already died, at a good age, soon after his defeat at Maclodio, but his nephew Sigismondo (who was never to be accused of excessive gentleness) was just making his first appearance on the stage of history, an arrogant adolescent, repudiating his engagement to the daughter of the disgraced Carmagnola. But Sigismondo, at fifteen, had still his military reputation to earn, and so had his future rival, Federigo of Urbino, at this date a boy of ten or eleven, held hostage in Venice. Federigo di Montefeltro, Sigismondo Malatesta, and Bartolomeo Colleoni demand full individual treatment in their turn, but for the moment, while the spotlight is focused on Sforza, they must make their occasional entrances and exits as supporting characters. It is important to remember, however, that they were all contemporaries, and that only between the oldest and youngest was there a very wide age-gap.

Before long, the Lombardy plain and the hill country surrounding Lake Garda and Brescia were to become again the battleground on which Sforza and Piccinino, Colleoni and Gattamelata, clashed in repeated conflicts. The death of Carmagnola was followed, though, by a short breathing-space. During the Emperor's visit to Italy a peace was patched up between Milan, Venice, and Florence, and Sforza's active services were not immediately required. The duke, with his habitual apprehensiveness, felt that he would be happier with the condottiere at a distance. There was never, indeed, any trust or liking on his part, but this did not inhibit him in his use of Sforza whenever it appeared advantageous. The first thing that now occurred to him was that Sforza could be employed against the new Pope, Eugenius IV, who was arousing widespread opposition by his reversals of Martin's policies and, as a native of Venice, was unlikely to prove a natural friend of Milan.

Filippo sent for Sforza. The atmosphere was, as usual, thick with menace and suspicion. Sforza's friends had warned him not to place himself in the duke's power. The duke, on the other hand, gave his envoys secret instructions that, if Sforza showed any hesitation in coming, it would be a proof

168 Cardinal Vitelleschi was a less successful Albornoz. He failed to hold the Adriatic cities for the Pope against Sforza's victorious advance.

of disloyalty and they must instantly put him to death. Sforza himself was either dangerously naïve, which is unlikely, or ready to run a calculated risk. He obeyed the summons promptly, and did not even take his body-guard. Filippo was reassured, at least for the time being. He outlined his scheme, or some of it, to his prospective son-in-law.

Sforza was to go on leave. It would be well to give some attention to his possessions in the Regno. Queen Joanna could not live for ever. Whoever happened to be her current choice of heir when she died, there was sure to be trouble in Naples. Sforza could count on Filippo's backing if he had to defend his interests against Alfonso of Aragon. Meanwhile, there were good openings for an enterprising condottiere in the papal territories, where many of the cities were in revolt against the unpopular new pontiff.

Sforza took the hint. He started southwards, but soon found plenty of business to detain him in the Marches round Ancona, where the Papal Vicar, the war-like Cardinal Vitelleschi, was making enemies on every side. Sforza was warmly welcomed. If those little hill-top cities had to bow to any master, they preferred the rough but kindly soldier. One after another they opened their gates to him – Ascoli, Osimo, even Recanati, the seat of Vitelleschi's own bishopric. Sforza occupied the famous pil-grims' town of Loreto, though not before the cardinal had stripped the shrine of all its treasures. By the end of 1433 Sforza had taken over a wide territory, making no bones about his defiance of papal authority. He even headed his letters, with cheerful impudence: 'From our castle of Fermo, in despite of Peter and Paul . . .'

264

Fermo remained for many years a convenient headquarters, secure in the rugged Marches overlooking the Adriatic, far from Milan and Venice and Naples, yet centrally situated so that he himself could ride north or south at will. On one occasion he hoped that his marriage to Bianca might take place there. There is a letter from his brother Alessandro Sforza, bidding his agent 'collect everything needful' – hay, litter, good beds, meat, chickens, game, fish, hams, kids, lambs, eggs, cheese, and so forth, and to muster cooks, smart lads to wait, and other temporary staff required for such lavish celebrations. But the duke made excuses to put off the marriage, and all the preparations were wasted. It was at Fermo, however, that Sforza's first son, Galeazzo, was born in after-years.

Sforza was altogether too successful in the Marches to please Filippo, who had originally diverted him in that direction but had intended any conquests to be passed over to himself. The next year or two saw a typical shuffle of relationships.

As a counter-balance to Sforza, Piccinino was sent into Romagna to encourage some of the cities there also to throw off the Pope's authority. With characteristic deviousness it was publicly given out that Piccinino was disgusted with the duke's ingratitude and was trying to build up an independent state. When this story had gained wide currency, Piccinino was able to issue an indignant repudiation and accuse the Pope of slandering him. Then, striking a high moral attitude, Piccinino handed over the captured cities to the duke as a demonstration of his own selfless loyalty.

Sforza, meanwhile, drew closer to the Pope. Eugenius felt no love for him, but badly needed friends. Even in Rome itself he was not safe. He was threatened by another of the Visconti condottieri, Niccolò Fortebraccio, a nephew of the famous Braccio, and it was this commander who, assisted by Piccinino, drove him from the city on a famous occasion in 1434. The Pope had to flee down-river in disguise, and, when recognized, was pelted by the hostile citizens. It was nine years before he dared return, and in the meantime he made Florence his headquarters. In these difficult circumstances he had little choice but to seek Sforza's goodwill by accepting the *fait accompli* in the Marches and investing Sforza with a veritable garland of honours and titles, Papal Vicar, Marquis of Fermo, Gonfalonier (or Standard-bearer) of the Church, and so forth. Sforza repaid these favours by defeating and killing Fortebraccio at Fiordimonte. The Pope's friendship, however, went only skin-deep. He could not forgive Sforza for seizing those towns in the Ancona region, and his rancour finally induced him to connive at a conspiracy to murder him, a scheme in which Piccinino appears also to have been involved. Luckily for Sforza, he had well-wishers even among the cardinals, and he received a warning in time. He was able to arrest the ringleader in the plot and clap him into a dungeon at Fermo, though he spared his life. Two of his own supporters then waited upon him and volunteered to set up a counter-plot for the liquidation of Piccinino. Sforza would have none of it, and drove them contemptuously from the room. The story seems to have got back to Piccinino, for, though his jealousy of Sforza remained undiminished, it is said that ever afterwards he spoke more generously of his rival, even when discussing him with the duke.

Developments in Naples produced yet another change of alignments. Joanna died in 1435, naming René of Provence as her successor. Alfonso, whom she had previously adopted and then disinherited, tried to occupy the throne by force of arms. His fleet was defeated by the Genoese, who took him prisoner and forwarded him proudly to their master in Milan. Filippo then did a remarkably uncharacteristic thing: he succumbed to the charm of his princely captive and switched his support from the Angevin side to the Aragonese. Alfonso was released without ransom, an action which so offended the Genoese that they threw off the overlordship of Milan and reasserted their independence. For Sforza this volte-face was equally vexatious, for it threatened all his interests in the Regno and underlined the hypocrisy of Filippo's earlier assurances. Alfonso, a fighting Spaniard himself, had little love for condottieri as a class, and when he finally captured Naples six years later he established a militia system to reduce his dependence on mercenaries. For Sforza personally he had an even greater antipathy. They were always on opposite sides, whereas, in the case of the duke, the Pope and the Venetian republic, Sforza could always boast that at one time or another he had given good service for, as well as against, them.

Now, as his relations with Filippo became more and more strained, and the prospects of his ever marrying Bianca grew dimmer and dimmer, it was to Venice that Sforza turned his eyes.

After their execution of Carmagnola, the Venetians had used various commanders for the defence of their mainland territories. Colleoni had remained in their service, and in 1434 they had engaged the elderly Gattamelata and his habitual colleague, Count Brandolini. One would like to know more of 'the Honeyed Cat'. The famous statue in Padua shows him as a strong, dignified, not unkindly character, while the effigy on his tomb in the Basilica of Sant'Antonio, not far away, suggests a straightforward honest nature, and is not at variance with the scanty biographical records. He is reputed to have been courageous, loyal, and a man of his word. Certainly his career with Venice ended more happily

266

169 Gattamelata (right) had something of Hawkwood's rugged professionalism, a quality which shows in Donatello's superb portrait head.

170 Gattamelata's son, Gian Antonio, also served Venice as a condottiere. He died only twelve years after his father and lies (left) beside him in the Santo at Padua.

than Carmagnola's, for the government presented him with an ornamental baton, two and a half feet long, wrought by a Venetian craftsman, as a token of their appreciation of his faithful service. After his death this baton was preserved as a relic in the church where he lies.

'Gattamelata and Count Brandolini', ran the *condotta* of 1434, 'are engaged as leaders of four hundred lances, with three horses to each lance as is the custom, and also of four hundred infantry. And after six months they shall have, additional to what is agreed above, fifty more lances for their two sons under them . . .'

Gattamelata's son was named Gian Antonio. He survived his father only by twelve years, and their tombs are side by side in the basilica.

The Venetian contract was on the usual detailed and businesslike lines, reminiscent of the agreements Hawkwood had been signing with Florence half a century earlier. 'Cities, lands, fortresses and their munitions', when captured, were to be regarded as the legitimate spoils of the republic, while ordinary plunder became the property of the troops, provided that they paid the Onoranza di San Marco, 'St Mark's Fee', a ten per cent tax on the value. Living captures were similarly graded into the important and the less important. Mindful of the trouble they had experienced after Maclodio, the Venetians laid down precise conditions: 'ruling princes and their brothers or sons, and rebels and traitors' were to be regarded as the prisoners of the republic, which also had an option to take over 'other condottieri and military commanders' on payment of half their ransom value to the captors. The mere rank and file were classed with the portable loot, and the victorious soldiers were welcome to them.

Gattamelata and Brandolini gave such satisfaction that they were jointly awarded the castle and lands of Valmarino, paying an annual tribute of ten pounds of wax on St Mark's Day. After a time Gattamelata bought out his comrade and became sole lord of the place, his name proudly registered in the *Libro d'Oro* with all the best families in Venice. It was an achievement for a baker's son from a little town in Umbria.

Full-scale warfare between Milan and Venice flared up again in 1438, with Piccinino commanding for the duke, at first against Gattamelata and Colleoni. The theatre of operations was the country round Lake Garda, midway between the rival cities. The Venetians held Brescia, well to the west of the lake, and Piccinino laid siege to what was, in Milanese eyes, a provocative outpost of their enemies' power. Filippo had managed to win over the support of a traditional enemy, Gonzaga of Mantua, which meant that the normal Venetian supply-line to Brescia – the highway skirting the southern shores of Garda – was cut by the Mantuan fortress of Peschiera rising at the corner of the lake. These were the factors determining the strategy of the war that raged through the next two or three years.

Sforza was not involved in the first phases, and the story of this particular struggle fits more conveniently into the study of Bartolomeo Colleoni, who was prominent in it from start to finish. Sforza was brought in as Captain-General for Venice when Gattamelata's health broke down. Gattamelata suffered a stroke and retired to Padua, where he died in 1443. He was given a magnificent funeral with the fullest honours that the Serenissima could accord him, though it was left to his widow, Giacoma Leonessa, to commission the Donatello statue in his memory.

Sforza's part in the operations round Lake Garda was a notable one. He was pitted, congenially enough, against his lifelong rival, Piccinino. In Colleoni he had a lieutenant he could depend upon. Some of the successes later attributed to Sforza might more fairly have been credited to Colleoni, and Sforza himself seems to have behaved honestly in giving him his rightful share of honour. On one occasion Sforza was engaged in an all-day battle at Cignano and would have been beaten had not Colleoni, then in Brescia, ridden promptly to his assistance.

171 At the Battle of Anghiari, 1440, the Florentines and Venetians under Sforza defeated the Milanese under Piccinino. It was long remembered with pride by

Piccinino was a redoubtable opponent. Having destroyed the fleet which the Venetians had managed, with superhuman efforts, to launch upon the lake, he sailed up to the northern end and found himself surrounded by Sforza's army near Riva. This was the oft-related occasion when he is said to have escaped through Sforza's lines in a sack, humped on the back of an outsize German soldier. Shortly after this episode, the wily little man made a surprise attack on Verona, the Venetians' key-position at the eastern approaches to the lake. Piccinino was helped by a deserter's information and by the shortness of the November days: he was in Verona before Sforza knew that he had left his base, and the whole city except for the riverside castle was swiftly overrun by the Milanese. Sforza, encamped at the northern end of the lake, reacted vigorously. He led a night march across the intervening mountains, already covered with the first snows of winter. The cold was intense. Some of his troops later lost fingers and toes through frostbite. But the march was accomplished, and to the utter amazement of the still-exulting Milanese Sforza burst into Verona only three days after its fall. Piccinino lost two thousand men as prisoners in the rout that followed.

Florence, being depicted not only in this panel from the school of Uccello, but also by Leonardo's lost fresco in the Palazzo Vecchio.

His luck had gone. In the following summer he invaded Tuscany. Ostensibly it was to create a diversion, to threaten the Florentines, and draw Sforza away from Lombardy. Piccinino had also a more personal motive. At the back of his mind was an idea to imitate his old commander and fellow townsman, and make himself lord of Perugia. But that proud city did not fancy another condottiere as despot. The people made him a generous donation but firmly indicated that they 'preferred to honour him as a countryman rather than hate him as a prince'.

The Tuscan expedition ended disastrously at Anghiari, an ancient walled village, once a Roman camp, above the upper Tiber valley. Piccinino's army, leavened with anti-Medici Florentines, clashed with Sforza's on 29 June 1440, and was crushingly defeated. Piccinino lost half his men as prisoners and all his baggage. Machiavelli afterwards ridiculed this affair as a condottiere battle without bloodshed, and the casualties were certainly light, which was all the more credit to Sforza's generalship. Nor was the engagement without important consequences, for it removed a threat to the Medici supremacy in Florence, and made Filippo Visconti more anxious to bring the war to a close.

Piccinino, on whom he had relied, was now a spent force. He had been wounded several times and the old ardent spirit could no longer transcend his physical handicaps. He murmured continually at his master's lack of appreciation. He was ready to retire and wanted to be given the town of Piacenza as a reward for his past services. Several other Milanese commanders were troubling Filippo with similar requests. It would be better, the duke decided, to cut his losses and satisfy his enemies rather than his supporters. He sent Sforza an urgent proposal: if he could influence the Venetians and Florentines to make peace, the long-postponed marriage to Bianca would be arranged without further delay, and her dowry would include the cities of Cremona and Pontremoli.

So it was that the Peace of Cavriana was signed in 1441, and in the same year Sforza became Filippo's son-in-law and presumptive heir.

Filippo's final and grudging assent to the match was to some extent influenced by the girl herself. Bianca Maria knew her own mind. She wanted no one but Sforza, and she had evaded two other proposals.

She was sixteen, fair-complexioned and tall, and carried herself well. She had a temper, and her fine white hands would flutter with exasperation, but the storms were soon over. She liked splendid clothes but her taste was too good for garish ostentation. She did not care for servile respect. Even in her greatest days she was impatient of all the cap-doffing in the street and of men kneeling to her. Like Sforza, she was open-handed. Her generosity became a legend. Much of it was displayed in charity – she was devout and walked barefoot to church at night. 'Better to spend,' she said, 'than to hoard and forget God.' She was intelligent and Sforza was often to consult her, in later years, especially on questions affecting the people of Milan, where her popularity as a Visconti was one of his greatest political assets.

It was her mother who brought her to the wedding. This took place at Cremona, one of the cities included in her dowry, some fifty miles south-east of Milan, a little set back from the banks of the Po. It was then a lovely Lombard town of mellow brick and terracotta, dominated by one soaring thirteenth-century tower, the Torrazzo. The marriage ceremony took place not in the ancient cathedral with the rose window but in the church of San Sigismondo just outside the city. This church was largely rebuilt, twenty-two years later, in thanksgiving for the happiness that stemmed from the union solemnized that day. After the service, the couple entered the city in procession, and the day was given over to banquets and sports for citizens and troops. Cremona was *en fête*. 'The very walls of the town', recorded Giovanni Simonetta, 'seemed to breathe delight.'

172 The wedding of Bianca Maria Visconti and Francesco Sforza, Cremona, 1441. The bride was sixteen, the bridegroom forty, but it was a lasting and happy marriage.

Even if the hyberbole of an official biographer be discounted, it is true to say that the Cremonese loved Bianca – and so did her husband. It might be a marriage of the utmost political convenience: it was also one of deep affection. 'I have many things to thank God for,' Sforza once declared, 'but the greatest blessing bestowed on me was a peerless wife.' He was solicitous for her health and would urge her not to overtire herself. This was necessary, for in moments of crisis Bianca did not allow her home responsibilities to prevent her playing a man's part. Once, when Sforza was campaigning at Brescia, some rebels seized the castle of Monza. Refusing to have her husband distracted, she collected a band of armed men and led them on foot to Monza, where her determination and authority produced an immediate surrender. On another occasion she arrived in Sforza's camp when he was about to abandon a siege because of the wet weather. She insisted that two fresh cannon should be brought up and the wall bombarded ceaselessly, day and night, until it collapsed into the moat and the defenders gave in to avoid being taken by storm. Such incidents were typical of her spirit. In the ordinary way, though, she was not one to interfere or to exploit her popularity with the troops by constant visits to her husband on active service. She loved the *ambiance* of a military headquarters, but mostly she kept away.

Sforza was forty when they were married. He was an experienced lover with many affairs behind him – and some, it must be admitted, still ahead. Some of his bastard children were older than Bianca. Polissena was married to Sigismondo Malatesta a little while before her father married

173 Sigismondo Malatesta, the husband of Sforza's illegitimate daughter Polissena.

174 Francesco Sforza was often compared to classical heroes; in this flattering picture he is shown (centre) conversing with Fabius, Scipio, Pompey, Julius Caesar, Hannibal, Epaminondas, and Themistocles.

Bianca. Sforza's acknowledged bastards eventually totalled twenty-two. He used them, as public men were wont to do, to strengthen his web of political and military connections. One daughter, Drusiana, married Piccinino's son, Jacopo. His son, Tristano, found a wife among the Este children.

Bianca accepted Sforza's occasional infidelities as calmly as she could, holding them to be 'the habit of men and particularly of princes'. As her own existence sprang from the habit, it was hard for her to argue too strongly against it. Once, however, her jealousy became more than she could bear. Sforza was showing too much interest in one of her maids of honour, Perpetua, a girl of virtuous reputation whose marriage nevertheless became suddenly a matter of urgency. She was married quickly to a complaisant groom and whisked off to a distant castle on the same day. She was not seen again, and unpleasant rumours circulated. The child she had borne was in due course added to the nursery and grew up with the name of Polidoro Sforza.

Bianca herself bore Sforza some notable children. Galeazzo Maria, his heir, came into the world at the castle of Fermo in 1444. The famous Lodovico il Moro arrived a few years later. Others included Ascanio, who became a cardinal, and Ippolita, who married Alfonso of Aragon. Ippolita's girlish gift for Latin oratory was her father's pride. Indeed, most of the Sforza children were enthusiastic reciters and speech-makers to their indulgent parents at Christmas and on other festive occasions.

By the standards of the period the marriage at Cremona, and the family life that developed from it, were harmonious and virtuous to a noteworthy degree.

All this felicity belonged, however, to the years that were still to come. In 1441 Sforza had secured his bride, but nothing else in his world was yet secure.

Filippo's obsessively suspicious nature seems to have made him completely unable to choose a line and stick to it. Having finally committed himself to Sforza as his son-in-law, he did not use the alliance to make his duchy strong. Instead, he continued to listen to the murmurs of Piccinino and other disgruntled elements, and manœuvred to weaken Sforza's position, which he had himself just helped to build up.

Once more the fighting broke out, up and down the peninsula. Once more Sforza had to fight Piccinino – the envious little man now so broken down physically that he sat on his horse with difficulty and leaned heavily on a companion's arm when he walked. This last contest between them took place in the Marches, where Sforza was being driven out of his possessions by the combined forces of the Pope and Alfonso, by this time firmly installed as King of Naples. Filippo egged them on against his son-in-law and lent them Piccinino as general.

Sforza won the first round at Montelauro. Piccinino was preparing to seek his revenge when Filippo, inconsistent as usual, asked the Pope to send him back to Milan. The condottiere obeyed the order reluctantly and with misgivings, leaving his son, Francesco, in command with precise orders to avoid battle. There were tears in his eyes as he passed through the lines on his departure. The men cheered him. Those who saw him as the temporary papal commander shouted, 'Chiesa!' in loyalty to the Church, but the rest saluted him not with his own name but with that of the legendary leader whose tradition he had kept alive for twenty years. 'Braccio!' the cry rose, 'Braccio!' In Milan the news he had dreaded caught up with him. After his departure, Sforza had attacked and routed his army. Francesco Piccinino and the Papal Legate were prisoners, though his other son, Jacopo, had escaped. This disaster was the last straw. Piccinino died a few days later. His had been a curiously disappointing and ineffective career, for while he had been deservedly rated among the foremost condottieri he had achieved none of the ambitions gnawing at his heart.

As was only to be expected, Filippo's peace with Venice did not survive the strains induced by these fresh developments. War broke out again. In 1446 the Venetian forces swept westwards across the Adda. Sforza, still striving to hold his estates in the Marches, viewed their success with mixed feelings. He did not mind the discomfiture of his father-in-law. On the other hand, if one day soon he were to inherit the duchy, he did not want to find it hopelessly weakened and dismembered by the Venetians.

He still did not know how he stood with the toad-like recluse in the Porta Giovia. The birth of his son had pleased the duke, who had asked for a traditional Visconti name for the baby, Galeazzo Maria, and authorized Sforza to add the family viper to his arms. Yet how much did these favours signify? Since then, the duke had propounded the interesting idea that Cremona had never been part of Bianca's dowry, merely a security for money owed to her bridegroom, and should now be returned. He had even sent Bartolomeo Colleoni to take possession of the city, that condottiere having joined his service – and then, before any more tiresome embarrassments could develop, he had evaded the crisis by unaccountably casting Colleoni into jail. Sforza might well reflect, with wry amusement, that he was not the only person who did not know where he was with the duke from day to day. Meanwhile, he made his dispositions to ensure that he should not lose possession of so important a city. He also took the precaution of giving secret orders that, whatever forces helped him to defend Cremona, it should not be his Venetian friends. No Venetian soldier was to enter the city. One form of far-sightedness was the capacity to keep watch in two opposite directions at the same time.

The summer of 1447 found the Venetian army dangerously close to Milan. Sick and frightened, Filippo sent to Sforza, appealing for aid. This appeal was backed by a letter from Sforza's friend, Niccolò Guarna, in Milan: 'Consider what the state of things is, and how you will be placed if our lord dies and you are not here.' That was on 13 August. Two days later he was writing again to say that the duke had just died. Sforza was already on the march, gathering all the forces he could. The news reached him when he had halted at Cotignola. Hard on the messenger's heels came another letter with the same announcement and a similar appeal to hurry. This second letter, from another well-wisher, Antonio Guidoboni, declared: 'As soon as you are here, half the game is won.'

The game was a complicated one. Malign and perverse to the end, Filippo had done everything he could to prevent that smooth transfer of power at which the Visconti family had become adept in earlier crises. He had provided his son-in-law with no clear title to succeed: Sforza based his claim on a document, never produced, said to have been drawn up a year earlier. In any case, only a day before he died, Filippo had named Alfonso of Aragon as his heir, and the castle, along with other key-positions, had been immediately occupied by troops favouring the Neapolitan king. A third claimant was the Duke of Orleans, son of Gian Galeazzo's beloved daughter, Valentina, who had married the King of France's brother in 1391.

Yet another factor now entered into the situation. The city of Milan was not lacking in men of spirit and ability. It occurred to such men that, if their counterparts in Venice and Florence were competent to manage their own affairs, there was something absurd and degrading in their submitting to any one of these three distant and alien masters, whether a French duke, a Spanish prince, or even an Italian condottiere from Romagna. The Visconti male line had been broken. Why not seize this excellent chance to end despotic personal rule? They accordingly proclaimed a constitution for what – harking back to the city's patron saint – they named the 'Golden Ambrosian Republic', headed by officers known as the 'Captains and Defenders of the Liberty of Milan'.

For a short time all went well. The garrison was weaned from its loyalty to Alfonso by a timely distribution of 17,000 florins, the condottieri present in the city were sufficiently impressed by the demonstrations of popular unity to swear allegiance to the new government, and the castle was enthusiastically demolished, like some earlier Bastille, as a symbol of the Visconti tyranny that had vanished for ever.

It looked as though Sforza had missed the prize that had glittered so long, if so uncertainly, before his eyes. But the newly born republic had not the solid qualities needed to back its idealism. As Machiavelli wrote: 'Nothing could make Milan free, being altogether corrupt, as was evident after Filippo Visconti's death, when she wanted to establish liberty but had neither the ability nor the knowledge to maintain it.'

The most pressing need was to do something about the victorious Venetians. The Milanese might have been wise to buy them off, for the moment, at almost any price. Instead, they played into Sforza's hands by asking him to become their Captain-General. They promised him Brescia and Verona for himself, if he could take them from the Venetians. Sforza hesitated, then accepted, partly on the advice of his friend, Cosimo de' Medici, who shrewdly saw that for the present it was his best way to stay in the game. He had sound advice also from his wife throughout this period. Bianca knew her Milanese.

278

175 Bianca Maria Sforza was in her own right a woman of notable intelligence and determination. Sforza's success in first gaining and then keeping the dukedom of Milan was in large measure due to her support.

Sforza took up his command and threw all his energies into re-establishing the situation in Lombardy. Piccinino's two sons, with characteristic professional detachment, agreed to serve under their father's lifelong opponent. Sforza asked the Milanese also to engage Colleoni, which they did.

The other Lombard cities had little enthusiasm for the Golden Ambrosian Republic. Some declared their own independence. One such was Piacenza, and was singled out by Sforza as a grim example. He subjected the city to a gruelling bombardment, heavier than any experienced by an Italian population up to that date. Then he stormed the breaches and gave the place over to his soldiers. After that terrible November day in 1447 Piacenza lay for some time deserted, and eventually it required compulsory settlement to repeople its ruins.

Pavia, ever jealous of Milan, also chose independence. The castle, however, was held by Bianca's mother, Agnese del Maino, and she persuaded the citizens to submit to her son-in-law personally, on the understanding that this would imply no subjection to the Milanese. This arrangement did not please the Golden Ambrosians, but they were in no position to upset it. A little while afterwards, when Tortona surrendered to Sforza, they gratified their injured dignity by ordering Colleoni to occupy the town himself and send away Sforza's garrison. Sforza thought it best to ignore this rap on the knuckles as a fair enough *quid pro quo*.

Cremona remained safe in his own hands all the time, stoutly defended by his wife. When a Venetian force approached the city, Bianca mustered her adoring supporters and rode out with them, spear in hand. It is even said that she threw the spear at a Venetian soldier, hit him in the mouth, and killed him. Whether or not she is justly credited with this exploit, the Cremonese certainly repelled the enemy with numerous casualties.

The claims of Alfonso and the Duke of Orleans had receded into the background. The triangle of forces was now composed of Sforza, the Ambrosian Republic, and Venice.

Early in 1448 the two governments talked of peace. Sforza's interests demanded that the war be kept going, and he managed to sabotage the negotiations. Hostilities were resumed in May, but the Milanese lacked money to pay their generals, so Colleoni changed sides. Sforza remained loyal, if that is the word, to Milan, having more at stake than a mere salary.

A few months later his army was surprised by the Venetians at Caravaggio on the road between Brescia and Milan. Sforza was either at Mass or at breakfast when the enemy attacked in the early morning light. He had no time to put on his armour. Undismayed, he rapped out his orders. He sent a strong cavalry force through the woods to take the enemy in the rear while he held their frontal assault in check as best he could. The manœuvre worked, and a crushing defeat was inflicted on the Venetians. Sforza took thousands of prisoners, far too many to feed, and at once released all the rank and file. The distinguished captives, including three generals and two high Venetian officials in their crimson gowns, were sent in triumph to Milan.

After this setback the Venetians concluded that it would be more immediately effective to strike a bargain with Sforza personally than with the Ambrosian Republic. On 18 October, therefore, at a small village called Rivotella, near Peschiera, an agreement was made whereby Sforza should change sides or (according to interpretation) Venice should back his claim to the duchy of Milan. Whatever formal phrases were used to justify the change of front, the fact was that Sforza acquired Venetian support to the tune of four thousand cavalry, two thousand infantry, and

13,000 ducats a month. If this aid enabled him to become master of Milan, the River Adda should form the future boundary between the states. The Venetians did not seriously expect him to take Milan, or indeed wish him to, but they felt that this agreement would split their enemies and scare the Milanese into accepting terms.

The next year brought no swift clarification to the complex affair. The mind grows dizzy, striving to keep track of the ever-changing relationships, with Sforza, Colleoni, and the two Piccinini now friends, now foes, and a fresh distraction introduced by an invasion of six thousand bloodthirsty Savoyards, whose defeat belongs more appropriately to the story of Colleoni.

Eleven months after their deal with Sforza, the Venetians achieved their original intention by making peace with Milan behind his back. The news was not broken to him until three days afterwards.

Now the final stage opened in Sforza's tireless struggle for Milan. It was Sforza against the rest – Sforza against the republican government, against the Venetians who swung their support behind that government, against Colleoni, against Sigismondo Malatesta, against all the condottieri and their companies that were sent against him.

176 Bartolomeo Colleoni played an important part in the struggle for Milan, being employed in turn by Filippo Maria Visconti and the Venetian republic. He was finally out-generalled by Sforza.

His strategy was to reduce Milan by blockade. His command of the Adda prevented supplies reaching the city from Venice: one river-crossing at Trezzo was dominated by a castle already in his possession; another, upstream at Brivio, was easily neutralized. Enterprising attempts to break his blockade at other points – a spirited dash by young Sigismondo Malatesta, an outflanking march through the mountains round Como by Bartolomeo Colleoni – had no success. As 1449 passed into 1450, Sforza tightened his stranglehold on the city. His own men were hungry, but the Milanese were hungrier, and he knew that his disciplined troops would not be the first to crack. Also he knew that he had his friends inside Milan, and that many people there were disenchanted with the Golden Ambrosian Republic.

As is often the way with revolutions, it was a trivial incident that touched off the explosion of discontent essential to his plans. A street-corner argument, one February day, attracted a crowd of disgruntled and war-weary townsmen. A rumour spread that the slum area of the Porta Nuova was under arms. Someone, whether authorized or not, began to ring the alarm-bell. Soon, a movement that had been spontaneous fell under the direction of Sforza sympathizers and was deliberately built up. Gaspare da Vimercate appeared on the scene, a respected figure who had himself served under Sforza and was a leader of those who favoured him. Vimercate and his friends led the crowd, growing minute by minute, to the Corte d'Arengo, the old palace close to the cathedral where the widowed duchess had installed herself after the demolition of the citadel. The Venetian ambassador met them at the head of the staircase. He was howled down as the representative of Milan's traditional enemy, and more recently the false friend that had proved unable to save the city from famine. The unfortunate ambassador was lynched, and the mob took over the palace.

The idealistic republicans had no strong man to restore the situation. The 'Captains and Defenders of Liberty' made themselves scarce. Under the guidance of Vimercate and the other pro-Sforza elements, an emergency mass meeting of citizens was called in the church of Santa Maria della Scala. Vimercate addressed this gathering and convinced it that there was no chance of independence and the sensible course was to negotiate a fair settlement with Sforza. Otherwise, they would all have died of starvation before the Venetians or anyone else could save them. This argument was received with acclamation and Vimercate was nominated as spokesman to go out and discuss terms.

Sforza had won, but he used his advantage with tact and moderation. He was ready to sign guarantees of the city's existing liberties. He acknow-

177 Although Sforza had married the Visconti heiress, Milan did not pass smoothly to him by inheritance. Not only did Venice oppose him, but the Milanese themselves formed a republic and refused to admit him. It was eventually a pro-Sforza party within the city, led by Gaspare da Vimercate (right), which made his accession possible.

ledged that he was receiving the dukedom by the gift of the people, not from any emperor. He promised to spend not less than eight months of every year in Milan.

On 26 February he made his first entry into the city. He ordered the troops to load themselves with bread, and to hand it out to the famished crowds who streamed out to meet him, cheering and shouting, 'Sforza! Sforza! Duca, Duca!' He rode in through the Porta Nuova, modestly declining the white canopy edged with cloth of gold which the citizens brought forward in honour of the occasion. Such shows, he said, were fit superstitions for kings, but he was going to pay homage to the Lord of the Universe, in Whose eyes all men were equal. He proceeded to the cathedral, where the press was so great around him that, it is said, horse and rider were carried bodily through the great door of the church. A little while later he came out into the piazza again and the multitude hailed him as Duke of Milan. It must have been a sweet moment after the years of doubt and deferment. But he did not linger. He paused just long enough to accept a cup of wine and a piece of bread outside a friend's house, without even dismounting from his charger, and then rode back to his camp outside the city.

The ceremonial entry followed on 22 March. This time Bianca rode with him, and his six-year-old heir, Galeazzo Maria, and his brother, Alessandro Sforza, lord of Pesaro. This time, too, he did not deprive the people of the pageantry they expected. He was invested with the ducal insignia on a dais erected outside the cathedral. He wore robes of shining white velvet for the ceremony. Vimercate carried the sceptre. In the distribution of honours that immediately followed he was rewarded for this, and no doubt for other services of even greater political value, by being made Count of Valenza. Little Galeazzo was created Count of Pavia.

So, on this day, the son of Muzio Attendolo completed his transformation from condottiere to one of the considerable princes of Europe. Not all foreign powers were quick to recognize him in his new role: Frederick III held that the dukedom was something only the Emperor could give and the King of France was still supporting the claim of Orleans. But most of the ambassadors representing the other Italian states hastened to offer their congratulations. The natural exceptions were Naples, where Alfonso held to his own claim, and Venice, where the Council was even then debating a businesslike offer to arrange for Sforza's poisoning.

Sforza, however, survived to die peacefully in his bed after sixteen years of constructive and enlightened government. His family life was no less successful. A conscientious parent, he wrote out in 1457 his *Suggerimenti di Buon Vivere* for the guidance of his heir. 'Galeazzo,' he began, 'you know that until now we have never been angry with you or given you a single blow . . .' He went on to offer ten moral precepts on the right attitude towards every one from Almighty God to personal servants. Galeazzo was admonished that he must learn to do without anything that he could not obtain by honest means. Never must he practise deceit or tell lies . . .

From Sforza the advice was perhaps a little cool, but he was not the first father whose precept was better than his example.

178 Francesco Sforza ruled Milan peacefully and efficiently for sixteen years, taking his place among the great humanist patrons of the Renaissance.

Bartolomeo Colleoni had a shrewd eye for his own immortality when he asked for a statue of himself to be put up in Venice. Although the laws of the Serene Republic denied him the site he would have preferred, in St Mark's Square, sufficient tourists seek out Verrocchio's masterpiece in the quieter setting of San Giovanni e Paolo to make sure that the general's name and features are still known throughout the world.

A year older than Francesco Sforza, Colleoni was born in 1400 at Solza, a small village on the Adda some six miles from Trezzo. He was thus a native of that region where the Lombard plain runs up into the Alpine foothills and where, for most of his lifetime, the conflicts of Venice and Milan were staged.

The Colleoni family was of Guelf sympathies and long established in Bergamo. Bartolomeo's father, Paulo, more commonly known as 'Puhò', was a gentleman of modest means. He owned the little castle at Solza and another at Chignolo, but such places were two a penny and implied no considerable status. His wife was Ricardona Valvasori dei Sanguini.

By the time Bartolomeo was toddling and framing his first coherent words, the death of Gian Galeazzo had plunged all the Milanese dominions into confusion. Puhò, like many other opportunists, helped himself to what lay handiest.

In this case it was the neighbouring and vastly superior castle of Trezzo, built by Bernabò Visconti, who had been attracted by the strategic value of the site, a promontory made almost an island by the bend of the swift green river. He had raised a splendid fortress which unfortunately Carmagnola was later to destroy. The bridge joining it to the other bank of the Adda was a three-decker affair. Honoured guests rode into the castle on the top level, the garrison and servants used the next, and the lowest passageway led conveniently straight to the dungeons. High above, a man standing on the battlements could look one way to Bergamo, lofty on its

179 Bartolomeo Colleoni: detail of the head of Verrocchio's equestrian monument.

own hillside, and the other way to Milan cathedral, pricking the flat horizon to the west.

Delighted with this more spacious accommodation, Puhò was ill-advised enough to offer hospitality to four of his cousins, whom the disturbed political situation had driven from Bergamo. They expressed their gratitude by attacking him one day as he sat playing draughts, and murdered him. His wife they threw into a dungeon. The little boy was snatched away by a schoolmaster who took him into the hills, keeping him safe for a year until his mother had been allowed to go back to her previous home at Solza, when Bartolomeo was restored to her. Even then the orphan was not left undisturbed. He was seized and held hostage by Giorgio Benzone, lord of Crema, until a debt could be repaid out of his mother's dowry. It was a fitting prelude to his adventurous life.

When he was old enough for training as a page, Colleoni was accepted into the household of Filippo Arcelli, lord of Piacenza. His education was not markedly intellectual or aesthetic, and he never became much of a scholar, but in adult life he enjoyed good conversation and could hold his own in literary and scientific discussions, bringing his matter-of-fact approach to arguments that sometimes lost themselves in excessive subtleties. Physically, he was growing up into a tall, athletic youth, dark-eyed and swarthy, holding himself well, destined to be equally famous for his stamina as a soldier and his susceptibility as a lover.

It was during his years as a page that Filippo Visconti succeeded to the dukedom and Carmagnola set to work with draconian harshness to establish his authority. Colleoni was sixteen when he heard that Carmagnola had taken Trezzo and ejected those treacherous cousins who had killed his father. There was little comfort in the news: Carmagnola had not captured the place in order to give it to Puhò's son, whose title anyhow was almost non-existent. Soon enough, too, the youth had more pressing problems. Carmagnola marched against Piacenza. Colleoni's master defied him, until his own son and brother were paraded in sight of the garrison and savagely executed. Broken in heart and will, Arcelli and his wife abandoned the defence and fled into exile. They did not take Colleoni with them. The boy had to look after himself. He slipped from the abandoned city and crossed the Apennines to seek his fortune in the south. It was the time when Braccio da Montone was supreme. Colleoni enlisted in his company.

Braccio knew nothing of his background. Casually, he enrolled the newcomer among the stable-lads. Colleoni was piqued. Not only was he of superior birth and upbringing but by now he was old enough to want a man's work. As soon as he could, he transferred himself to Jacopo

Caldora, a Neapolitan baron who had become something of a condottiere and was just then fighting on the other side under Muzio Sforza. He gave Colleoni a command of twenty lances, later raised to thirty-five. It is said, and is wholly credible, that the striking features and proud bearing of the young officer caught the fancy of the amorous Queen Joanna. He regularly afterwards used the badge she granted him, a pair of lions' heads joined by a red band, between two narrower bands of white.

Colleoni stayed with Caldora for several years and won a good reputation in the final campaigns against Braccio. After the battle at Aquila, when Caldora helped to destroy Braccio, the Neapolitan was anxious to take over some of the territories in the Marches previously held by the dead man. Caldora's son, Giovanni Antonio, was nominally entrusted with this enterprise, but as he was relatively inexperienced he was given Colleoni to help and supervise him. The successful discharge of this assignment still further enhanced Colleoni's reputation.

In 1429 he transferred to the service of Venice. Carmagnola, then commander-in-chief, gave him forty lances. It was Colleoni who, during Carmagnola's curiously inert siege of Cremona in 1431, led the party that seized the outlying fortress of San Luca. Colleoni was actually the first man to mount the battlements. He held the place for two days, until lack of support from Carmagnola compelled him to evacuate it.

In the campaigns that followed Carmagnola's execution Colleoni steadily improved his standing with the Venetians. At first his supreme commander was Gian Francesco Gonzaga, Marquis of Mantua, until that not-very-successful general was replaced by Gattamelata. Colleoni showed special skill in the mountain country. When Piccinino won a victory over the Venetian forces at Lecco, where the Adda flows out of Lake Como, it was Colleoni who with Gattamelata re-formed the survivors and marched them to safety along the mountain paths of the Valsassina. Later, when Gonzaga was nervously retreating before Piccinino's superior forces, Colleoni urged a more resolute strategy and, when the Milanese attacked them in the rear, helped to extricate the army from the battleground known afterwards, not inappropriately, as 'the Field of Fear'. This left Bergamo exposed. Accordingly, he led a column in that direction and harassed Piccinino from the hills, so that he sheered off and made for Brescia. Having removed the threat to his family's native city, Colleoni rode quickly to assist Brescia. His zeal pleased the Venetians, and they sent commissioners to offer him another hundred lances.and the command of their infantry.

For prestige and for practical reasons alike, Venice could not bear to lose Brescia. Its possession was vital to Doge Foscari's mainland policy, but became very difficult when, the Marquis of Mantua having been replaced by Gattamelata, the traditional friendship between Mantua and Venice was interrupted and the Mantuan fortress at Peschiera threatened the lifeline to Brescia. Hunger was the primary problem when Gattamelata and Colleoni were besieged there in 1439. Piccinino held the plain. There was no way in and out of the city except through the hills behind. The people were eating their dogs and horses. The historian, Soldo, recalls seeing a hundred children in the piazza crying, 'Bread, bread, for the love of God!' Unable to supply all their own troops, the two condottieri decided to reduce the garrison to the minimum needed to hold the place, and to withdraw with the remainder. Leaving sixteen hundred men in Brescia, they slipped away northwards into the mountains past Lake Idro and, repelling a Milanese force under Ludovico dal Verme, won through to the safety of Veronese territory in the upper valley of the Adige.

Following this incident, the Venetians made their famous and imaginative attempt to break the blockade by establishing a fleet on Lake Garda to destroy the Milanese control of that water. This bold conception meant towing the galleys up the fast-flowing Adige and then manhandling them over the mountains so that they could be launched at Torbole, at the northern end of the lake. The operation took fifteen days, two thousand oxen, and vast expense, but it was accomplished – and in winter conditions. To the consternation of the Milanese, six Venetian galleys and twenty-five smaller craft appeared on Garda. Colleoni won most of the credit for this miracle, and no doubt it was due largely to his determination and to that sceptical, pragmatic approach which was noted in his discussions with intellectual friends. But, Churchill-like, he needed an expert to galvanize with his own spirit, and a Venetian engineer, Niccolò Sorbolo from Crete, filled this indispensable role. It was unfortunate that the effort was all in vain, and the Milanese were able to annihilate the flotilla.

The luck, however, was changing. There followed the defeat of Piccinino on land (and the little man's personal escape in a sack) and Sforza's triumphant recapture of Verona. The Venetians were able to establish themselves again on the lake, Peschiera fell, and in June 1440, the long siege of famished Brescia was ended. Colleoni rode back into the city at Sforza's side.

The next year brought peace, Sforza's marriage, and his *rapprochement* with Filippo Visconti. Colleoni was left in an advantageous position with his Venetian employers, for his other senior colleague, Gattamelata, had retired sick to Padua and clearly would never fight again. A decree of the senate recorded Colleoni's exemplary services and named him as one of

180 A fifteenth-century map showing Lake Garda (left) and the River Adige (right). The Venetians succeeded in transporting a flotilla of galleys overland from the river to Torbole, the town at the corner of the lake.

the principal condottieri of the republic, essential to its safety. He was awarded a little group of castles, Romano, Antegnate and Covo, confiscated from the rebel Count of Covo.

This was agreeable enough as far as it went, but Colleoni was less pleased when the Venetians began to effect the economy measures they thought permissible now that peace had come. The *provedditore* or inspector entrusted with making the cuts was an admirable but tactless man named Gherardo Dandolo. He reduced the size of Colleoni's command and, when the general complained about pay-arrears totalling 34,000 ducats, snubbed him with the arrogance inbred in a family that had produced four doges. This was short-sighted behaviour. Colleoni visited Milan early in 1443 and was accorded remarkable attention by the duke, who invited him more than once to dinner and engaged him in lengthy private conversations. Colleoni's wife, Tisbe, was presented with jewels, and Filippo invested the condottiere with the castle of Adorno, a singularly magnanimous gesture towards one who had consistently since boyhood fought against his armies. The Venetian intelligence service, normally so good, met its match in the secretive Visconti, and the sequel to this hospitality seems to have taken the authorities by surprise. In Sanuto's records there is a pained entry under the date 28 September 1443: 'News arrived of the flight of Bartolomeo Colleoni from our dominions and his defection to the Duke of Milan. In the beginning he had no more than three lances, and the republic gave him 200 and 150 hired infantry. What is more, he is our subject.'

A condottiere had to look after himself. It was not always easy to give due notice and proffer a dignified resignation. Employers were arbitrary and were just as ready to break the rules. Thus, when the duke fell out with Sforza, Colleoni was ordered to recover Cremona, but before he could proceed he was arrested and thrown into prison at Monza. His possessions at Adorno were removed to Pavia, along with his wife and daughter. The whole affair was wrapped in mystery. The duke sent Colleoni's tenants a curious letter, which was tortuous even by Visconti standards:

> Our beloved, lest you be surprised and distressed by anything that has been done against the person of the honourable Bartolomeo Colleoni, we are advising you that what has been done has not been done because we have any intention of doing him harm. . . . Be of good cheer, for in a little while he will be in favour, with better prospects than before, and you shall be reassured and satisfied . . .

Despite these soothing words, Colleoni was still in prison eleven months later when Filippo died. The proclamation of the Golden Ambrosian Republic did not, for all its talk of liberation, produce any immediate benefit for him, and he resolved to escape. He pretended illness and obtained a quantity of linen bandages, with which he made a rope; he then tied it to a bench, and lowered himself into the ditch. The alarm was given at once. The tocsin was rung, the townspeople turned out with weapons in their hands, and the whole vicinity of the castle was in confusion. Colleoni was able to climb out of the ditch unseen and lose himself in the excited throng. Almost immediately he was fortunate enough to run into one of his old soldiers, who provided him with a horse. Colleoni then galloped to Landriano, where some of his troops were quartered. They welcomed him back with delight. His wife and daughter were at Pavia, which Sforza was holding in defiance of the new Milanese govern-

181 Colleoni, seen here in a somewhat naïve miniature from a history of his 'Life and Deeds', belonged to the north Italian gentry and learned his profession in the Neapolitan wars. He entered Venetian service in 1429, under Carmagnola, transferred to Milan in 1443, and back to Venice when Filippo Maria Visconti died.

ment. Colleoni rode thither with his troops, was reunited with his family, and for the time being threw in his lot with Sforza.

Such associations were apt to be brief in the fluid situation that then existed. Soon Colleoni was persuaded to go over to the Venetian side again, taking the fifteen hundred troops he commanded. He fought Sforza at Caravaggio, when Sforza so unexpectedly snatched a triumph out of imminent disaster. Then it was Sforza who changed sides, linked up with Venice against Milan, and the two men were comrades-in-arms once more.

In the following year, 1449, Filippo's widow helped the Ambrosian Republic to an alliance with her brother, the Duke of Savoy, who had the backing of the King of France. Early in the year the French general, Jean des Compeys, appeared in the region of Novara, not far west of Milan, heading an army of six thousand Savoyards and Picard archers. Sforza was busy besieging Vigevano, so Colleoni was sent to deal with this new menace. He joined battle on 1 April and took Compeys prisoner, with some hundreds of his men, but without destroying the main army. There was another fiercely contested encounter three weeks later, just south of Lake Maggiore. Colleoni's troops had to cope with the novel tactics of the French archers, who tethered their horses and fought from behind a row of pointed stakes, rather like the English longbowmen at Crécy. Finally, however, the invaders gave way, and Colleoni chased them for two miles, taking a thousand prisoners. Sforza gave him a triumphal welcome back and praised him generously. These successes won Colleoni a high reputation far beyond the boundaries of Italy.

Soon, through no choice of their own, the two generals were on opposite sides again. Venice had made peace with Milan behind Sforza's back – and Colleoni's contract was with Venice. So, when Sforza blockaded Milan, Colleoni did his duty and tried to break through to relieve the city, making one of those circuitous mountain marches with which he sometimes fore-shadowed the genius of Garibaldi, yet failing, in spite of it, to prevent the collapse of the Ambrosian Republic.

Sforza was now Duke of Milan, yet Colleoni had the mortification of seeing himself undervalued in Venice, where he was not included in the trio of generals chosen to share the supreme command. He made no secret of his dissatisfaction but let it be known that he was considering resignation from the Venetian service. Venice seemed genuinely anxious to keep him – negotiators were sent to his camp on the border of the Mantuan marshes, where he was supervising the construction of a fortress. As he appeared adamant, the Venetians asked the Pope and the King of Naples to add their persuasions. Then, mindful that he had suddenly deserted them once before, they sent troops to arrest him.

Colleoni also would have done well to remember that earlier occasion. He allowed himself to be taken by surprise. He heard the tramp of armed men and knew they were not his own. They were coming to seize him, and if he delayed an instant he might share the fate of his old chief, Car-magnola. He managed to leap on a horse and, with only the three men in attendance at the time, gallop off along the road to Mantua. There was no chance to rally his troops – they had been surprised in their quarters and he saw at a glance that the camp was in other hands. Nor was there time to find his wife and daughters. He had to ride for his life, with pursuers hard on his heels. He managed to throw them off and finally reached Mantua safely, completing the journey bareback on a peasant's mule. Gonzaga of Mantua gave him a princely welcome, but his family remained prisoners of the Venetians, and it was two years before he saw them again.

Those two years were not happy ones. His own estates suffered badly in the confused, pointless warfare that raged to and fro. Near his castle at Covo he had reclaimed some waste land and made it fertile – now it was waste again, and some of the peasants, he knew, had suffered cruelly. He soldiered on, sometimes displaying a reckless personal bravery, as when he stormed the outworks screening a Venetian pontoon-bridge over the Adda, or when he fought on the snowy hillsides of the Val Seriana. But in his heart he felt that he was fighting on the wrong side. He could not bring himself to attack his ancestral city of Bergamo, which remained loyal to Venice. He did not want to see it delivered into Sforza's hands.

It was a happy day for him, as for countless others, when the Peace of Lodi in 1454 put an end to the struggle. That settlement agreed by Sforza, Cosimo de' Medici, Foscari, Pope Nicholas V, and a reluctant Alfonso of Aragon, achieved a kind of balance between the five great powers of Italy. The petty quarrels might continue, but with the Turks confronting Christendom with a terrible new threat in the east – it was the year after the stunning fall of Constantinople – there was a genuine move to close the ranks and stop the endless bickering between the cities.

Colleoni was able to rejoin his wife and daughters and make his own peace with the Venetians. On 10 March 1455, he had the satisfaction of being appointed Captain-General, and a few weeks later, at a parade in the piazza at Brescia, he was solemnly handed his baton. The same baton had been presented to Carmagnola in that same square just twenty-four years earlier, but the ominous parallel went no further.

The Lodi settlement wore well for about twenty years, and with the notable exception of Molinella (1467), when Colleoni fought a last battle against the courtly Federigo of Urbino, he was able to enjoy those twenty years as a peaceful country gentleman. He had many offers. Twice King Louis XI of France offered him a command. When he was sixty-eight he was pressed by Pope Paul II to lead a holy alliance against the Turks and even at seventy-two his services were sought by Charles the Bold of Burgundy. He took a natural pleasure in these flattering advances – he regularly used the titles 'of Anjou and Burgundy' and bore the golden lilies of Anjou granted by Duke René – but he was not to be lured from his peaceful country retirement.

Soon after his installation as Captain-General of Venice, he bought from the government the castle of Malpaga, which became his favourite home for the rest of his life and has continued in the possession of his descendants down to the present day. Malpaga stands on the banks of the Serio, a few miles from his beloved Bergamo. He took over a modest

182 Colleoni spent the last years of his life in relative peace
at Malpaga (above), which still remains in his family's possession.

thirteenth-century building, which the Venetians let him have freehold
for 100 gold ducats, and proceeded to enlarge and remodel it into a fine
residential castle, rather than a fortress, typical of the late fifteenth century.
He was, in these serene later years, immensely wealthy. When he died,
the Venetian valuers found a total in cash of 216,000 ducats, lodged in
various places and in different currencies, Venetian, Florentine, Neapolitan,
and even Hungarian. Apart from what he had already spent on the reconstruction of the castle he had busied himself with many other projects,
some concerned with estate betterment, others purely charitable. Canals
and irrigation-systems particularly appealed to him. He improved the
old canal leading from the Serio and later had a new one excavated, which
was lined with saw-mills, corn-mills and wine-presses. He was occupied
with further such plans until the day of his death. One of his charitable
schemes was the restoration of the ancient sulphur and mud baths at
Trescorre. He had the waters examined by doctors, the whole site cleaned

183 Malpaga, the inner courtyard. It was a medieval fortress, remodelled by Colleoni into a comfortable residence.

184 Colleoni, cleanshaven and on a white horse, goes hunting with his guest King Christian of Denmark, bearded and on a black horse.

up, and the nursing of patients undertaken by Benedictine nuns. Another of his endowments provided dowries for the girls of his native region, an appropriate gesture from a man whose wife had borne several daughters but no sons. There was no problem about finding suitable husbands for his own offspring: at the Battle of Molinella it is said that he had three sons-in-law fighting under him. But the daughter best known to posterity, because of the marble monument still to be seen in the Colleoni chapel at Bergamo, was his youngest, Medea, whose death at a tender age in 1470 was a heavy blow to him.

His life at Malpaga, or at least its more showy side, is depicted in the still extant if imperfect frescoes painted there by Romanino a generation later, to commemorate what must have been a highlight in the old soldier's closing years. This was the visit in March 1474 of the Danish King Christian, a remarkable sovereign who reigned over all Scandinavia and was then journeying to Rome as a pilgrim, laden with gifts for the Pope ranging from ermine to dried cod.

The Malpaga frescoes show Colleoni welcoming him at the draw-bridge and the subsequent festivities. There is a banquet scene, portraying the actual room in which the fresco is painted: the king sits at the head of the table, three decanters lined up before him, while Colleoni's grey-bearded seneschal carves a bird at his side; even the host sits below the salt, with one of his married daughters opposite and his little grandson on her knee; musicians play as another course is borne in by servants in procession, led by the butler, wand in hand. Another scene shows a tournament outside the castle, with Bergamo visible among the snow-clad hills and old Colleoni and the king sensibly watching from a covered loggia. Another illustrates the country sports offered the royal guest: a clean-shaven Colleoni on a white horse rides with the long-bearded Dane on a black, while hares are coursed and falcons flown in the middle distance. The king's departure is depicted with Colleoni's two trumpeters managing a fanfare. Before that, there is a scene in the courtyard with Colleoni sitting behind a table and handing out gifts of livery to the king's retinue, one of whom is doffing his cap in acknowledgment. By a most happy coincidence, the Colleoni colours were red and white, the same as the Danish.

It was a gratifying occasion for the condottiere. True, he had not achieved a dukedom and founded a dynasty like Sforza, but he had become a great man and a personage honoured far outside Italy, a man who could play host to a king. And where, after all, was Sforza now? Dead these eight years! Colleoni, his elder by a year, was still hale and hearty, rising with the sun and able to tramp for miles until his younger companions protested.

185 On his tomb in the Colleoni Chapel at Bergamo, the famous condottiere is shown as a warrior, holding the baton of the Venetian republic.

186 Below: the tomb of Colleoni's daughter Medea, who died in 1470, five years before her father.

He lived for another eighteen months after King Christian's visit. He was seventy-five when he died. At the end of October 1475, chilly and feverish, he felt that his end was near and made his will. A party of Venetian senators visited him. 'Never give another general as much power as you gave me,' he advised them. 'I could have done more harm with it!' After their visit he added a codicil, bequeathing to the republic 100,000 gold ducats for the war against the Turks, cancelling the arrears of pay due to him, and leaving to Venice another 10,000 ducats owed him by the Marquis of Ferrara. He humbly requested that the senate would erect a statue to him in St Mark's Square.

Having signed this, confessed and taken the sacrament, he called his friends round his bed, raised himself on his elbow and made his farewells. He died in his own room at Malpaga on 3 November 1475. On the following night his body was carried into Bergamo and laid in state before the altar of Santa Maria Maggiore, close to the cathedral where he was buried two months afterwards and where he still lies. This last fact, questioned in modern times, was confirmed in 1969 by the British scholar, Dr R. E. Linington, using a newly devised metal-detector which, being sensitive to the spurs still worn by the skeleton, located the coffin in an unsuspected compartment in the base of the ornate mausoleum. The baton was there too. Even Colleoni's dark red jacket with its button-decked sleeves had survived the passage of nearly five centuries. A large leaden plaque paid tribute in Latin to 'the undefeated general of the Venetian empire'.

It cannot be said that the Serene Republic showed excessive generosity to the man who had, on the whole, served it so loyally. True, the law may have compelled the relegation of his statue to a less conspicuous site. No law, however, compelled the Venetian treasury to seize another 90,000 ducats over and above the legacy freely bequeathed, or to rush through a decree taking back various lands Colleoni had been given absolutely and for ever, and restoring them for political reasons to the Pope. Still, as the shade of Carmagnola may have murmured, greeting his old lieutenant in the next world, who but a fool would expect generosity from the Venetians?

Riding triumphantly home to Bohemia after his coronation in Rome in 1433, the Emperor Sigismund was received with fitting festivities in the Italian cities through which he passed, and marked the occasion by conferring knighthoods on countless young men presented to him. At Rimini he knighted his namesake, Sigismondo Malatesta, who was barely sixteen but had become lord of that place a year earlier. At Mantua, some days further along the imperial progress, the candidates included the eleven-year-old Federigo, who was then living at the Gonzagan court as a hostage for the good behaviour of his father, the Count of Montefeltro and Urbino.

The lives of these two new knights were to run parallel for the next thirty years and more, their similarities as striking as their contrasts. Both were bastard sons of minor rulers on the eastern side of Italy. Both, none the less, inherited their fathers' dominions. Both supplemented their inadequate revenues by becoming condottieri and may be reckoned among the most famous members of that profession. Both were enthusiasts for culture and left visible memorials to their taste, the Tempio Malatestiano at Rimini and the Palazzo Ducale at Urbino. Otherwise, they were utterly unlike. Whereas Federigo, with all due allowance for the bias of his friends, seems to have been a pattern of chivalry and the beloved father of his people, Sigismondo won a reputation which, if only one half deserved, gives him a high place among the handsome monsters of the Renaissance. Murder, incest, rape, and sodomy were just four of the charges levelled against him. 'Of all men who have ever lived or ever will live,' asserted Pope Pius II confidently, 'he was the worst scoundrel.' Since Rimini and Urbino were little more than twenty miles apart, as the crow flies, it was inevitable that the two condottieri should clash. Their respective cities underlined the contrast between them: Rimini lay low beside the tawny Adriatic beaches, whereas Urbino, which the ancients had named 'the little garden town', perched fifteen hundred feet up in the mountainous hinterland.

Rimini, with its sombre and passionate history, was the right background for Sigismondo. His family had ruled there for a century or more, their apt nickname signifying 'Evil-head'. The dynasty had started with Malatesta di Verrucchio, Dante's 'old mastiff'. His son, Giovanni the Lame, had married Francesca da Rimini. The tale of her affair with his handsomer brother, Paolo, and Giovanni's murder of them both, was only one, if the most famous, episode in a gory family chronicle.

Sigismondo himself, however, was born at Brescia on 19 June 1417. His father, Pandolfo, had seized that city when Gian Galeazzo died, and Sigismondo was the child of his local mistress, Antonia. Pandolfo had had to make his own way in the world, for Rimini was ruled by his brother, Carlo Malatesta, the condottiere who has already figured in the account of Carmagnola. And it was Carmagnola who threw Pandolfo out of Brescia when Sigismondo was two years old. The child and his parents went to Fano, another Malatesta possession on the Adriatic coast. Pandolfo died there when Sigismondo was ten. Carlo Malatesta, old now and childless – it was the year of his catastrophic defeat at Maclodio – gave Sigismondo and his two brothers a home at Rimini. That home was the old family fortress on the inland side of the city, a grim place beautified by frescoes painted a generation earlier by Ghiberti, just before he won the competition for the Baptistery doors at Florence. Sigismondo did not inaugurate the Malatesta tradition of art patronage.

It is possible that Sigismondo would have developed into a stabler, more controlled character if his uncle had lived longer, for Carlo was one of the more respectable members of the family. On the other hand, the wildness was already deeply planted in the boy, and the elderly soldier's austerity might have driven him into violent reaction. At all events, Carlo died two years after Sigismondo's arrival in Rimini, and the lordship of the place devolved upon the eldest of his three illegitimate nephews, Galeotto. This youth, Sigismondo's half-brother, suffered from religious mania. He joined the Third Order of St Francis, spent all his time in fasting and sick-visiting, and, after reluctantly taking as bride one of the Marquis Niccolò d'Este's illegitimate daughters, declared himself incapable of anything but a platonic association.

Such a ruler was of little use to Rimini, a small state ringed with greedy neighbours. Even the other branches of the Malatesta family were not to be trusted. Another Carlo Malatesta at Pesaro, just down the coast, soon leagued himself with the Count of Urbino to attack Rimini. Galeotto, lost in mystical ecstasies, would patently be useless on the battlements. It

302

187 Federigo da Montefeltro, Duke of Urbino, the most attractive and civilized of all the condottieri, is seen here in an altarpiece by Piero della Francesca.

was then that the thirteen-year-old Sigismondo gave precocious evidence of his military leanings. Doubtless he had the help and prompting of experienced men who despaired of the situation and could find no one else acceptable as their nominal leader. Whatever the precise value of Sigismondo's contribution, he certainly rode out of the city secretly by night at the head of a little army, crossed the River Foglio, surprised the invaders' camp and won the credit for dispersing them.

For two more years the growing boy fretted impotently while the titular lord of Rimini prayed, fasted, and kissed the ulcers of the sick, but ignored his wife and his healthy subjects. It is hard to believe that Galeotto could have survived much longer under the demanding conditions of political life at that time. But one sin, fratricide, Sigismondo was saved from committing. Galeotto virtually starved himself to death in his excessive piety. He died in October 1432.

Sigismondo succeeded him. Theoretically, he was under a regency exercised by Galeotto's virgin widow, Margherita d'Este, and by his aunt, Elisabetta Gonzaga. Sigismondo had his uses for women, but not as political mentors. He asserted himself from the start. Only a man, and a soldier, could save Rimini. He rode inland up the old Roman road to Cesena, another of the Malatesta cities, and there mustered a little army of supporters. Then he returned, drove off his kinsman, Malatesta of Pesaro, for the second time, and demonstrated to all the world that he, and no one else, was to be lord of Rimini. The new Pope, Eugenius IV, hastened to confirm his title. Martin V had already legitimized him and his brother.

It was in the following summer that Sigismondo knelt before the Emperor to receive the accolade. At sixteen he was tall and wiry. Pisanello's medallion makes it easy to imagine the head bowed in that moment of uncharacteristic humility – the sheen of the smooth hair, brushed and cut to a sweeping line that touched the ear-tips and curled under itself at the nape of the neck. The face, uptilted again as the newly dubbed knight regained his feet, was strongly featured with something of the falcon in the nose. Only the life in the eyes was beyond the art of the medal-designer. Sigismondo is said to have had small but brilliant eyes, with flattish lids that conveyed a snake-like impression. Falcon or snake? There was an element of both in his character.

It is harder to picture the child Federigo who was similarly honoured at Mantua, along with the Gonzaga boys, as the Emperor proceeded northwards. It is necessary to forget the familiar portraits of the good duke in maturity, kindly, balding, rather ordinary, his most striking feature the broken nose he had acquired in a tournament.

188 The tyrant Sigismondo Malatesta, lord of Rimini, forms a complete contrast to Federigo: a relief by Agostino di Duccio.

Federigo was born on 7 June 1422, his father being Guidantonio, Count of Urbino, and his mother an unnamed girl of that city. Federigo himself grew up as amorous as most of his contemporaries, but rather better at keeping his desires within reasonable bounds. His father later had a legitimate son, Oddantonio. Federigo was brought up with this boy and various sisters. As usual in that period, illegitimacy caused little concern, and in Federigo's case, as in that of the Malatesta boys, it was in due course expunged by an obliging Pope. Federigo's status as the count's son was so fully acknowledged from the start that, when the Venetians demanded a living pledge of his father's loyalty, he was accepted as adequate.

In Venice the little hostage seems to have charmed everyone, from Doge Foscari, who prophesied fame and fortune, down to the more matter-of-fact Venetian boys who invited him to join their exclusive fraternity, known as the *Calze* from the gay, parti-coloured hose that distinguished its members. After a year, however, there was an outbreak of plague in the city, and the doge considerately had Federigo transferred for safety to the court of Mantua.

Here he shared the education of the Gonzaga children and developed that love of all-round culture which was afterwards reflected in his own court at Urbino and immortalized in Castiglione's book. The marquis himself supervised the boys' riding, fencing, and other military training, while the more intellectual side was directed by the remarkable scholar, Vittorino da Feltre, whom he had attracted to Mantua a few years earlier. At once mild and firm, quiet and gay, Vittorino was an unworldly, dedicated little man, who went about in a peaked hood with a long gown trailing on the ground. Born poor, he had worked his way through the University of Padua, becoming footman to the professor of mathematics in the hope, vain as it proved, of obtaining free instruction. He had mastered Euclid by himself and learned Greek from the famous Guarino da Verona. With all his reverence for book-learning he combined a platonic belief in the balance of aesthetic and physical education with the intellectual. The marquis gave him a house in which to train the Gonzaga children and their playmates: Vittorino insisted on his right to exclude the unsuitable, however illustrious their parentage, and to admit the humblest if they had talent. Money meant nothing to him. When he died, he did not leave enough for his own funeral. The fees and gifts showered upon him by the wealthy were used to subsidize his poorer pupils. Nor had he any prejudice against girls: he had Cecilia Gonzaga writing excellent Greek when she was ten.

This was the environment in which Federigo passed two formative years. Of all the famous condottieri he was the only one who can be said

189 Vittorino da Feltre, one of the founders of Renaissance educational theory, was tutor at the Mantuan court when Federigo spent his formative years there. Study was balanced by exercise, intellectual guidance by moral.

to have been to a school – and it was the best available in Europe at that time, run by an idealist who held that 'the school-room must be a holy place'.

After those two years Federigo went home, his role as political hostage discharged. The next stages in his education were marriage and military service. At the end of 1437, being then fifteen and a half, he married Gentile, the orphaned daughter of Bartolomeo Brancaleone. Little is known of her except that she was very plump and that, her father having no male heir, she brought Federigo the fief of Mercatello and some other small townships to govern on her behalf. His military service was probably of more immediate interest to the youth.

Under which famous captain should he enrol for his initiation in the art of war? The choice lay between Francesco Sforza and Niccolò Piccinino. It was decided that he should join the latter, and at the end of May 1438 Federigo took leave of his bride. Piccinino gave him four hundred soldiers to command and soon he was taking part in the Milanese siege of Brescia. The rest of his apprenticeship was served in the Lombardy campaigns against Gattamelata, Colleoni, and Sforza, but it was not long before the aggressions of Sigismondo Malatesta against his father's territory drew him home and began the feud between the two young men that lasted almost all their lives.

307

190 Sigismondo Malatesta as a young man: a medal by Pisanello. Though totally unscrupulous he was, in a typically Renaissance way, a man of considerable artistic judgment, the patron of Alberti and Piero.

Sigismondo was by this time firmly established in Rimini.

He had called off, just in time, his marriage to the daughter of the disgraced Carmagnola, though he had retained the splendid charger and the silver helmet already given him by her father. Instead, he had married Ginevra d'Este, daughter of the Marquis of Ferrara, when he was seventeen and she sixteen. Their marriage, celebrated in Rimini with signal splendour, had been fruitless for three years. Then Ginevra produced a son, who did not live long. She herself died in 1440, and, though there was no scandal at the time and the marquis continued friendly, it was later alleged that Sigismondo had poisoned her. A year later he married Polissena Sforza, one of five children born to Francesco by his favourite mistress, Columbina, in his early Neapolitan days. This wedding took place in the camp, during the war then in progress, and Rimini had no chance to welcome the bride until the spring of 1442. Polissena bore a son in the following January, but lost him in infancy. Her marriage was no more fortunate than Ginevra's.

Through all those years Sigismondo was building a new castle on the foundations of the old. The design was his own and expressed his determination to possess a base from which he could defy the world. The moat was a hundred feet wide and each gate was defended by drawbridge and portcullis. The six main towers rose eighty feet high and there were numerous lower towers and bastions. Inside, the area was divided into three courtyards. He laid the first stone of the Castel Sismondo on 20 March 1437, and the work continued for the best part of a decade. The final effect was grim externally, but there was beauty within, a fit setting for the sophisticated court he gathered round him by his patronage. But the Ghiberti frescoes had gone for ever, sacrificed in the demolition of the previous building.

When not otherwise occupied, Sigismondo lost no chance of raiding the adjacent Montefeltro territories. Such harassments of one's neighbours were a tradition of the rough life in the Marches and Romagna. Guidantonio Montefeltro was drawing near the end of his days. His legal heir was young and, as the future was to show, not a very impressive character. Inevitably the count leaned more and more on his elder son, who had by now seen several years of fighting under Piccinino. Federigo came home and made forays into Malatesta territory by way of reprisal.

For some time Sigismondo's troops had held the little town of San Leo which, with its surmounting fortress, occupies a sheer and jagged crag near San Marino, a site of such romantic inaccessibility that it suggests an illustration to a fairy-tale more than a place where workaday people would make their homes. It was commonly assumed to be impregnable.

Federigo was persuaded that it could be taken. He had in his company an enterprising fellow named Matteo Grifone, a miller who later found a more congenial career as a commander in the Venetian service. Grifone was confident that, given twenty volunteers of the right sort, he could climb over the town wall at night and secure the foothold essential to victory. Federigo let him try. Helped by a rainy black night, the little party crept up the lower slopes with scaling-ladders, which they fitted together and placed against the ramparts. Even then it was evidently a daunting climb, for the story speaks of only one man going up the ladders with Grifone, and the rest waiting to be admitted through the gate. Grifone and his companion stole through the silent town. Chains customarily dangled outside the house doors. Their purpose is obscure: they could have been either for the tethering of beasts or, as was sometimes done, the barring of the narrow lanes to charging horsemen. Whatever their true function, Grifone used them to fasten the dormant citizens inside their own homes.

There was still the citadel, perched on the summit above another cincture of ramparts. Its garrison knew nothing until daybreak. Then, peering down as Federigo's trumpets suddenly sang out in triumph, they saw the town full of his banners as his main forces marched in. Of resistance there was neither sign nor sound, since the townsmen could not escape from their houses. The garrison mistakenly concluded that the whole place had willingly gone over to the enemy, an impression strengthened by their finding, when they sallied down to the upper gates of the town, that those gates were barred against themselves. Discouraged, they surrendered the citadel without striking a blow.

A few months after this victory, Federigo lost his father. Oddantonio succeeded to the Montefeltro possessions and was soon undeservedly advanced by Pope Eugenius to the rank of duke. He proved an unpopular and inefficient ruler, with a cruel streak and lascivious instincts. Sigismondo is credited with a subtle scheme to influence him, through his advisers, and indirectly encourage him to excesses that would provoke a revolution and pave the way for Sigismondo himself to take over Urbino. Things worked out rather differently.

The young duke did indeed make himself insufferable. A conspiracy was formed. Early on the morning of 22 July 1444, after two and a half years of misgovernment, Oddantonio and some of his cronies were assassinated in his own hall. 'The duke,' wrote one of the chroniclers, 'was killed by the citizens because he showed scant respect for their wives either by night or by day.'

Federigo had all this time been continuing his work as defender of the family territories. He was miles away down on the coast at Pesaro and the news was broken to him by the Bishop of Urbino, who intimated that the people wished him to take over the government but on the clear understanding that matters would be managed very differently in the future. That suited Federigo. The conception of some sort of social contract at the outset of his reign was quite inoffensive to one educated in the ideals of Vittorino da Feltre. He mounted and rode hurriedly to Urbino. He was not allowed to pass the gates until he had sworn to grant a general amnesty. Then he sat down with the leading citizens and discussed their demands. Apart from those usual on such occasions – lower taxes, reform of local government, and the payment of ducal debts – there were several of special interest. A health service was to be instituted, with two doctors paid out of public funds and bound to attend all citizens. There was similar provision for a schoolmaster and one assistant teacher. Federigo was delighted to agree. The proposals were embodied in a proclamation issued a week later. Delegations streamed in from the outlying towns, offering homage, while congratulations – sincere and otherwise – arrived from neighbouring rulers. Federigo had inaugurated what was to prove the golden age of Urbino and make that obscure mountain principality famous in the annals of Renaissance culture.

He was just twenty-two and he had his life before him.

'To the Lord Federigo of Montefeltro,' wrote Sigismondo from Rimini on 21 February 1445.

> Mighty Lord, Your Lordship is aware of the long-standing difference between us, and, if you judge fairly, you will see that the fault lies on your side, not mine. Patience is not one of my virtues, and, so far from showing willingness to make amends for your errors, you increase them every day. You have again written libels against me to the court of Rome and provoked slanders against me. I am determined to tolerate it no longer but to prove myself your better, man, to man . . .

The letter went on to nominate Sigismondo's chancellor as his second and to offer a safe-conduct to any representative Federigo chose to send. It was signed, 'Sigismondo Pandolfo di Malatesta, Captain-General of the illustrious Count Francesco Sforza', the lord of Rimini being still in the service of his father-in-law.

Federigo accepted the challenge. A meeting was arranged under the walls of Pesaro, but for some reason Sigismondo did not keep the appointment. He was a bundle of contradictory qualities, now recklessly brave, now shamelessly fearful, quite unable to control his impulses. He would whip out his sword in argument, no matter where he was, but he did not subscribe to Federigo's conventional code of honour.

Soon afterwards Federigo accepted a *condotta* from the Florentines to fight for them against Naples. Alfonso promptly engaged Sigismondo to come and help him, paying an advance of 30,000 ducats. Sigismondo then stayed at home and used the money to finance his private inroads on the Montefeltro lands. In a plausible letter to the king he explained that this was the best strategy to make Federigo hurry back from the main front. Federigo characteristically continued his campaign for the Florentines, trusting his sturdy subjects to defend their native hills until he could return. Alfonso pointed this out to Sigismondo and suggested that he should now make his belated appearance in the war he had been paid to fight. Sigismondo did so, but on the wrong side, selling himself and his two thousand soldiers to Florence, which made him temporarily a colleague of Federigo's, to the latter's considerable disgust. When Federigo's engagement expired, he took a contract offered him by Sforza, who by then had just achieved the dukedom of Milan. Sigismondo did his best by various intrigues to prevent his father-in-law and his rival from becoming friends, but his own credit with Sforza had dwindled to vanishing-point.

In 1449 Polissena Sforza died. For years Sigismondo had neglected her. From the early days of their marriage he had been passionately in love with

Isotta degli Atti, a beautiful and charming Rimini girl who had captivated him at first sight. She was then only twelve. At thirteen she was carrying his child. He gloried in flaunting a relationship which could only humiliate his wife. With a far-sighted enthusiasm typical of the Renaissance, he began almost at once to design a superlative tomb that should one day be worthy to enclose his inamorata. But it was Polissena who needed a tomb long before Isotta. There were ugly rumours about the manner of her death, and twelve years later Francesco Sforza was quite explicit in a letter to Pius II.

'The said Lord Sigismondo', he wrote, 'had my daughter, his wife, strangled by Count Antonio with a napkin, for no fault of hers.' Sigismondo had then sent for a friar and ordered him to swear that he had heard Polissena's confession of adultery. When the friar refused to perjure himself, he had been cast down into an oubliette. Sforza assured the Pope that he had eyewitnesses to back this story. 'She was our daughter,' he wrote with feeling, 'our own flesh and blood.'

If Sigismondo did murder his legal wife, as most people came to believe, it was not to free himself for a marriage with Isotta. Of his devotion to her there is no doubt, though physical fidelity was a notion that would hardly have occurred to him and he continued to indulge his instincts in a variety of ways. Whatever affairs he had, and whether Polissena lived in neglect or rotted in an obscure grave, his real consort in the eyes of the world was 'the sweet and sovereign Isotta'. She was more than he deserved, beautiful, intelligent, and cultured, loyal and discreet, often using her diplomatic skill to smooth over the trouble caused by his outbursts, never deserting him even when his situation seemed beyond hope. What was good in him, this woman brought out. He poured forth poems to her, his courtiers joined in the chorus, and a whole anthology, *The Book of Isotta*, was compiled by his laureate, Basinio Parmense. In spite of all this, for years after Polissena's death, Sigismondo declined to marry again. In 1453 Isotta was writing to him on campaign in Tuscany, and, while accepting his protestations at their face value, concluding with the plea: 'I ask a favour of your lordship – marry me as soon as possible.' It was another three years before the favour was granted, and then so unobtrusively that some historians have doubted whether the ceremony ever took place.

Such perversity was in key with his character. He would proclaim his passion, he would entwine their initials in the badge, I.S., worn by his soldiers, and he would design for her that magnificent tomb, resting on the Malatesta elephants, which remains one of the outstanding features of the Tempio at Rimini – yet he was grudging in the matter of a simple wedding-ring. He himself cared nothing for the Church's blessing or indeed for

191, 192 Left: Isotta degli Atti, the girl with whom Sigismondo fell in love when she was only twelve, and to whom he remained faithful, in his fashion, for the rest of his life. Below left: a *putto* in the Tempio Malatestiano with the initials I and S intertwined.

193 Below: the castle of Rimini, begun by Sigismondo in 1437.

194 Bottom: transforming the old church of S. Francesco into Alberti's splendid new 'Tempio'.

Christianity, preferring the Neoplatonism of a recent Byzantine philosopher, Gemistus Plethon. His outstanding artistic monument, the Tempio, was pagan in inspiration, though he converted it out of an old Franciscan church, ransacking Ravenna and other sites for rare marbles, and enlisting the genius of Leon Battista Alberti, Matteo de' Pasti, and Agostino di Duccio to realize his dream.

His unorthodox views and the scandals of his private life furnished all the ammunition needed by his political enemies. He was formally denounced before Pius II in 1460. Federigo and Alessandro Sforza, Francesco's brother and now lord of Pesaro, were present in Rome that Christmas to add to the long list of charges. Sigismondo was accused, in absence, of everything from forgery and coining to blasphemy and heresy. He was said to have had one wife poisoned and the second strangled, to have committed incest with his daughter, to have raped numerous people of both sexes, and even on one much-quoted occasion to have violated the fresh corpse of a young German lady killed in the mêlée when her attendants resisted his attempt to abduct her.

How many of these fantastic stories were true? A proportion, no doubt, for it was a fantastic age and Sigismondo a fantastic character. But a knowledge of twentieth-century propaganda methods encourages scepticism. Sigismondo's unforgivable offence was political, his opposition to the Pope, and Pius had long been urging his representatives to concentrate on means to ruin this enemy. A show was made of an impartial inquiry, months were devoted to the leisurely judicial processes of the papal courts, but the result was a foregone conclusion: Sigismondo was found guilty on all counts, excommunicated, and condemned to be burnt at the stake as a heretic. Not unnaturally, the lord of Rimini declined to come to Rome for the ceremony, and the authorities had to make do with burning a handsomely robed effigy on the steps of St Peter's, labelled 'Here am I, Sigismondo Malatesta, son of Pandolfo, king of traitors, hated by God and man, condemned to the flames by sentence of the Sacred College.'

Against the flesh-and-blood Sigismondo, the Pope could only pursue his struggle by conventional means – with Federigo as his sword-arm.

The Duke of Urbino was the ideal person to pit against the lord of Rimini. He was much more than a traditionally hostile neighbour, he was by this time one of the most esteemed commanders in the whole of Italy. He was known as a man of honour, and, apart from a few marginal infidelities, his private life was unblemished. The begetting of a mere four bastards did not constitute any scandal in the eyes of his contemporaries, but was accepted as reassuring evidence of a popular gentleman's vitality.

His first wife, Gentile, had died in 1457 after twenty years of childless marriage. In 1460 he married Battista, the daughter of Alessandro Sforza, who in the next twelve years provided him with a family of seven. She had lost her mother early and had spent much of her childhood at the court of her uncle in Milan. There she had shared in the warm and stimulating family life of the Sforzas – the duke and duchess liked children to be heard as well as seen, there was much acting and reciting and speechifying, and the bed-time appearance to say 'good night' was no unwelcome formality. It was Francesco Sforza who suggested the betrothal when Battista was only thirteen, a petite figure apt to astound distinguished guests by greeting them with fluent Latin orations. The wedding followed at Urbino a year later, Federigo being then thirty-seven. Battista contributed much more besides pattering footsteps – her cultured background and practical ability helped her husband immeasurably in transforming a minor court into one famous throughout Europe. Battista's tragedy was that all her first children were girls and she obviously wore herself out in childbed to provide the boy, Guidobaldo, who was born only five months before her untimely death. 'Being both of them resolved to leave nothing untried,' wrote the Abbot Baldi, 'on the recommendation of competent physicians they unceasingly made use of powerful remedies, calculated to invigorate them and to supply, as far as practicable, the defects of nature.' It was fever that carried her off – Federigo, far away, rode night and day through the July heat and reached her side just in time – but it is hard to

195 Battista Sforza, niece of Francesco, who became the second wife of Federigo of Urbino in 1460.

196 Federigo delighted in the new learning of the humanists. Here he and his young son Guidobaldo attend a lecture in the Ducal Palace.

escape the conclusion that seven, possibly eight, pregnancies by the age of twenty-six had weakened her.

Apart from her family responsibilities Battista had to run the government of the Montefeltro territories during her husband's periodical absences. Federigo was a condottiere not solely from choice but also from necessity: His miniature state measured only forty miles by forty. It was a rugged, poverty-stricken land. Sombre pine-forests climbed the mountain-sides, woods of oak and chestnut clothed the lower slopes, and seasonal torrents carved their way down through narrow valley-bottoms to the sea. There was nothing valuable to mine and no easy livelihood for the peasant. Military service was the invisible export that balanced the budget.

So for thirty-four years, with hardly an interlude, Federigo earned a continual income to finance his government, his court, and the artistic projects dear to him. Much of the money went straight to his soldiers and so filtered back to the individual households in his duchy. In that period he served as Captain-General to three Popes, two Kings of Naples, two Dukes of Milan, the republic of Florence, and several alliances. He had a life-pension from Naples for past services, and the allied command he held at the end of his life brought him 165,000 ducats when on active service and a retainer of 65,000 ducats a year in time of peace. Venice he never fought for, but in that final year the Most Serene Republic offered him 80,000 ducats merely to keep out of the contest. He declined, and, when someone showed surprise, he explained: 'Keeping faith is better still, and worth more than all the gold in the world.' Not only cash but symbolic honours were showered upon him. The Pope awarded him the Golden Rose, Naples gave him the Order of the Ermine, far away in England Edward IV conferred the Garter. He was Gonfalonier of the Church, bearing the white banner of the Papacy with its crossed gold keys.

He took pleasure in those honours. He had their emblems, the Ermine, the Garter, and the rest, embodied in the carvings that adorned his new palace at Urbino. The architect was Luciano Laurana, who used a creamy limestone from his native Dalmatia, producing a palace of noble staircases and elegant salons with gilded doors, carpets and brocades. Loggias and windows commanded panoramic views of looming Monte Carpegna, the twin points of the Sassi di Simeone, the triple peaks of San Marino, and the rest of that craggy amphitheatre soaring to five thousand feet and higher.

To the left of the great courtyard was his beloved manuscript library, its tall windows admitting a cool northern light, its inlaid armchairs inviting the reader. Federigo was an avid book-collector, but he loved literature even more, and if he could not buy the volume he coveted he would settle for a copy. He had thirty-four transcribers on his pay-roll in Florence and other cities. His biographer, Vespasiano, records: 'I compared the catalogue with those he had obtained from other libraries, the Vatican, Florence, St Mark's, Pavia, down to the University of Oxford in England, and I found that all the others had deficiencies and duplicates.' Federigo insisted on perfect copies, written on vellum and bound in crimson with silver clasps. He was himself a good Latinist. By welcoming refugee scholars from Constantinople, he made Urbino one of the earliest centres of Greek studies in the West.

No exaggerated reverence for ancient classics or Early Fathers lessened his encouragement of living writers, but he was unlucky in his patronage. No Petrarch or Boccaccio was drawn to his court, and his shelves collected more and more mediocre verses with fulsome dedications. His secretary, Angelo Galli, turned out three hundred and seventy-six poems and songs in Italian, but who remembers them? It was different with the artists he befriended. Piero della Francesca, Alberti, Pisanello, Justus of Ghent (who painted Federigo in his Garter robes) and others did good work at Urbino. Piero's pupil, Melozzo da Forlì, spent three years there.

Not only authors and artists buzzed round this honey-pot. The guests included men with the noblest names in Italy, Orsini, Colonna, Farnese, Doria, and della Rovere. Their boys were sent to Urbino as a school of manners. Federigo had to maintain an appropriate household. A list of his staff runs to three hundred and seventeen, including '4 transcribers of MSS for the library' and '5 readers during meals', and ending with '1 keeper of the camelopard'. Battista had her separate entourage, with '6 staid and elderly gentlemen' and numerous other attendants, no doubt equally indispensable.

Federigo's routine, when at home, is vividly preserved in Vespasiano's biography. It tells how in summer the duke loved to be in the saddle at dawn, riding out into the country with a handful of friends and unarmed servants, and returning when others were just waking up. He would hear Mass and then sit in the garden until breakfast-time, available to all comers. Later, he might go down into the town, strolling informally through the streets, diving into shops and workrooms for a chat, pausing to discuss some unfinished house with the builder, or joking with the peasants in the market. He put on no airs, but treated high and low with equal courtesy, doffing his cap so often that his nephew, Ottaviano Ubaldini, told a bustling friend that he was 'as busy as Federigo's bonnet'. Soldiers

197 The intarsia panelling of his 'studiolo' reflects Federigo's range of interests. Everything seen here is represented in cunning perspective on a flat wall. The duke himself appears extreme right.

on parade were addressed as 'gentlemen' or 'honoured brothers'. Even on ceremonial occasions the duke would break through protocol with some friendly inquiry.

A ruler, he believed, should set an example. Once he discovered that a trader was in difficulties because of the money owed to him by various important customers, including the ducal household. 'Sue me,' said Federigo. It was difficult to convince the man that he meant it, and then to find an officer willing to serve the summons. But it was arranged, and as Federigo came out of his palace he was duly accosted and cited to appear before the magistrate next day. He thereupon beckoned the master of his household and said distinctly, for all to hear: 'Please give instructions so that I don't have to spend every day attending this tribunal or that.' The hint was not wasted on Urbino society. Similarly, wishing to reduce brawls, he asked the *podestà* to ban the carrying of swords in the town. He arranged to encounter the town-crier just as the proclamation was being made. 'Our *podestà* must have a good reason,' he said, 'and it is only right that he should be obeyed,' whereupon he unbuckled his sword and sent it back to the palace by a servant, his companions having no choice but to imitate him. He was a man of sly good humour, which he used to talk his subjects out of unreasonable demands and intolerant attitudes, rather than apply the weight of his authority.

He took an interest in everybody. He paid regular visits to the convent of Santa Chiara and would have long talks through the grating with the old Mother Superior, asking after the welfare of her nuns. In the cool of the evening he liked to go down to the field and watch the boys of his court at their games, chatting to them between the wrestling bouts and other events. Then, after supper, all business done and the last audience granted, he would retire to winter fireside or summer loggia overlooking the blue bowl of twilit valley, and there relax with his intimate friends, talking of books and art and affairs. 'To hear him converse with a sculptor', it was said, 'you would have thought he was a master of the craft.' Vittorino would have been proud of his pupil and of what he had done with the broad education given him long ago in Mantua. Castiglione, whose classic book is based on the life of the court as it continued under Duke Guidobaldo in the same cultured and humane manner, pays tribute to Federigo 'of glorious memory, who in his day was the light of Italy'.

In 1462 'the light of Italy' had to come down from the ivory towers of Urbino and deal with 'the disgrace of Italy', as Pope Pius described the newly excommunicated Sigismondo, who 'surpassed all barbarians in cruelty' and deserved to be 'enrolled as a citizen of Hell'.

This unflattering view of Sigismondo was not unanimously held. There were those still glad to do business with him. One such was Jacopo Piccinino, the thoroughly shifty son of the famous Niccolò. Working for the Angevins, who refused to relinquish their hopes of recovering Naples, Piccinino subcontracted the lord of Rimini to move down the Adriatic coast and invade the most northerly part of the Regno. Federigo reacted promptly. Making forced marches through the August heat, he intercepted Sigismondo at Senigallia, arriving just an hour too late to prevent the surrender of the city. The Malatesta forces had not even moved in, but were still in the entrenched camp from which they had besieged it. Nonplussed by Federigo's swift appearance, Sigismondo made diplomatic overtures, suggesting that it would better suit the interests of Urbino if Rimini, rather than Rome, controlled Senigallia. Federigo retorted that this was not a point he could very well discuss, since he was acting not as ruler of Urbino but as Captain-General to Pius II.

Sigismondo did not care to risk a battle, weary though Federigo's troops must have been, after marching thirty miles. He did not even fancy being besieged in the town he had just taken. Accordingly, just before midnight, he quietly struck camp and began to retreat along the Fano road, assisted by the light of a full moon. He assumed that, even if Federigo was wakened with news of the manœuvre, he could not possibly get his troops on the move before daybreak.

He underestimated the toughness and resilience of his opponent. How tough Federigo was is indicated by his continual triumph over wounds, accidents, and illnesses. He might lose an eye and break his nose in a tournament, wrench his back riding so that he fought one battle swathed in bandages and unable to put on his armour, break an ankle and nearly lose a leg from gangrene after the collapse of a balcony, sustain various wounds and suffer several bouts of malaria, yet he remained an energetic commander until he died on active service at the age of sixty.

On that summer's night at Senigallia he did not hesitate for an instant. He mustered a small party and rode off in pursuit, ordering the main body to follow as soon as possible. Some of his officers suggested that he was taking a chance. He pointed out that it had been in this same neighbourhood, under closely parallel conditions, that Claudius Nero had followed and annihilated the army of Hannibal's brother, Hasdrubal. An apt classical reference was the surest way to clinch an argument in that book-respecting society. Without further demur, they galloped on beside the moonlit sea.

They caught up with the enemy rearguard at the Cesano, one of the many little rivers that crossed their road to enter the Adriatic. This slightly spoilt the classical parallel – it was the next river, the Metauro, that had witnessed the defeat of the Carthaginians. Federigo, however, was no pedant. He sounded a trumpet to let Sigismondo know he was coming, and his opponent, confident that he had only a small advance-guard to deal with, swung round to give battle. He had miscalculated again. They were still only three or four miles from Senigallia, and, while the Malatesta forces took up their positions along the river, Federigo's were continually arriving to join their leader. As soon as he felt that he had enough, Federigo made a determined charge across the dried-up river-bed. Sigismondo's unready forces broke in confusion. Daybreak found them straggling along the northward road, Sigismondo himself in flight to Fano and his bastard son, Roberto, later a condottiere of some achievement, taking refuge in the castle of Mondolfo.

This was the beginning of the end for Sigismondo. Within little more than a year Federigo had overrun most of his territory. The Angevins would give Sigismondo no more financial backing, only the Venetians still foresaw a use for him. They hired him some supply vessels, and escorted them with their own galleys, so that he could send provisions to Roberto, who had by this time taken over the defence of Fano, completely blockaded by Federigo on the landward side. These supplies did not affect the issue. Federigo stormed the town. Roberto retired to the citadel with his sisters and mother, Vanetta Toschi, Sigismondo's mistress before the days of Isotta. The women, knowing Federigo's chivalrous reputation, persuaded Roberto to surrender. Sure enough, though the other captains and the Papal Legate urged Federigo to hold them as hostages, he insisted on letting them all go free, Roberto included. He escorted them personally to the harbour and watched them sail away to join Sigismondo in Rimini. Prudently, however, they told the captain to alter course and made for Ravenna.

Sigismondo was down but not quite out. If there was one enemy the Pope hated more, it was the Turks. Pius was near his end and longed to realize his dream of a crusade against the infidel, still triumphantly installed in Constantinople ten years after its capture. He was in haste to settle the internal quarrels of Italy so that a united front could be created, and he was prepared to stop short of Sigismondo's complete annihilation. Sigismondo skilfully encouraged this mood of compromise by making it clear that, if he was shown no mercy at all, he was prepared to offer his remaining territory as a bridge-head for an invasion by the Turks and even to fight on their side.

A settlement was agreed. Sigismondo was stripped of all his territories except Rimini. He was to recant his heresy publicly in Rome and admit all

321

his crimes. He finally wriggled out of this extreme humiliation by sending a proxy to speak for him in St Peter's, but he could not avoid making the declaration in person at Rimini in front of his own subjects, kneeling before the high altar of the cathedral.

Oddly enough, when all had been said, it was only he who went off to fight the Turks. The Venetians were the one major power with a selfish practical interest in the crusade. They tried to hire Federigo and Colleoni, who both declined, and had to offer the command to Sigismondo. He signed a two-year *condotta* at 300 ducats a month and received the blessing of the dying Pope, who could find no one else to bless. For those two years, 1464 and 1465, Sigismondo fought creditably in Greece, where he captured Sparta from Omar Bey and only just failed to take the old Byzantine

198 Sigismondo's son, Roberto (below) was a condottiere in his own right; he succeeded to the lordship of Rimini and married a daughter of Federigo.

199 Sigismondo Malatesta died in 1468 and was buried, as he wished, in the Tempio Malatestiano. This relief is from his tomb. His last years had been spent fighting the Turks on behalf of a pope who did not trust him.

capital, Mistra. But the odds were against him and his successes transitory. He sailed home with little to show for the expedition except the bones of his favourite Neoplatonist philosopher, Gemistus Plethon, which he buried in Rimini cathedral to the scandal and vexation of the godly.

For all his enforced shows of repentance, he was still the same Sigismondo. Summoned to Rome, he found that the new pontiff, Paul II, was as much his enemy as the last. Paul asked him to surrender even his own city of Rimini, exchanging it for the unimportant inland town of Foglino. Sigismondo's passionate reaction was a resolve to kill the Pope at their next interview, smuggling his weapon into the audience-chamber under a black velvet cloak. This was prevented by a significant postponement of the meeting, and, realizing that he was suspected, he wisely abandoned the idea. In the end, by humbling himself completely, he was allowed to keep Rimini.

He died there on 9 October 1468, aged fifty-one. The Pope tried to take over the territory, but Roberto Malatesta moved faster. There was some fighting with the papal forces but they no longer had Federigo's leadership. This time Federigo owed Rome no allegiance and was free to consult the interests of Urbino. He quite liked Roberto and did not wish the Pope's power to grow stronger in that neighbourhood. He threw in his weight on Roberto's side, and Rimini remained under the banner of a Malatesta.

200 Federigo da Montefeltro passed his life as a condottiere, earning in this way the money that he spent on his palace at Urbino. This miniature shows him on active service before the besieged city of Volterra.

Much had happened elsewhere during those closing years of Sigismondo's life. Jacopo Piccinino had married one of Sforza's illegitimate daughters, Drusiana, but soon afterwards, in 1465, while on a mission to Naples had been treacherously murdered by Alfonso's successor, King Ferrante, an act which infuriated Sforza and did nothing to improve his ever-uneasy relations with the House of Aragon. But in the following year, on 8 March, Sforza himself died at the age of sixty-five after only two days' illness. The dukedom he had secured by such long and determined efforts was held fast for his son, Galeazzo Maria, by the decisive action of Bianca. She rose to the emergency despite shock and passionate grief and took control of a difficult situation until her son could hasten back, incognito and at great risk, from his service with the King of France. A third event which demands mention was the Battle of Molinella on 25 July 1467, which brought old Colleoni into the field for the last time and pitted him against Federigo.

This was a gentlemanly affair between two of the most punctilious condottieri, a fact which misled Machiavelli in later years to ridicule the battle as one in which two mercenary armies buffeted each other for hours without a single fatal casualty. In fact, some hundreds were killed on both sides, and Federigo might easily have been one of them. He led the first charge himself, lance in rest, supported by his future son-in-law, Giovanni della Rovere, and was brought down by an enemy foot-soldier, who got under his horse and gave it a mortal gash. Federigo was rescued with some difficulty. The fighting went on for hours. It was intensely hot and both armies had previously marched some distance. Darkness was falling and it was obvious that no one was going to score a decisive victory. Trumpets sounded for an interval, and it was quickly agreed to call it a day. Colleoni's troops resumed the pitching of their camp, which they had begun before Federigo attacked them, and this enabled them to claim a technical success, since it was Federigo's men who quitted the field to set up their tents three miles away. Before Federigo himself rode off to his supper, he advanced into the light of Colleoni's camp-fires and shook hands warmly with his opponent. As the whole affair had been prompted by Florentine exiles trying to upset the Medici régime, and the interests of other states were not so deeply involved as to make it worth upsetting the peace of Italy, the two commanders felt they had satisfied their consciences and the campaign was allowed to peter out without a return match.

For fifteen years after that – fourteen years after the death of his old rival, Sigismondo – Federigo held first place among the condottieri still active in Italy. His last war was fought in 1482.

In April of that year he was given a three-year *condotta* to defend Ferrara against Venice and Pope Sixtus IV. Federigo became Captain-General of a combined force contributed by Florence, Naples, Milan, Mantua, and

201 Roberto di Sanseverino was one of the condottieri employed by Venice and Pope Sixtus IV against the Florentine forces led by Federigo. The scene here is his wedding to a girl of noble family in Siena.

Bologna. The enemy, having vainly tried to secure his services, made do with Roberto Malatesta, now his son-in-law, and another much-esteemed condottiere, Roberto di Sanseverino. The young Malatesta, however, went south to defend Rome against the Neapolitan forces under the Duke of Calabria, so that he was not directly involved in fighting Federigo.

The latter rode out of Urbino for the last time accompanied, for the first few miles, by a whole band of his literary and artistic friends. There was an under-current of concern for him. How much longer could the elderly warrior go on like this? Yet Federigo's spirit and ability seemed unimpaired. When he turned to his nephew, Ottaviano, and charged him with the protection of his young heir, Guidobaldo, it was no more than the sensible precaution of any soldier leaving for a distant front.

Lorenzo de' Medici came as far as Sansepolcro to meet him. At Florence itself, where he was gratefully remembered for past victories, the magistrates turned out to welcome him at the doors of the Palazzo Vecchio. Civilities were showered upon him, but it was a different matter when he reached the theatre of war and appealed for the reinforcements vital to his task. Neither Florence nor Milan would give him enough troops. Sanseverino was besieging Ficarolo, the last town masking Ferrara itself fifteen miles away, and there was a danger that he would link up with a fleet of five hundred shallow-draught boats which the Venetians were sending up the Po to join him. All that Federigo could do was to occupy La Stellata, the fortress on the other side of the river from Ficarolo, and bide his time.

That summer malaria decimated the armies. Federigo himself had an attack but recovered. Seeing no immediate hope of taking offensive action, he moved most of his troops to a healthier spot, and remained in La Stellata with only a token force of four hundred men. Soon the fever left only a tenth of these fit for duty, and nothing but his iron will made Federigo one of them. He was begged to transfer his headquarters to a villa in Ferrara that had been made ready for him. Characteristically he refused. But early in September he had a relapse and sensed that this was the end. His mind was clear to the last. He made his final military dispositions and formally resigned his command, at the same time submitting suggestions for a safe withdrawal. On 10 September he died, fortified – it was no empty phrase in his case – by the last rites of the Church in which he believed.

Roberto Malatesta had just died at Rome after scoring a victory for the other side. His wife, Elisabetta, heard of his death and of her father's on the same day, and retired grief-stricken into a nunnery. The life of a condottiere might be hard, but that of his womenfolk could be even harder.

The last of the Condottieri 21

At one corner of the Piazza San Lorenzo in Florence, aloof above the gay-canopied stalls and the parked cars, sits Baccio Bandinelli's statue of Giovanni de' Medici, variously designated in his own day as 'the Invincible', as 'Italy's Giovanni' and, most often of all, as 'Giovanni of the Black Bands' – Giovanni delle Bande Nere. Had his contemporaries but realized it, they might have given him yet another label, 'the Last of the Condottieri'.

He was born on 6 April 1498. Four months later, Columbus caught his first glimpse of the American mainland. That coincidence of dates is merely a convenient reminder that Giovanni was born just as one historical epoch was drawing to a close. There were other factors, more immediately obvious and relevant than the discovery of the New World, that brought an end to the era of the condottieri. The development of a more effective artillery and a more disciplined infantry reduced the role of the armoured knight who had so long dominated the Italian battlefield, and the political changes in the peninsula meant that there was no market for the free-lance general, selling his services to any one of half a dozen or more independent republics and duchies. That Italy died finally with the Sack of Rome in 1527. Giovanni delle Bande Nere's short and colourful life coincides precisely with this closing phase.

Of all the Medici he was the only one who took to soldiering. So far as heredity and upbringing are concerned, it is far more significant that his mother was a Sforza – Caterina, granddaughter of the great Francesco and a handsome, passionate 'virago' in the family tradition. She was three times married, first to Count Girolamo Riario, son of Pope Sixtus IV, then (after his assassination) to the son of her own castellan at her home in Forlì, and finally (after the murder of this second husband) to Giovanni de' Medici. This Giovanni belonged to the junior branch of that famous house, being descended from Cosimo's brother. His more illustrious

327

relatives had just been expelled from Florence in the 1494 uprising. On all counts the political advantages of Caterina's marriage were not obvious, yet quite unpredictably the child born of it, another Giovanni, our Giovanni delle Bande Nere, was to be the Medici who carried on the dynasty and the ancestor of all those Grand Dukes who ruled in Florence until the eighteenth century. Caterina's husband did no more than beget the child and unknowingly transmit the great inheritance: the future condottiere was only four months old when his father was taken ill at Pisa and left Caterina, at thirty-five, a widow for the third and last time.

That was the summer in which Cesare Borgia renounced the priesthood and the cardinal's hat bestowed on him by his father, Alexander VI, and entered upon a more congenial career as a soldier, his first plan being to subdue the once papal, now virtually independent, cities of Romagna and weld them into a dukedom for himself. Forlì was on his list. Caterina defied him and defended the town in the true Sforza way. Finally she tried to blow herself up with the powder-magazine, but this heroic gesture did not come off, and Cesare took her prisoner, sending her to Rome to the Castel Sant'Angelo. Giovanni, by this time eighteen months old, had long before been lodged in a place of safety with a Medici uncle outside Florence.

He was three when his mother returned to him, prematurely grey and aged by the harsh treatment she had endured in Rome. She now made her home in the Villa di Castello, one of the Medici houses overlooking the city, set about with woods and gardens, a property which she claimed through her last husband but finally secured only after a long battle in the law-courts. At one stage she was driven out and took lodging in a convent. Later still, the little Giovanni had to spend his ninth year with the nuns, dressed as a girl and sharing lessons with the real girls, to conceal his whereabouts from his father's brother, a 'wicked uncle' of story-book villainy. As Caterina had lost two husbands by assassination, and suffered appalling hardships herself, she wisely took no chances.

The year with the nuns was but an interlude. The boy's education until he was eleven was otherwise entirely in Caterina's hands – and there was nothing effeminate about it.

She was well equipped to serve as both mother and father. No one could have questioned her womanly attributes: before her incarceration in the Castel Sant'Angelo she had been renowned for her beauty and she took care of her fine complexion to the end of her life. In her last year she added a new formula for a face-lotion to her private book of recipes, which included everything from sunburn remedies to abortifacients and slow-working poisons. She was a good needlewoman, kept careful household

202, 203 Giovanni de' Medici,
'Giovanni delle Bande Nere' (above),
sprang from a union of the two most
powerful families in Italy. His father
was descended from Cosimo de'
Medici's brother. His mother (right)
was Caterina Sforza, granddaughter
of Francesco. Giovanni was the only
Medici to become a condottiere and,
as it proved, was to be the last of his
profession.

accounts, danced gracefully, and spoke with charming eloquence, which only degenerated into a tirade when she lost her temper. Her three husbands (and certain others, it was rumoured) could have testified that she was well endowed with the normal feminine instincts. At the same time, she was a Sforza, and when the occasion called for a man she would appear in armour, sword in hand. Once, with a conspiracy to put down, she galloped through the night like any soldier, though she was far gone in pregnancy at the time.

It delighted her that Giovanni was growing up a Sforza too, 'all fire, arms and horses', not loans and ledgers (she might have added) like the Medici. The fire was in his temperament. He was headstrong and unmanageable, not surprisingly after such a disturbed childhood, but the warmth was in his heart too, for he was affectionate and open-handed. He adored this firm but essentially approving mother. Only she could handle him. The earlier children who survived had long been out of her care and were now grown up. Giovanni, only child of her last marriage, seemed like an only child in the fuller sense. All her hopes were centred on him, but she did not mean him to be spoilt.

He rode, he swam, he revelled in every type of physical exercise and weapon-training suited to his years. She went to great pains to get him the best tutors possible, though she was a poor woman relatively – she had sold her jewels to meet the legal costs of her battle over the villa – and she could not offer high pay or future prospects. Few people shared her own blind faith that one day this boy would command armies and rule a state, and that therefore it was a duty to educate him for the task.

Giovanni delighted in riding and swordsmanship, the traditional knightly skills, but he grew up well aware that great battles were won now by other means. Alberico da Barbiano's belief in the cavalry charge must now be qualified, the quibbles of the Sforzeschi and the Bracceschi had become almost irrelevant. The later condottieri had had to come to terms with gunpowder. They were now expected to capture fortified places which earlier commanders would have left alone. Federigo had attached great importance to his siege artillery. In 1478 his dispatches to the councillors of Siena were full of requests. The powder sent was 'not fit to be fired . . . let me have as soon as possible some that will do the business'. And again, 'there being hereabouts great scarcity of stones for the bombard, I send your lordships the measure of its height, from which you can have them prepared, since you have the diameter'. The bombard may have been the one cast by a bell-founder, Pietro of Siena, which had a barrel nine feet long and fired stone cannon-balls weighing three hundred and seventy-five pounds. These guns had fanciful names, like 'the Cruel',

204 The old style of warfare changed completely with the development of heavy artillery, first employed on Italian soil at the Battle of Marignano in 1515.

'the Desperate', and 'None of Your Jaw'. Such monsters required long lines of draught animals to shift them, and another of Federigo's letters appealed for all the buffaloes and bullocks in the neighbourhood to be commandeered for the purpose. Despite all their comic and tragic break-downs, the guns worked. Giovanni's mother could assure him of that from bitter experience, remembering how Forlì had gone down before Cesare Borgia's bombardment.

Such artillery could not be used in mobile warfare, but gradually the problem of lighter fire-arms was being overcome. Colleoni himself is credited with the invention of a small cannon, mounted on a carriage, and firing balls not much larger than a walnut. He used these against Federigo at Molinella. But the Italians witnessed the full dreadful power of massed field-guns only in 1515 at Marignano, when the French artillery cut bloody swathes through the Swiss pikemen. Giovanni, by then a youth of seventeen, obsessed with military matters, must have heard and pondered the full details of that encounter.

The hand-gun or arquebus was another innovation now well estab-lished. Bembo, writing in Venice in 1490, mentioned imports of this weapon from Germany. The government appointed instructors to towns and villages throughout the republic. Annual shoots were arranged and prizes offered, as in England in the heyday of the longbow.

331

Such weapons would, for generations, remain short in range, inaccurate in aim, and perilously slow to reload. Useful though they were, they could not by themselves repel the onslaught of determined troops using cold steel. At Marignano the Swiss kept up the struggle for a day and a half against a combination of cannon, arquebusiers, armoured knights, and mercenary pikemen rather like themselves, their hated rivals, the *landsknechte* from Germany. The Swiss had neither cavalry nor guns. They lost twenty thousand men, but they did not break until the French king was joined by his Venetian allies at sunset on the second day. That was another lesson not lost on Giovanni. He, more than any of the preceding condottieri, grasped the potentialities of good infantry.

It was for other reasons outside his control that he was the last of his profession. It was not that he – or, for that matter, Colleoni or Federigo before him – was unadaptable or blind to technical change. All three demonstrated that they had open minds. It was rather because the future wars in Italy were to be larger in scale and waged by foreign invaders striving for a knock-out victory. The change had really begun just before Giovanni was born, when Charles VIII of France swept down the peninsula, his troops shocking the Italians because they fought to kill, not to earn ransom-money. The future lay with such Frenchmen, with the ferocious *landsknechte* from Bavaria, Tyrol, and the other Teutonic regions, and with the Spanish pikemen whom Gonzalo de Cordoba forged into the finest military weapon sixteenth-century Europe knew. The long subjugation of Italy to the foreigner had begun. Soon only

332

205, 206, 207 The improvement of guns spelt the end of the condottiere system. These three illustrations show early examples of the new weapons.

Far left: troops using the arquebus at the Battle of Pavia in 1525. The men in the foreground are reloading.

Left: heavy cannon being employed against a fortified city, from a textbook on warfare published in 1521.

Right: German *landsknechte* fighting the Swiss in the early 1530s.

Venice, aloof in her corner, would remain of the old truly independent powers. Emperors and kings would still use mercenaries, even the Popes would hire Swiss halberdiers for their bodyguard, but the true condottiere, the commander with his own small army under contract, would have no place in the new scheme.

This change was much harder to grasp than the mere technical innovations. Giovanni could scarcely be blamed for not seeing something which in fact, while he lived, was not an inevitable development. He had no reason to doubt, as he grew up, that a long career as a soldier of fortune lay before him.

Caterina died when he was eleven. She appointed as his guardians Jacopo Salviati and his wife, Lucrezia. Salviati belonged to one of the leading Florentine families and Lucrezia's father had been Lorenzo the Magnificent. They had a palazzo in the centre of the city and a small daughter, Maria, a year younger than Giovanni. The two children were brought up like brother and sister, but their eventual marriage was probably planned from the start.

The Medici fortunes, lately in eclipse, were shining brightly again. The mild republican government which had ruled Florence since the death of Savonarola had displeased the bellicose Pope Julius II and he encouraged the restoration of the Medici exiles. The Florentines objected. They mobilized their civic militia. Machiavelli had a touching faith in this kind of force and believed it could prevail against rude soldiery who fought

333

only for pay. He was wrong. The militia were routed by Spanish pikemen at Prato, eleven miles away, and Florence made no more resistance. Lorenzo's son, Giuliano, entered the city in triumph. Giovanni thought it 'a fine sight'. He could share whole-heartedly in the rejoicings. Was he not a distant cousin of Giuliano's – and was not this new ruler of Florence the brother of Lucrezia Salviati? And another, even greater, triumph for the Medici family was on its way. Within a few months Julius II was dead, and Lucrezia's other brother (confusingly enough, yet one more Giovanni de' Medici) was elevated to the throne as Pope Leo X. 'God has given us the Papacy, let us enjoy it,' he told Giuliano. That sentiment was probably general throughout the family.

Meanwhile, the young orphan grew to manhood in the Palazzo Salviati, lively, quick-tempered, increasingly absorbed in military interests. He brawled with a more experienced swordsman and wounded him. For this misdemeanour he was rusticated by the authorities and forbidden for a time to come within twenty miles of Florence. His guardian used part of this period to take him on a journey to Rome and Naples. Back in Florence, at the age of sixteen, he made his début in one of the spectacular tournaments for which the Piazza Santa Croce provided so perfect a setting. He distinguished himself with a run of victories. It is possible now to picture him as described by his biographer, Gian Girolamo Rossi, his half-sister's son. He was of more than average height, muscular, broad-shouldered and narrow-waisted. Of fresh complexion, he had fine features recalling those of his remarkable mother.

In the following year, 1515, Pope Leo called his kinsman to Rome. Leo was enjoying his papacy as he had intended. Surrounded by poets and other writers, by musicians and artists of every kind, he was brightening the atmosphere of the Vatican with the grace of Medicean Florence. Whether all this culture made much appeal to Giovanni is doubtful. What he wanted was a military commission.

He had not long to wait. Leo had a scheme to install his brother as ruler of Urbino as well as Florence. Since the death of Duke Federigo, that happy little mountain-city had suffered more than one violent change of possession and had become a regular award to papal relatives. First, Federigo's son, the invalid Guidobaldo, had been driven out by Cesare Borgia, only to return on the crest of a popular insurrection. On his early death, the duchy had passed to his nephew, Francesco Maria della Rovere, who enjoyed the additional advantage of being nephew to the new Pope, Julius II. Now Julius was dead and Leo filled the apostolic throne. What more natural than to dispossess della Rovere and add Urbino to the domain of Giuliano de' Medici?

334

208 Maria Salviati, wife of Giovanni delle Bande Nere. It was their son, Cosimo, who was to become the first Grand Duke of Tuscany.

The ethics of the matter did not concern Giovanni. What he cared about was the first command, of one hundred cavalry, that he was now given in the army Giuliano led off into the mountains. The expedition proved to be little more than a pleasant springtime excursion. By the end of May della Rovere was in flight, and Giovanni and his comrades were riding up the hill into Urbino. The campaign had lasted just long enough for him to display his abilities, to make himself popular with his men, and to be allotted a larger command.

His marriage to Maria Salviati took place in the following November. They were eighteen and seventeen respectively, mature by the standards of their time. Maria was attractive in both appearance and character. Vasari, who knew her well, portrayed her in the Palazzo Vecchio. Her personality is enshrined in her letters, still preserved in the Florentine archives. They have been described as 'models of sense, wisdom, and the strongest affection'.

The marriage unfortunately involved a good deal of letter-writing, for Giovanni was now launched on the career he wanted, and he was seldom at home. 'Home' indeed continued to be the Palazzo Salviati in which the couple had grown up together. Giovanni had neither time nor money nor interest to expend on a suitable household of his own. He was back on active service at the first opportunity. Soon the Pope offered him a size-able command to mount an attack on the free city of Fermo. He took four thousand infantry and a mere handful of cavalry – a disproportion that would have astounded the condottieri of an earlier generation. But the operation was a success, and the report of that success, written in Giovanni's own bold hand, is also preserved in the archives in Florence.

He was twenty-one before Maria bore him the son, Cosimo, who was later to make himself the first Grand Duke of Tuscany. Entering the courtyard of the Palazzo Salviati one day, and seeing Maria with her baby looking down from a window, Giovanni insisted that the child be thrown down for him to catch, the idea being to inculcate fearlessness from an early age. The unfortunate mother protested but finally obeyed, and the experiment was conducted without mishap. Its ultimate effects are debatable. Cosimo was never famous for personal courage, never risked his skin in battle, and always surrounded himself with a bodyguard. Perhaps the lesson he learned as a baby, flying through the air, was not so much courage as the inadvisability of trusting people, even one's own mother.

That same year, 1519, saw the death of Giuliano de' Medici, leaving only a daughter, the future Catherine de' Medici. For the time being the government of Florence was carried on by an illegitimate Medici, that cardinal who later became Pope Clement VII. This failure of the male line on the senior side of the family turned many eyes upon the young condottiere. Though no strict rights of inheritance came into the matter, Giovanni could claim that he – apart from Pope Leo – was the foremost survivor of the house. Had he been more politically minded, he could have exploited the fact. But for the time being, at least, Giovanni had no thought for anything but his military career, and he took no steps to build up his position in Florence. That was left to Cosimo when he grew up.

The chief Italian theatre of war at this time was once again Lombardy. The French had held Milan since Francis I's hard-won victory at Marignano. Pope Leo made a bargain with the newly elected Emperor Charles V: the French were to be expelled, the Sforza dynasty restored. Giovanni was given command of a papal force, subordinate to an elderly, cautious, and conservative general, Prospero Colonna. The association led to friction, Giovanni's tactics being altogether too dashing – and successful. He won his first nickname, 'the Invincible', which did nothing to improve his relationship with Colonna. It was Giovanni who frustrated the French sorties from Parma, made a breach in the walls, and led the storming party, only to have his gains nullified by Colonna's insistence on a withdrawal. It was Giovanni who later threw the French into confusion by swimming the Adda with his entire force, each cavalryman helping a foot-soldier to cross the river. This achievement enabled the papal forces and their Imperial allies to move rapidly against Milan, which the French evacuated without a battle.

Leo was overjoyed, but Giovanni's contribution did not bring him the advancement he might have expected. The Pope, already unwell, caught

336

a chill during the victory celebrations and quickly died. It was then that Giovanni, bidding his troops wear mourning bands over their armour, acquired his permanent sobriquet, 'delle Bande Nere'.

He was right to mourn Leo. The next Pope was the Flemish mystic, Hadrian VI, who knew no Italian and had no interest in Italian affairs. Giovanni could hope for no employment from him. And when Hadrian died, after less than two years, he was succeeded by Cardinal Giulio de' Medici, who despite the distant relationship had no love for the young soldier. Indeed, just because of the relationship, and Giovanni's undeniable position in the family, the new Pope Clement would have preferred him dead.

Giovanni spent the short pontificate of Hadrian in reluctant idleness, keeping a large force together in camp at Reggio Emilia, sure that before long the French would be back in Lombardy. He had three thousand infantry, six guns, and only a small number of cavalry, paying them as best he could out of his own pocket. Only a dedicated soldier would have done it. Giovanni was prepared to give up everything else. Maria protested, but always ended by – metaphorically – dropping the baby over the balcony. Giovanni was idolized by his men. So long as he could offer them a minimum to live on, none wished to leave his service.

He paid short visits home to Maria, but he could not be absent from his headquarters for long. At Reggio, when not drilling his troops or supervising their welfare, he amused himself with sport and good company. Very likely it was during this interlude that he sat for Titian. All kinds of visitors were attracted to his camp, for his reputation had spread far and wide, even to England. Of all these guests the most congenial was Pietro Aretino, the satirist whose lubricious verses matched his life.

Pietro had just overstepped the mark. He had written an obscene sonnet-sequence to be printed with illustrations by Giulio Romano. *The Twenty-six Positions* proved a best-seller in Rome but led to the printer's imprisonment and the poet's hasty departure from the city. He arrived at Reggio and a firm friendship developed between him and Giovanni. The soldier delighted in his irreverent wit and named him 'the Scourge of Princes'. In return, the poet gave Giovanni an affection as genuine as any his cynical nature was capable of feeling. He encouraged him in loose living – not that Giovanni needed any extra encouragement, as poor Maria was well aware – but he respected and admired, almost worshipped, him as a military hero.

The peaceful interlude did not last long. Francis sent his troops back into Italy. The new Pope began by opposing them. He refused Giovanni a major command but could not avoid employing him. Giovanni harried the French with guerrilla attacks and won a new nickname, 'the Great Devil'. Clement heard of these exploits with mixed feelings. If the young man got himself killed, so much the better.

Dissatisfied with the poor success of his armies, Francis appeared in person with a large force and quickly occupied Milan. Clement changed sides and made a secret pact to help the French against the Emperor. Giovanni was part of the deal and was sent over, with his troops, to join the king he had been fighting. As a good condottiere, he was untroubled by the move. Francis showed him every possible honour and he was given a high place in the councils of the army. Giovanni presented his poet friend to the king, who was delighted with him and gave him generous presents. He too enjoyed literature and lechery.

As the winter drew to a close, Francis decided to move against Pavia, then held for the Emperor by an army of Spaniards and Germans. While on reconnaissance outside the city, Giovanni nearly met the fate that Clement desired for him. His right leg was broken by a shot from an arquebus. Just such a shot had killed the Chevalier Bayard, striking him in the spine, less than a year before. Giovanni was luckier, but even a leg-wound, in the then prevailing conditions of surgery, could easily have been fatal.

Fire-arms were destroying the old concepts of chivalry, yet something of the spirit remained. Genuinely distressed by this mischance to their late ally and current adversary – such things should not happen to gentlemen – the Emperor's generals begged Giovanni to accept a safe-conduct by boat down the river to Piacenza, where he could benefit from the skill of a famous Jewish doctor sent by the Marquis of Mantua. This courteous gesture probably saved his life. While he lay there, *hors de combat*, the Imperial forces surprised and annihilated the French at the Battle of Pavia. 'All is lost but life and honour,' lamented Francis as he was led away into captivity. But he always used to say, in after-years, that he would never have lost the battle if Giovanni had not been incapacitated only a week before.

While convalescent, Giovanni thought of little but keeping his troops together and fighting another day. His letters to Maria were full of requests that she should raise money 'to buy fresh horses, arms and equipment in Florence'. He could get no pay from Clement. Maria, her patience sorely strained, tried to make him face facts. 'There will be no Popes like those who are gone,' she wrote. 'Will you never cease to be at others' bidding, and return home and look to your own interests, now there is time? God alone knows the future. Think of Pope Leo, how he died without warning . . .' Yet having made her point, the loyal wife

338

travelled to Rome herself, saw Clement, and made him disgorge 6000 ducats which she forwarded to Giovanni for his men. The Pope also made him lord of Fano on the Adriatic coast.

Soon the war was resumed. Francis, having secured his release from captivity, broke his word and joined a fresh league against the Emperor. There seemed a chance that, if the states of Italy closed their ranks in time, the threat of Spanish domination might be averted. Machiavelli was urging such action in letters he wrote in March 1526. 'I think that, however things develop, war in Italy is inevitable – and soon. . . . We must make some resistance, concealed or open, or we shall wake up one morning and find it is all over.' He wanted to see Giovanni delle Bande Nere as supreme commander of an allied Italian army, for he was quite the best general available, 'brave, aggressive, with grand conceptions and able to appreciate great causes'. Machiavelli knew his man, and, however they might disagree on theories, the two got on well together. Bandello tells an anecdote about a visit by Machiavelli to Giovanni's camp. The men were training and Giovanni mischievously invited his guest to try out on the ground some of the formations he had described in *The Art of War*. The author accepted with delight, and in the course of the next hour reduced the troops to a chaos of puzzled and perspiring humanity, whereupon Giovanni tactfully intervened, murmuring that it was a very hot day and past dinner-time, unravelled the tangle with a few decisive orders, and quickly produced the disposition Machiavelli had been trying to achieve.

Clement still stubbornly refused to let Giovanni hold the supreme command. This went to Francesco della Rovere, that same Duke of Urbino whose brief expulsion, ten years before, had been the objective of Giovanni's first campaign. Once more the brilliance of the young condottiere was subordinated to the indecision and inefficiency of his superior. Giovanni's own command was a considerable one – he had under him all the papal and Florentine infantry, as well as a thousand cavalry – but there was not much he could do by himself. The Duke of Urbino was outgeneralled at every turn by the Constable of Bourbon, the renegade Frenchman commanding the Imperial forces. Those forces included many thousands of fierce German *landsknechte*, full of the new Lutheran ideas, breathing fire and slaughter against the Pope, whom their leader, Frundsberg, declared himself ready to hang with his own hands. Ideology was entering into warfare. Added to the growth of nationalism, it was yet another nail in the coffin of the condottiere system.

It was a *landsknecht* who fired the fatal shot which shattered Giovanni's right leg again. There had been four days of heavy fighting in bleak

November weather along the banks of the Mincio. On the fourth day, as he rode towards the enemy's position, Giovanni was hit on the thigh by a three-pound cannon-ball.

He was carried to Mantua, where the same Jewish doctor attended him. This time, the wound was far worse. Pietro Aretino had the task of breaking the news to him. There was nothing for it but amputation. 'Do it at once,' said Giovanni.

The horrors of surgery, before anaesthetics and antiseptics, have been described too often to need repetition. Giovanni, consistent to the last, was less afraid of the pain than of displaying weakness. He refused the men who would have held him down while the surgeon sawed through the ruined limb. He insisted on taking a candle in his own hand to provide extra light for the operation.

He survived the shock, but gangrene quickly set in, and he realized that he had not long to live. He made his will, sent a farewell message to Maria, composed an address to his soldiers. Pietro Aretino remained all the while at his bedside, talking to him, noting his wishes, and reading to him to take his mind off his pain and help him to fall asleep. It was Aretino who recorded his last hours, and how, after confessing and receiving the sacrament, he insisted on being taken from his bed and laid upon a camp cot. Soon after that, he died in his sleep. He was buried in Mantua, wearing the black armour in which he had fought.

A few months later the wild host of Imperial invaders swept down the road to Rome, unhindered by the inept Duke of Urbino, largely uncontrolled even by their own commander, the Constable of Bourbon – yet another leader who was about to be cut off by an impersonal shot from an arquebus. Many believed that there need have been no Sack of Rome if Giovanni delle Bandè Nere had lived and been given his chance. With his initiative and disciplined followers he would never have let the ill-organized *landsknechte* and their assorted allies come within a hundred miles of the city.

That may be so. Yet if Giovanni had survived to save Rome and even temporarily deflect the course of history, he would still have been the last of the condottieri. He could have continued successfully only as Machiavelli dreamed of his doing, not as a soldier of fortune but as a national leader, 'Giovanni of Italy', rallying the dissident peoples of the peninsula. The role of the condottiere no longer corresponded with the needs of the time. The nature of warfare had altered too drastically, and so had the political situation in Italy.

Whatever allowance is made for the prejudice of contemporary historians like Machiavelli and Guicciardini, with their exaggerated contrasts

340

between the kid-glove combats of the fifteenth century and the sanguinary struggles that began with the French invasion of 1494, there is no denying that wars had become bloodier (by Italian standards) and bigger in scale, something beyond the scope of the private army and the professional contractor. The condottiere system had been the logical last stage in the evolution of medieval warfare. For all Hawkwood's bowmen and Federigo's cannon, its basis had remained the mobile man-at-arms, highly trained, well equipped, experienced – and relatively few in numbers, so that a powerful striking force need not be prohibitively expensive to maintain. Its code of conventions derived from the general rules of chivalry. Its assumption of a ransom-system, accepted by both sides, depended on mainly hand-to-hand conflict: it was inapplicable to the new kind of battle, in which the combatants could be slain from a distance by cannons and hand-guns, and in which, even when it came to push of pike or cavalry charge, there was no guarantee that the other side would either grant quarter or ask for it. Booty, fairly shared in strictly regulated proportions, had been another essential economic element, but, while looting continued as in every war that has yet afflicted mankind, it was now incidental. The improvement of artillery had stimulated interest in the art of fortification and the cities hugged their wealth behind thicker walls with angle bastions from which to rake their attackers. Condottieri had never liked long and difficult sieges, and such operations were becoming even less attractive. For loot, their soldiers had depended more upon the open countryside and the smaller, undefended towns, and it had often paid them better to accept a lump sum, as protection-money, and leave the civilians poorer but in peace. Conditions changed after the French invasion of 1494. J. R. Hale, in the *New Cambridge Modern History*, reminds us that a scorched-earth policy was recommended by Robert de Balsac in his book, *Nef des Princes et des Batailles*, based partly on his experience in the Italian wars and published in 1502. And it is Hale again, in *Italian Renaissance Studies*, who cites the appalling atrocities of the French and Swiss, followed by the Spaniards after 1503 and the Germans after 1509. There might have been some black entries in the annals of the condottieri, especially in the earlier period – Cesena springs to mind – but wholesale and wanton destruction was not in their interests. It savoured too much of killing the goose that laid the golden eggs. Guicciardini had some justification when he wrote that 'this way of making war, not having been practised in Italy for many centuries, filled the whole country with the greatest terror'. In such a ravaged countryside, over which thousands of foreign invaders had passed like locusts, what regular livelihood was there for the old-style condottiere and his band?

Machiavelli and Guicciardini did their countrymen less than justice when they depicted them as sapped of martial quality. 'The wars', wrote C. M. Ady in the *New Cambridge Modern History*, 'show many instances of skill and bravery on the part of individual Italians. . . . Although the Italians produced no military genius equal to Gonzalo de Cordoba or Gaston de Foix, they had among them distinguished generals.' J. R. Hale shares her view, writing in the same volume: 'Italy's weakness was not that she relied on mercenaries, nor that her wars smacked more of the chessboard than the shambles; Italian troops had already shown at the Ponte di Crevola in 1487 that they could defeat the Swiss, her artillery was not so seriously inferior in quality to that of the French – whose instructor she had been – as her embittered historians suggested: it was in disunity, in divided command, in excessive reliance on political action that the weakness lay. . . .'

Disunity. That surely was the decisive factor, as so often in the long history of the peninsula. Disunity put the Italians under various foreign rulers for the next three centuries. But it was that same disunity that had made possible the profession of the condottiere and if, by some miracle, Italy could have achieved unity in the sixteenth century and repelled her external enemies she would have removed at the same time the old *raison d'être* of her mercenary captains. Whatever the outcome of the struggle, the era of the free-lance was at an end.

What epitaph should be pronounced upon the condottieri? Not as fulsome as the eulogies pronounced at their funerals, yet perhaps not too uncharitable. Granted, these men were violent, ambitious, sometimes cruel and treacherous, but often they compare favourably with those they served. True, they had a vested interest in war, but it would be more accurate to say that their interest lay rather in defence expenditure than in carnage. War was unquestioningly accepted by everyone, including the Church, as a part of life. The condottieri did not cause, or particularly exacerbate, the conflicts of the Italian states. They merely did most of the fighting, leaving the civilians to get on with their daily lives. On the whole, the battles between patriots or partisans were far bloodier. If it be accepted that wars were inevitable in the peninsula at that time, it may be argued that the condottieri, with their professional attitudes and conventions, their ideological detachment, and their preoccupation with ransom-money, rendered those wars more humane and less destructive than they would have been if waged by zealous citizens.

It would hardly be fanciful to say that, if only in this negative sense, the condottieri played their part in making possible the artistic and cultural achievement of the Italian Renaissance.

342

209 A French map of 1515 (right) shows the Alps and the passes by which foreign armies entered Italy. Beginning in 1494, these invasions introduced a new and bloodier phase of Italian warfare, in which the condottieri could have no part.

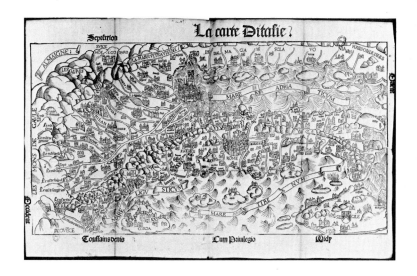

210 Below: Italy, showing the main sites of condottiere operations mentioned in this book.

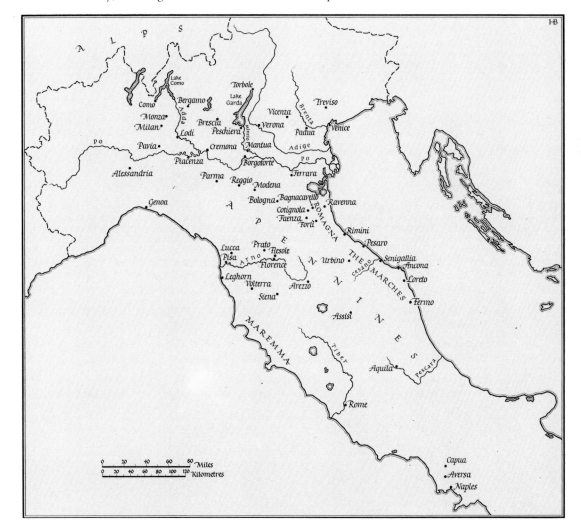

Principal personages

The following brief notes on recurring characters
and their dates may be convenient for quick reference.

POPES

1352–62	Innocent VI	Diverted mercenaries from Avignon to Italy.
1362–70	Urban V	Tried unsuccessfully to restore the papacy to Rome.
1370–78	Gregory XI	Continued at Avignon.
1378–89	Urban VI	His controversial election began the Great Schism. Hawkwood's uncongenial superior, Cardinal Robert of Geneva, 'the butcher of Cesena', became the Anti-Pope Clement VII – at Avignon.
1389–1404	Boniface IX	Concentrated on establishing papal authority in Rome.
1404–10	Several short-lived Popes and their rivals.	
1410–15	John XXIII	Baldassare Cossa, a Neapolitan soldier and corsair, who most unsuitably became a prince of the Church. Fought Ladislaus of Naples. His deposition led to end of Great Schism.
1417–31	Martin V	Rebuilt political power of papacy. Bitter enemy of Braccio da Montone.
1431–47	Eugenius IV	Much involved in the wars of the time, including a struggle with Sforza for possession of the Marches.
1447–55	Nicholas V	Great humanist. Less effectual as a peace-maker.
1455–58	Calixtus IV	
1458–64	Pius II	The sophisticated scholar, Aeneas Sylvius, inveterate foe of Sigismondo Malatesta.
1464–71	Paul II	
1471–84	Sixtus IV	Commemorated by the Sistine Chapel. He employed Roberto Malatesta as his condottiere, and had Federigo of Urbino against him.
1484–92	Innocent VIII	
1492–1503	Alexander VI	Cesare Borgia's father.
1503–13	Julius II	Himself a robust military campaigner.
1513–21	Leo X	Giovanni de' Medici, Lorenzo's 'clever' son. 'As God has given us the Papacy, let us enjoy it.'
1522–23	Hadrian VI	
1523–34	Clement VII	Giulio de' Medici, whose political misjudgments resulted in the Sack of Rome in 1527.

ALBERICO DA BARBIANO. Died 1409. A condottiere from Romagna who from 1379 onwards made himself the champion of the native Italian mercenary against the foreigner, and, after Hawkwood's time, restored the supremacy of the cavalry. Regarded by Italians as their first great captain.

ALFONSO THE MAGNANIMOUS. Aragonese claimant to the throne of Naples, which he held from 1442 until his death in 1458. A cultured and in many ways attractive character, one of the statesmen who tried to pacify Italy with the Lodi settlement in 1454.

ATTENDOLO, MUZIO. 1369–1424. Earned the nickname Sforza ('Force') which was passed on to a dynasty. A rough and illiterate Romagnol condottiere, one of Alberico da Barbiano's two great disciples.

BANDE NERE, GIOVANNI DELLE. 1498–1526. The only Medici to become a condottiere. In his brief life he won a brilliant reputation. Machiavelli regarded him as the military hope of Italy.

BRACCIO DA MONTONE. 1368–1424. Exiled Perugian aristocrat. Comrade-in-arms, and subsequently lifelong professional rival of Muzio Attendolo Sforza, he was Alberico da Barbiano's other famous pupil and developed his own tactical theories that were always contrasted with Sforza's.

CANE, FACINO. Died 1412. Piedmontese condottiere, mainly serving Milan, where in his closing years he was supremely powerful because of Giovanni Maria Visconti's inadequacy.

CARMAGNOLA, FRANCESCO BUSSONE. 1390–1432. Piedmontese shepherd's son, who became a great condottiere, first with Milan, then with Venice. Executed for alleged double-dealing.

CARRARA, FRANCESCO. Died 1393. Ambitious lord of Padua, a city the Carrara family dominated for nearly a century. His son of the same name, distinguished as 'Francesco Novello', was Hawkwood's nominal commander at Castagnaro.

CHARLES VIII, KING OF FRANCE. 1470–98. His invasion of Italy in 1494 was regarded (and somewhat exaggerated) by contemporary Italian commentators as introducing a new and more savage era of warfare and the end of the old polite conventions of the condottieri.

COLLEONI, BARTOLOMEO. 1400–75. Famous Venetian condottiere who also for a time served Milan. Born near Bergamo.

ESTE, NICCOLÒ D', MARQUIS OF FERRARA. 1383–1441. Outstanding member of the ancient family which dominated Ferrara. He commissioned Muzio Sforza and for a time had Francesco Sforza educated with his own children.

FOSCARI, FRANCESCO. c. 1372–1457. Elected Doge of Venice in 1423 as exponent of the controversial 'mainland' policy and confounded his enemies by his longevity.

GATTAMELATA, ERASMO DA NARNI. c. 1374–1443. Baker's son from Umbria, a dependable condottiere who served many masters and ended as a much-respected servant of Venice.

HAWKWOOD, SIR JOHN. c. 1320–94. The great Englishman who dominated Italian warfare for the last thirty years of his life.

JOANNA II, QUEEN OF NAPLES. 1371–1435. Succeeded her brother, Ladislaus, in 1414. Her amorous and irresponsible character, added to the perennial dynastic disputes and unrest of her kingdom, provided ample employment for condottieri such as Braccio and Muzio Sforza.

LADISLAUS, KING OF NAPLES. 1379–1414. Joanna's brother and predecessor on the throne of Naples, which he occupied effectively from 1400. He employed Alberico da Barbiano and then Muzio Sforza, and blocked Braccio's personal ambitions at Perugia. He was himself an active soldier.

MACHIAVELLI, NICCOLÒ. 1469–1527. The famous Florentine was, in J. R. Hale's phrase, 'a keen armchair soldier' and his writings have greatly influenced later historians. It is now evident that his bias against condottieri and his advocacy of a civic militia on the ancient Roman model led him to misrepresent some aspects of mercenary warfare.

MALATESTA, SIGISMONDO. 1417–68. Lord of Rimini and most notorious member of a family which for generations combined the rule of a small state with the profession of condottiere.

MEDICI, COSIMO DE'. 1389–1464. The founder of the great Florentine ruling family was a friend, counsellor, and backer of Francesco Sforza, and with him one of the architects of the Lodi peace settlement.

MICHELOTTI, BIORDO. Assassinated 1398. Perugian exile who became a condottiere and returned to rule his native city.

MONTEFELTRO, FEDERIGO DA. 1422–82. Duke of Urbino and eminent condottiere, lifelong opponent of his neighbour, Sigismondo Malatesta. Patron of art, whose cultured court inspired Castiglione – a generation later – to write *The Courtier*.

PICCININO, NICCOLÒ. 1386–1444. Perugian of humble birth, miniature size, and great spirit. His military abilities never won him the reward he deserved. A pupil of Braccio, he was in continual rivalry with Francesco Sforza. His sons,

Jacopo and Francesco Piccinino, were also well-known condottieri.

SFORZA, FRANCESCO. 1401–66. The most noteworthy example of a condottiere who made himself head of a powerful state. Son of the illiterate Muzio, Francesco was cultured and a sophisticated statesman as well as an able soldier. Helped by a Visconti marriage, he managed in 1450 to make himself Duke of Milan.

VERME, JACOPO DAL. Came to prominence in 1378, when Gian Galeazzo Visconti made him Captain-General. He was the best-known member of a Veronese family of professional soldiers. He assisted Gian Galeazzo in his coup against Bernabò and served him loyally throughout his reign. He finally quitted the Milanese service in despair and is thought to have died fighting for Venice against the Turks in the first decade of the fifteenth century.

VISCONTI, BERNABÒ. Died 1385. The apparently all-powerful despot of Milan until deposed by his nephew, Gian Galeazzo. A great employer of condottieri, several of whom (including Hawkwood) were given his bastard daughters as wives.

VISCONTI, FILIPPO MARIA. 1392–1447. Third Duke of Milan from 1412. A neurotic recluse and highly devious statesman. Hired most of the chief condottieri, from Carmagnola to Piccinino and Sforza, who married his daughter, but trusted none of them.

VISCONTI, GIAN GALEAZZO. 1352–1402. Count of Virtù and first Duke of Milan, after seizing power from his uncle, Bernabò. Step by step he advanced to the control of nearly all northern Italy, but on his sudden death from plague the whole fabric collapsed in disunity.

Guide to further reading

A truly comprehensive bibliography on this subject, in all its ramifications, would be almost impossible to compile. The following are probably the most useful books, available in English, to the general reader.

For the condottieri as a class and for military matters at that time:

Oscar Browning *The Age of the Condottieri* (London 1895)

D. M. Bueno de Mesquita 'Some Condottieri of the Trecento', *Proceedings of the British Academy* XXXII (1946)

E. R. Chamberlin 'The English Mercenary Companies in Italy', *History Today* (May 1956)

J. J. Deiss *Captains of Fortune* (London 1966)

M. H. Keen *The Laws of War in the Late Middle Ages* (London 1965)

R. Ewart Oakeshott *The Archaeology of Weapons* (London 1960)

Sir Charles Oman *A History of the Art of War in the Middle Ages* (Oxford 1898, revised ed. 1924)

Lynn White, Jun. *Medieval Technology and Social Change* (Oxford 1962)

For biographical details of individual condottieri and others:

C. M. Ady *History. of Milan under the Sforza* (London 1907)

Horatio Brown *Studies in Venetian History* (London 1907)

Oscar Browning *Life of Bartolomeo Colleoni* (London 1891)

D. M. Bueno de Mesquita *Giangaleazzo Visconti* (Cambridge 1941)

L. M. Collison-Morley *The Story of the Sforzas* (London 1932)

J. Dennistoun *Memoirs of the Dukes of Urbino* (London 1851; new edition, ed. E. Hutton, London 1908)

Fritz Gaupp 'The Condottiere John Hawkwood', *History* (March 1939)

Edmund G. Gardner *The Story of Siena* (London 1904)

Lina Duff Gordon *The Story of Assisi* (London 1900)

E. Hutton *Sigismondo Malatesta* (London 1906)

F. Marion Crawford *Gleanings from Venetian History* (London 1907)

D. Muir *History of Milan under the Visconti* (London 1920)

E. Noyes *The Story of Milan* (London 1908)

Margaret Symonds and Lina Duff Gordon *The Story of Perugia* (London 1898)

J. Temple-Leader and G. Marcotti *Sir John Hawkwood*, trans. Leader Scott (London 1889)

For general historical background:

Hans Baron *The Crisis of the Italian Renaissance* (Princeton 1955)

Cambridge Medieval History, vols. VII (Cambridge 1932), VIII (Cambridge 1936)

E. R. Chamberlin *Everyday Life in Renaissance Times* (London 1965)

J. R. Hale *Machiavelli and Renaissance Italy* (London 1961)

E. F. Jacob (ed.) *Italian Renaissance Studies* (London 1960)

J. Lucas-Dubreton *Daily Life in Florence in the Time of the Medici* (London 1960)

New Cambridge Modern History, vol. I (Cambridge 1957)

Iris Origo *The Merchant of Prato* (London 1957)

Peter Partner *The Papal State under Martin V* (London 1958)

J. H. Plumb (ed.) *The Horizon Book of the Renaissance* (London 1961)

Daniel Waley *The Italian City-Republics* (London 1969)

List of illustrations

12 Emperor Frederick II. From his own treatise on falconry, *De Arte Venandi cum Avibus*, 1248. Biblioteca Apostolica Vaticana, Ms. Pal. Latino 1071, f. 1v.

13 The right and the wrong way to hold a falcon on horseback. From *De Arte Venandi cum Avibus*, 1248. Biblioteca Apostolica Vaticana, Ms. Pal. Latino 1071, f. 89v.

14 The right and the wrong way to hold a falcon on foot. From *De Arte Venandi cum Avibus*, 1248. Biblioteca Apostolica Vaticana, Ms. Pal. Latino 1071, f. 103.

15 Charles of Anjou, King of Naples and Sicily. Statue attributed to Arnolfo di Cambio (d. 1302). Museo Capitolino, Rome. Photo Mansell-Anderson.

16 Templar seal, 1259. Archives Nationales, Paris.

17 Templars in battle. Detail of a map of Crusader Jerusalem, late twelfth century. Koninklijke Bibliotheek, The Hague.

18 Templar knight, thirteenth century. Parish church of Villalcazar de Singa, Spain. Photo Mas.

19 Knight killing a Saracen. From *Codice de los Usatjes*, thirteenth century. Escorial Monastery, Madrid. Photo Mas.

20 Plan of Acre. From *Secreta fidelium crucis* by Marino Sanuto Torsello, 1321–24. Bodleian Library, Oxford, Ms. Tanner 190, f. 207.

21 Crusader knights in battle. Linen wall-hanging from Bishop's Palace, Sitten (Valais), Switzerland. North Italian, second half of fourteenth century. Historisches Museum, Basel.

22 Map of Byzantium. From *Liber insularum Archipelagi* by C. de Bondelmontius, 1422. British Museum, Ms. Cotton, Vesp. A XIII, f. 36v.

23 Emperor Michel VIII Palaeologus. From *Codex Monacensis*, fourteenth century. Staatsbibliothek, Munich, Ms. Grec. 442, f. 174.

24 Tomb monument of Cangrande della Scala (d. 1329), Verona. Probably by a Tuscan artist, fourteenth century. Photo Max F. Chiffelle, Chexbres.

25 Tomb monument of Mastino II della Scala (d. 1351), Verona. Probably by a Venetian artist, fourteenth century. Photo Mansell-Alinari.

26 Joanna I of Naples. Fresco by Roberto de Oderisio, 1370. Chiesa dell'Incoronata, Naples. Photo Mansell-Alinari.

27 Battle of Sluys, 1340. From a history of the world. French, illuminated in Italy, fourteenth century. British Museum, Ms. Roy. 20 D 1, f. 258.

28 Edward III endows his son, the Black Prince, with the province of Aquitaine. From a copy of the grant, 1362. British Museum, Ms. Cotton, Nero, D VI, f. 31.

29 Soldiers pillaging a house. From *Chroniques de France ou de Saint Denis*. French, late fourteenth century. British Museum, Ms. Roy. 20 C VII, f. 41v.

c. 1335–40. British Museum, Ms. Add. 42130, f. 147v.

48 Soldiers using scaling-ladders to enter a town. From *Liber de Casibus Troie* by G. delle Colonne. Italian, fourteenth century. Biblioteca Ambrosiana, Milan, Ms. H 86 Sup., f. 35v. Photo Courtauld Institute of Art, London.

49 Fourteenth-century battle scene. Detail of *Battle of Val di Chiana* by Lippo Vanni. Fresco, 1373. The Sienese under Giordano Orsini beat the English Compagnia del Cappello under Niccolò da Montefeltro, ancestor of Federigo da Montefeltro, in 1363. Palazzo Pubblico, Siena. Photo E.P.T., Siena.

50 English knight. From *Luttrell Psalter*. East Anglian, c. 1335–40. British Museum, Ms. Add. 42130, f. 202v.

51 Italian knight. Relief, fourteenth century. Victoria and Albert Museum, London.

52 Rape scene. From *Effects of Bad Government* by Ambrogio and Pietro Lorenzetti. Fresco, c. 1340. Palazzo Pubblico, Siena. Photo E.P.T., Siena.

53 Condottiere in his tent. From *De Bello Pharsalico* by Lucan, 1373. Miniature by Niccolò da Bologna. Biblioteca Trivulziana, Milan, Ms. 691, f. 86v.

54 The hill of Fiesole. From the Codex of M. di Bartolomeo Rustici, 1448. Biblioteca del Seminario Centrale, Florence. Photo Soprintendenza alle Gallerie, Florence.

55 Design for the painted monument of Sir John Hawkwood. Drawing by Paolo Uccello, 1436. Uffizi, Florence. Photo Mansell-Anderson.

56 View of Florence. Detail of *Madonna della Misericordia* by an anonymous artist. Fresco, fourteenth century. Loggia del Bigallo, Florence. Photo Mansell-Alinari.

57 Money-changers. Detail of *Calling of St Matthew* by Niccolò Gerini. Fresco, 1395. S. Francesco, Prato.

58 Mercenary captains receiving their pay. *Biccherna* cover, 1464. Archivio di Stato, Siena.

59 Doge Giovanni dell'Agnello of Pisa awaiting the arrival of Pope Urban V at Leghorn, June 1367. From *Cronica* by Giovanni Sercambi, completed 1400, no. CLXVII. Archivio di Stato, Lucca.

60 View of Milan. From *Cronaca di Milano* by G. Fiamma. Milanese, early fourteenth century. Biblioteca Trivulziana, Milan, Ms. 1438, f. 6.

61 Bernabò Visconti. Detail of monument by Bonino da Campione, before 1363. Castello Sforzesco, Milan.

62 Lionel, Duke of Clarence. Detail of the tomb of Edward III, c. 1377–80. Westminster Abbey, London. Photo Royal Commission on Historical Monuments (Crown Copyright).

63 Subject cities paying homage to Milan. Detail of the tomb of Azzone Visconti by Giovanni da Balduccio,

c. 1340. S. Gottardo in Corte, Milan. Photo Federico Arborio Mella, Milan.

64 Allegorical figure of Milan holding a shield and a helmet bearing the Visconti family emblem, a viper or dragon swallowing a man. From *De natura deorum et De divinatione* by Cicero. Italian, fourteenth century. This book belonged to the Visconti family library. Bibliothèque Nationale, Paris, Ms. Latin 6340, f. 901v.

65 Cardinal Albornoz receiving homage from the conquered cities of Rimini, Pesaro, Fano, Senigallia and Ancona. Italian miniature, fourteenth century. Biblioteca Apostolica Vaticana, Ms. ARM 35, Vol. 20, f. 6v.

66 Mounted soldier. Detail of *Crucifixion* by Barna da Siena. Fresco, c. 1350–55. Chiesa della Collegiata, S. Gimignano. Photo Scala.

67 Capture of a town. Detail of *Battle of Clavigo* by Altichiero. Fresco, c. 1370. Oratorio di S. Giorgio, Padua. Photo Scala.

68 Design for a siege machine. From *Taxaurus Regis* by Guido da Vigevano, 1335. Bibliothèque Nationale, Paris, Ms. Latin 11015, f. 11.

69 Bombard. Italian, fourteenth century. Museo Nazionale dell' Artiglieria, Turin.

70 *Bombardella*. Italian, late fifteenth century. Museo Bardini, Florence. Photo Pineider, Florence.

71 Rocca Malatestiana, Cesena. Begun by Galeotto Malatesta, early fourteenth century. Photo Ciganovic, Rome.

72 Coronation of Robert of Geneva as Pope Clement VII. From *Chroniques de France ou de Saint Denis*. French, late fourteenth century. British Museum, Ms. Roy. 20 C VII, f. 208v.

73 Muzio Attendolo Sforza. From *Vita di Muzio Attendolo Sforza* by Antonio Minuti, 1491. Miniature by a follower of Giampietrino Birago. Bibliothèque Nationale, Paris, Ms. Italien 372, f. 4v.

74 Tomb of Ostasio da Polenta, 1396. S. Francesco, Ravenna.

75 Rocca da Ravaldino, Forlì. Erected by the Ordelaffi family, late fourteenth century. Photo Ciganovic, Rome.

76 Rocca Malatestiana, Rimini, begun by the Malatesta family, thirteenth century.

77 Hawkwood's Tower, Cotignola, the remains of Hawkwood's fortifications, destroyed in the Second World War. Photo E.P.T., Ravenna.

78 Cleaning out the wine-barrels. From *Historia Plantarum*. Lombard, fourteenth century. Biblioteca Casantense, Rome, Ms. 459, f. 106.

79 Convent of S. Antonio, Florence. From the Codex of M. di Bartolomeo Rustici, 1448. Biblioteca del Seminario Centrale, Florence. Photo Soprintendenza alle Gallerie, Florence.

80 Tuscan countryside. Detail of *Allegory of Good Government* by Ambrogio and Pietro Lorenzetti. Fresco, *c.* 1340. Palazzo Pubblico, Siena. Photo Grassi, Siena.

81 Castello Visconteo, Pavia, begun by Galeazzo Visconti 1360–65, and completed by Gian Galeazzo Visconti. Photo Chiolini, Pavia.

82 Gian Galeazzo Visconti leading troops on a military expedition. Detail of his tomb by Cristoforo Romano, 1493–97. Certosa, Pavia. Photo Mansell-Alinari.

83 Courtyard, Castello Visconteo, Pavia. Photo Chiolini, Pavia.

84 Caterina Visconti, wife of Gian Galeazzo Visconti, by Benedetto Briosco, *c.* 1490. Certosa, Pavia. Photo Chiolini, Pavia.

85 Gian Galeazzo Visconti. Relief by Antonio da Carrara, 1490. Certosa, Pavia. Photo Chiolini, Pavia.

86 The Christ Child crowning Gian Galeazzo Visconti. From *Elogium on Gian Galeazzo Visconti* by Pietro da Castelleto, 1403. Miniature by Michelino da Besozzo. Bibliothèque Nationale, Paris, Ms. Latin 5888, f. 1.

87 God blessing the lands and deeds of the Visconti. From the *Ofiziolo* of Filippo Maria Visconti, 1420. Miniature by Belbello da Pavia. Biblioteca Nazionale, Florence, Codex Landau-Finaly 22, f. 41.

88 Storming the 'Castle of Love'. Back of an ivory mirror case. French, mid fourteenth century. Victoria and Albert Museum, London.

89 View of Verona. Seal on parchment, 1410. Archivio di Stato, Verona.

90 Castle and fortified bridge of the Scaligers, Verona, 1354–75 (detail). Photo Mansell Collection.

91 Francesco Carrara the Elder. Detail of *Adoration of the Magi* by Jacopo da Verona. Fresco, 1397. S. Michele, Padua. Photo Museo Civico, Padua.

92 Francesco Novello da Carrara. From *De principibus Carrariensibus et gestis eorum* by Vergerius Petrus Paulus, fourteenth century. Museo Civico, Padua, Ms. BP. 158.

93 *Carroccio* led by oxen. From *De re militari* by Roberto Valturius, 1472. British Museum.

94 Paduan knight. Detail of the Lupi di Soragna family tomb by Andreolo dei Santi, 1377–84. Oratorio di S. Giorgio, Padua. Photo Perissinotto, Padua.

95 Veronese soldier. Detail of *The Cavalli family presented to the Virgin by St George, St Martin and St Jacopus* by Altichiero. Fresco, *c.* 1369. S. Anastasia, Verona.

96 Camp scene. Drawing by a Veronese artist, late fourteenth century. British Museum, Department of Prints and Drawings.

97 Coronation of Gian Galeazzo Visconti. From *Missale Ambrosianum*, fourteenth century. Miniature by Annovelo da Imbonate. Biblioteca Ambrosiana, Milan, Ms. M.6.

Biadajolo by Domenico Lenzi, 1320–35. Biblioteca Laurenziana, Florence, Ms. Tempi 3, f. 58.

116 Richard II of England. Detail of recumbent effigy by Nicholas Broker and Godfrey Prest, 1394–96. Westminster Abbey, London. Photo Warburg Institute, London.

117 Alberico da Barbiano ravaging the lands of Florence and taking prisoners. From *Cronica* by Giovanni Sercambi, completed 1400, no. CCCCLXXV. Archivio di Stato, Lucca.

118 Biordo Michelotti of Perugia appointed Captain-General of the Florentines. From *Cronica* by Giovanni, Sercambi, completed 1400, no. CCCCLXIX. Archivio di Stato, Lucca.

119 Pope Boniface IX. Statue by an anonymous artist, fourteenth century. S. Paolo fuori le Mura, Rome. Photo Mansell-Anderson.

120 Pope settling a dispute. From *Decretals of Pope Gregory IX*. Bolognese, late fourteenth century. Österreichische Nationalbibliothek, Vienna, Cod. Vindob. 2040, f. 88.

121 View of Perugia. Detail of *Removal of the body of S. Ercolano from S. Pietro to the cathedral of S. Lorenzo, Perugia* by Benedetto Bonfiglio, 1454–70. Galleria Nazionale di Umbria, Perugia. Photo Mansell-Alinari.

122 Porta Marzia, Perugia. Detail of *Siege of Perugia by the Goths* by Benedetto Bonfiglio, 1454–70. Galleria Nazionale di Umbria, Perugia. Photo Mansell-Anderson.

123 Painted wooden chest used for the election of civic officials. Fifteenth century. Palazzo dei Priori, Perugia. Photo E.P.T., Perugia.

124 Banner of Perugia, griffin holding a sword. From *Matricola dei Notai di Perugia*, 1343. Biblioteca Augustea, Perugia, Ms. 972, f. 3.

125 Rocca Maggiore and Rocca Minore, Assisi, with the Tiber Valley beyond. Photo Mansell-Alinari.

126 Montecchio Castle, Emilia. Photo E.P.T., Reggio Emilia.

127 Suit of Italian armour, *c.* 1400. The Metropolitan Museum of Art, New York. The Bashford Dean Memorial Collection. Gift of Helen Fahnestock Hubbard, 1929, in memory of her father, Harris C. Fahnestock.

128 Italian knight with a raised visor. Detail of tomb of Count Tiberto VI Brandolini (d. 1397). S. Francesco, Bagnacavallo. Photo E.P.T., Ravenna.

129 Gian Galeazzo Visconti presenting a model of the Certosa to the Virgin. Detail of *Gian Galeazzo and members of the Visconti family kneeling before the Virgin* by Ambrogio Bergognone. Fresco, 1488–90. Certosa, Pavia. Photo Martinotti, Milan.

130 Construction of the Certosa. Detail of *Christ carrying the cross with monks of the Certosa* by Ambrogio Bergognone, 1494. Museo Civico, Pavia.

131 Façade of the Certosa, fifteenth century. Photo Chiolini, Pavia.

132 Gian Galeazzo Visconti. Detail of his tomb by Cristofozo Romano, 1493–97. Certosa, Pavia.

133 Gian Galeazzo Visconti's body transported to the Certosa. Detail of façade of the Certosa by Benedetto Briosco, 1501. Photo Mansell-Alinari.

134 Grape harvesting. Detail of *Occupations of the Months* by an anonymous artist. Fresco, *c.* 1415. Castello del Buon Consiglio, Trento. Photo Rensi, Trento.

135 Rape scene. Detail of *Rape of Helen* by a follower of Fra Angelico. Probably a *cassone* panel, *c.* 1450. Courtesy of the Trustees of the National Gallery, London.

136 Braccio da Montone. Anonymous portrait. Uffizi, Florence. Photo Mansell-Alinari.

137 Muzio Attendolo Sforza. Fresco by Bernardino Luini, 1522–26. Castello Sforzesco, Milan.

138 Sforza family coat of arms, 1410. Casa Sforza, Cotignola. Photo E.P.T., Ravenna.

139 Pisanello. Medal·attributed to Pisanello (*c.* 1395–1455/56). Bibliothèque Nationale, Paris. Photo Giraudon.

140 Guarino da Verona. Medal by Matteo dei Pasti, *c.* 1440–46. British Museum.

141 Niccolò d'Este. From *Geneaologia dei principi d'Este*. Ferrarese, *c.* 1474. Biblioteca Nazionale Vittorio Emanuele, Rome, Ms. 293, f. 6.

142 Anti-Pope John XXIII. Detail of his tomb by Donatello and Michelozzo, 1425–27. Baptistery, Florence. Photo Brogi.

143 Leonello d'Este. From *Geneaologia dei principi d'Este*. Ferrarese, *c.* 1474. Biblioteca Nazionale Vittorio Emanuele, Rome, Ms. 293, f. 6.

144 View of Naples. From *Cronica di Partenope* by Giovanni Villani, 1481. Pierpont Morgan Library, New York, Ms. 801, ff. 116v–117.

145 Ladislaus of Naples. Detail of his tomb by Andrea da Firenze, 1428. S. Giovanni a Carbonara, Naples. Photo Mansell-Alinari.

146 Joanna II of Naples. Detail of the tomb of Ladislaus of Naples by Andrea da Firenze, 1428, erected by Joanna. S. Giovanni a Carbonara, Naples. Photo Mansell-Anderson.

147 Castel dell'Ovo, Naples. Photo Alinari.

148 Niccolò Piccinino. Medal by Pisanello, *c.* 1441. Bargello, Florence. Photo Mansell-Alinari.

149 View of Rome. Fresco by Taddeo di Bartolo, 1414. Palazzo Pubblico, Siena. Photo E.P.T., Siena.

150 Pope Martin V. Detail of his tomb by Donatello and Michelozzo, 1433. S. Giovanni in Laterano, Rome. Photo Mansell-Alinari.

151 Design for a medal of Alfonso of Aragon. Drawing by Pisanello, 1448. Louvre, Paris. Photo Giraudon.

152 Giovanni Caracciolo. Detail of his tomb by Andrea da Firenze, 1433. S. Giovanni a Carbonara, Naples. Photo Mansell-Alinari.

153 Arms and portrait of Louis III of Anjou. From *Codice della Confraternità di Santa Maria*, 1424. Archivio di Stato, Naples.

154 Castle, Aquila. Photo E.P.T., Aquila.

155 Francesco Sforza. From *Commentarii rerum gestarum Francisci Sfortiae* by Giovanni Simonetta, 1490. Miniature by Giampietrino Birago. Biblioteca Riccardiana, Florence, Ms. E.R. 428, f. 1v.

156 *Death of Braccio da Montone at the siege of Aquila*, 5 June 1424. Fresco by Papacello (Tommaso Bernabei 1500–59). Palazzo dei Priori, Perugia. Photo E.P.T., Perugia.

157 Filippo Maria Visconti. Relief by Benedetto Briosco, 1497. Certosa, Pavia. Photo Chiolini, Pavia.

158 View of Carmagnola. From *Theatrum statuum Sabaudiae ducis* by Johannis Blaeu, 1682. Museo Civico, Carmagnola. Photo Comune di Carmagnola.

159 Francesco Bussone, Count of Carmagnola. Photograph of anonymous engraving. Museo Civico, Carmagnola. Photo Comune di Carmagnola.

160 Beatrice di Tenda, first wife of Filippo Maria Visconti. Relief by Benedetto Briosco, *c.* 1490. Certosa, Pavia. Photo Chiolini, Pavia.

161 Battle of Arbedo, 30 June 1422. From *Lucerne Chronicle* by Diebold Schilling, 1513. Zentralbibliothek, Lucerne.

162 Doge Francesco Foscari receiving the Statutes from the head of the Carpet-Makers' Guild. From *Mariegola dei Calaforti*, 1577. Museo Correr, Venice.

163 Map of the River Adda showing all crossing points. From *Decretum super flumine Abduae* by Carte Pagnani, 1520. British Museum.

164 Niccolò da Tolentino at the Battle of San Romano, 1 June 1432. Detail of *Battle of San Romano* by Paolo Uccello, 1450–59. Courtesy of the Trustees of the National Gallery, London.

165 Bianca Maria Visconti. Detail of *Privilegio di Bianca Maria Visconti* by an anonymous artist, 9 September 1465. Biblioteca Trivulziana, Milan, Perg. min. no. 4.

166 Piazza S. Marco, Venice. From *Description de Venise*, late fifteenth century. Musée Condé, Chantilly, Ms. 799, 1344. Photo Giraudon.

167 Design for an equestrian monument of Francesco Sforza. Drawing by Antonio del Pollaiuolo, 1489. Courtesy of the Robert Lehman Collection, New York.

168 Cardinal Giovanni Vitelleschi. Anonymous portrait. Uffizi, Florence. Photo Mansell-Brogi.

169 Gattamelata (Erasmo da Narni). Detail of monument by Donatello, 1447–53. Piazza del Santo, Padua. Photo Mansell-Brogi.

188 Profile of Sigismondo Malatesta supported by two elephants by Agostino di Duccio, after 1450. Tempio Malatestiano, Rimini. Photo Sansoni.

189 Vittorino da Feltre. Medal by Pisanello, *c.* 1446. British Museum, London.

190 Sigismondo Malatesta. Medal by Pisanello, 1446. Staatliche Museen, Berlin.

191 Isotta degli Atti da Rimini. Medal by Matteo dei Pasti, 1446. National Gallery of Art, Washington, D.C. Samuel H. Kress Collection.

192 *Putto* with the initials of Isotta da Rimini and Sigismondo Malatesta by a follower of Agostino di Duccio, 1447–57. Tempio Malatestiano, Rimini. Photo E.P.T., Forlì.

193 Rocca Malatestiana, Rimini. Medal by Matteo dei Pasti, 1446. Staatliche Museen, Berlin.

194 Construction of the Tempio Malatestiano, Rimini. From *Hesperidos* by Basinio Parmense, fifteenth century. Bodleian Library, Oxford, Ms. Oxon. Can. Class. Lat. 81, f. 137.

195 Battista Sforza, Duchess of Urbino. Painting attributed to Francesco di Giorgio (1439–1502). Palazzo Ducale, Urbino. Photo Mansell-Alinari.

196 *Lecture at the court of Urbino.* Relief attributed to Justus van Ghent and Pedro Berruguete, *c.* 1470. Royal Collection, Hampton Court. Reproduced by gracious permission of Her Majesty Queen Elizabeth II.

197 Intarsia panelling in the 'studiolo' of Federigo da Montefeltro by Baccio Pontelli, 1479–82. Palazzo Ducale, Urbino. Photo Edwin Smith.

198 Roberto Malatesta. Relief by a north Italian artist, 1484. Louvre, Paris. Photo Giraudon.

199 Sigismondo Malatesta. Detail of his tomb by a follower of Agostino di Duccio, fifteenth century. Tempio Malatestiano, Rimini. Photo Mansell-Anderson.

200 Federigo da Montefeltro in front of besieged Volterra. From *Storia di Firenze* by Poggio Bracciolini, 1472. Biblioteca Apostolica Vaticana, Ms. Urb. Lat. 491, f. 2v.

201 Wedding of Roberto di Sanseverino and Lucrezia di Agnolo Malavolti. Detail of a cover of a register of taxes by Sano di Pietro, 1473. Archivio di Stato, Siena.

202 Giovanni delle Bande Nere. Detail of monument by Baccio Bandinelli, 1540. Piazza S. Lorenzo, Florence. Photo Mansell-Brogi.

203 Caterina Sforza Riario. Medal by an anonymous artist, fifteenth century. Victoria and Albert Museum, London.

204 Battle of Marignano, 1515. Watercolour by an anonymous artist, sixteenth century. Musée Condé, Chantilly. Photo Giraudon.

205 Troops using the arquebus at the Battle of Pavia, 1525. Detail of a Flemish tapestry, sixteenth century. Museo di Capodimonte, Naples. Photo Alinari.

Index

Italic numerals denote pages on which the reference occurs only in a picture-caption. In the case of constantly recurring place-names, such as Florence and Milan, only the more important references are listed.